Geography and Travels of Jammu, Kashmir and Ladakh

GEOGRAPHY AND TRAVELS OF JAMMU, KASHMIR AND LADAKH

Edited by:

Usha Sharma

RADHA PUBLICATIONS
NEW DELHI 110 002

First Published 2001

ISBN 81-7487-061-X

Published by

RADHA PUBLICATIONS
4378/4-B, Ansari Road,
Daryaganj,
New Delhi 110002
Phones: 3261839, 3254306

PRINTED IN INDIA

Published by Smt. Radharani Garg for Radha Publications, 4378/4-B, Ansari Road, Daryaganj, New Delhi 110002 and printed at Tarun Offset Press, Delhi.

Preface

The State of Jammu and Kashmir is situated between 32°17' and 36°58' north latitude and 73°26' and 83°30' east longitude. It covers an area of 22,22,236 sq km. Its boundaries extended to Russian Turkistan in north, Tibet in east, Punjab in south and Pakistan in west. Geographically, the State can be divided into four zones. First, the submontane and semi-montane plain commonly known as *Kandi belt;* the second, hills including Siwalik Ranges; the third, mountains of Kashmir Valley and Sir Punjab range; and the fourth, Tibet tract of Ladakh, Kargil, Gilgit and Skardu.

In the east of this region flows the river Ravi and in the west the river Jhelum. Jammu, the winter capital of this State, stands on the spur of a hill overlooking the picturesque small Tawi. Both the Tawi and the Ujh, another small river flowing nearby are chiefly dependent on rain which often floods them during the monsoons. The Chenab issues from the mountains into the plains near the town of Akhnur and flows through parts of the Jammu district before entering the plains of Punjab.

The Valley of Kashmir nestled securely among the Himalayas at an average height of 1800 metres, is approximately 134 km. in length and 32-40 km. in breadth. The mountains which surround Kashmir are infinitely varied in form and colour. To the north is a veritable sea of mountains dominated by the mighty Nanga Parbat (7980 metres), to the east stands Haramukh (5,150 metres) to the south in Mahadeo and the lofty ranges of Gwasha Brari (5425 metres) and the peak of Amarnath (5,280 metres) on the south-west in the Panjal range with peaks of 4,500 metres.

Kashmir is also a land of lakes, rivers and springs. For its fresh water lakes and tarns, the State is celebrated all over the world. Those in the Valley are Wular, the Dal and Manasbal. Beside these lakes which are fed by springs and snow-fed streams striking down the mountain sides, there are a number of tarns formed by glacial action. Hence the Valley is a happy combination of mountains and lakes.

Srinagar, the capital of the State, is sitnated in the centre of the Valley. One of the oldest cities of India, its history goes back to the reign of Asoka who is credited with having founded it during his visit to Kashmir. Srinagar with its numerous canals and adjacent lake is aptly called the "Venice of the East" and is a centre of trade and commerce.

Situated between 32°15/to 36/ latitude and 75° 15/to 80° 15/ longtitude, the major part of Ladakh is a desert of bare crags and granite with vast, and tableland of high elevations. Cowley Lambert writes in his *A Trip to Cashmere and Ladak* (1877) "the prevailing features of this country are bare rocky mountains, bare gravel slopes and bare sandy plains-------."

Indus, the principle river of Ladakh locally known as 'Singge-Chhu' (lion river) has two principle tributories—Shyok and Nubra. A number of lakes have been formed on the rivers. The lakes are land-locked and their water is blackish. Hot springs abound in Ladakh of which Puga and Panamig are well known

Ladakh is said to be very rich is minerals which are still to be exploited. It includes borax, chromite, lime, gold, platinum, gypsum, sulphur, copper etc.

However, owning to its majestic mountains, gleaning glaciers, placid rivers, large lakes, scenic grandeur etc. Kashmir, from ancient times, was attracted by a galaxy of travellers who is turn, expressed their travels in the form of beautiful memoirs.

The material for this volume has been collected from a number of sources lying at various institutions/libraries. I feel much beholden to the authorities and staff of these institutions/libraries which have been consulted by me during the completion of this work.

Dated: 23 May, 1996

Editor

Contents

Introduction

The State of Jammu and Kashmir is one of the largest states of the Indian Union. It is situated between 32^0 17' and, 36^0 58' north latitude, and 73^0 26' and 83^0 30′ east longitude. It covers an area of 22,22,236 sq. km. It has boundaries extended to Russian Turkistan in north, Tibet is east, Punjab in south and Pakistan in west. It includes, besides the celebrated Valley, the areas of Jammu, Ladakh, Baltistan, Gilgit, Hunza and Nagar. It is mostly mountainous, rising in several tiers from the plains in the south to the high altitude valleys and peaks in the north, and enclosing some of the loftiest inhabited helmets in the world.

The State has a chequered history which is chronicled in Sanskrit verses in the *Rajatarangini* (literary the "River of Kings."). Dr. Stein, an eminent Oriental scholar said that "Kashmir can claim the distinction of being the only region of India which possesses an uninterrupted series of written records of its history reaching back beyond the period of the Muhammadan conquest and deserving the name of real chronicles".

Kalhana relates the story of Kashmir till the 14th century when Buddhist and Hindu rulers ruled over it. After four centuries of Muslim rule it was conquered by Maharaja Ranjit Singh of Punjab in 1819. Soon after his death in 1839, the East India Company defeated the then Sikh ruler of Punjab who ceded Kashmir to the Company in lieu of Rupees one crore. The Company sold Kashmir to Raja Gulab Singh, the Dogra Government of Jammu. The Dogra dynasty ruled over the state till 1949. However, on the transfer of power in 1947, the State of Jammu and Kashmir acceded to India, and Ladakh, a part of that State became an integral part of India.

Kashmir has been famous as a seat of learning. "The people of Kashmir" wrote Yuan Chwang, the renowned Chinese traveller who visited the Valley in 631 A. D. "love learning and are well cultured. For centuries, learning has been held in great respect in Kashmir". Later, when during the medieval times Persian was introduced as medium of education and learning, Kashmir acquired fame as a centre of Persian scholarship and was known all over the East as *Iran-i-Saghir* or Little Iran.

The State, no doubt, has been a land of unrivalled beauty and charm. Its snow-capped mountains, green valleys, fresh water lakes, springs and countless streams etc. have always an enchanting attraction for tourists. This superbly beautiful land abounds in a variety of delicious fruits. The luxuriant gardens grow flowers of a number of colours and of varrying fragrance. Its scenic beauty, rich vegetation and abundant water resources have turned it into a paradise for tourists.

This magnificent land is also famed for the exquisite craftsmanship of its artisans whose skilled hands have produced some of the finest works of arts. They are well-known both within and outside the country for their delicate, and splendid products in wood, silver, silk, pashmina etc. These artisans have earned their name for matchless works in embroidery and *paper mache*.

It may be observed that the State owing to its strategic and unique position has become an important issue in Indian and international politics today.

Heritage of Jammu, Kashmir and Ladakh, seeks to provide a detailed account of the history, geography travels, political development and economic life of these mountainous areas—Jammu Kashmir and Ladakh, and the magnificent contributions of each of them to the India as a whole.

The material for these volumes has been culled from a number of sources which are lying at numerous institutions/

libraries. I feel much beholden to the authorities and staff of all these institutions/libraries consulted by me during the completion of this project. I am also thankful to all those whose contributions have been included in these volumes.

Editor

Dated: 23 May, 1996

1

Geography and Topography of Kashmir and Ladhak

Political Geography

The territories of the Kashmir State comprise two provinces, Jammu and Kashmir, each of which is administered by a Chief Officer, or Governor, Styled *Hakim-i-ila*. The districts of Baltistan or Skardu and Ladak are included in the province of Jammu; and the district of Gilgit, including Astor in Kashmir. The territory of Punch is administered by Raja Moti Singh, who holds it under a grant from the Maharaja.

Boundaries

When the treaties of 1846 were made, Gulab Singh held, as Raja of Jammu, the hill chiefship around Jammu in a more or less complete state of subjection, and Ladak and Baltistan by right of conquest, and Gilgit had become an appendage of the Sikh governorship of Kashmir. The general and practical result therefore of the Treaty of Amritsar was to confirm Gulab Singh in what he already possessed, and to transfer to him the province of Kashmir with its newly-acquired authority over Gilgit.

Treaty Provisions

The clauses in the treaties of 1846, which relate the boundaries of the Kashmir State, are as follow:

I. By the 4th Article of Treaty of Lahore, dated the 9th March 1846, the Maharaja of Lahore ceded to the East India Company "in perpetual sovereignty, as equivalent for one crore of rupees, all his forts, territories, rights, and interests in the hill countries which are situated between the rivers Beas and Indus, including the provices of Kashmir and Hazara."

II. By the first Article of the Treaty of Amritsar, dated the 16th March 1846, the British Government transferred and made over "for ever, in independent possession to Maharaja Gulab Singh, and the heirs male of his body, all the hilly or mountainous country, with its dependencies, situated to the eastward of River Indus and westward of the River Ravi, including Chamba and excluding Lahoul, being part of the territories ceded to the British Government by the Lahore State, according to the provisions of Article IV of the Treaty of Lahore, dated the 9th March 1846".

III. The 2nd Article of the Treaty of Amritsar provided that the eastern boundary of the tract transferred by the Article just quoted should be "laid down by Commissioners appointed by the British Government and the Maharaja Gulab Singh respectively for that purpose", and should be "defined in a separate engagement after survey".

IV. The 4th Article of the Treaty of Amritsar stipulated that "the limits of the territories of Maharaja Gulab Singh shall not be at any time changed without the concurrence of the British Government".

The Eastern Boundary

From the valley of the Chandra Bhaga to the Gya peak (lat 32^0 31', long. 78^0 28') the boundary line has been defined by Commissioners, as it here divides the territories of the British and the Kashmir Maharaja. From the Gya peak northwards the Chinese territories adjoin the Kashmir State. The following is an extract from the Commissioner's Report:

> "In 1830, when Captian A. Cunningham surveyed the Lahoul districts, the boundary between the States of Kulu and Chamba was formed by the Nalda and Chugam nalas, two tributaries of Chandra Bhaga, the one on its left and the other on its right bank. From the head of the Chugamnala the Commissioners determined that all the country to the eastward, which is drained by the Bhaga, the Chandra Bhaga, and their tributaries, belonged to the British district of Lahoul; and that the boundary between Lahoul and the Zauskar district was the snowy Range (called Paralassa by Dr. Gerard) dividing the drainage of the Bhaga and Chandra Bhaga from that of the Zauskar river.
>
> "Beyond the Bara Lacha pass to the eastward, the Commissioners found that there was an old well-known boundary stone, called Phalang Danda, which marked the limit between Lahoul and Ladak. This stone is noticed by Moorcroft (I.,p.220). It stands in the midst of an open plain on the right bank of the Yunam rivers. As there was no known or recognised boundary mark on the other side of the stream, the Commissioners selected a remarkable cream-coloured peak, called Turam, as the northern limit of the British territory on the left bank of the river. As this peak is situated at the end of one of the spurs of the great snowy chain, already determined as the northern limit of the Lahoul district, it forms a natural continuation of the boundary line from the westward. The bearing of the Turam peak from the Phalang Danda is 9^0 to the northward of west.
>
> "As it appeared that the country to the eastward of the Phalang Danda belong to Spiti, the Commissioners determined that the boundary

> between Spiti and Ladak on the westward should be the Yunam river. A straight line was accordingly drawn from the Phalang Danda to the junction of the first *nala* on the right bank of the Yunam, from which point the Yunam river forms the boundary as far as the junction of the Ts-arap river.
>
> "Almost due north-east form this junction there is a remarkable square rock on the top of the hill, which from its resemblance to a fort, has received the name of Lanka. This curious and well-known peak was selected as another fixed point in the boundary, to which a straight line should be drawn from the junction of the Ts-arap river."

The following passages from Captain Cunningham's journal also describe a portion of the boundary:

> "*Monday, 7th September*—To mouth of Ts-arap river, 6¼ miles. Road good, over a long level, alluvial plain, in the midst of which was a square block of micas late thickly imbedded with large crystals of quartz. This stone, which is 8 feet square and 12 feet high above the ground, is called Lingti by the people of Kulu according to Moorcroft, and *Phalang Danda* by the Ladakis. The only name that we could learn was *Phalang Danda*, which means the boundary stone, the stone being a well-known boundary mark between the States of Kulu and Ladak. Almost due east from the junction of the Ts-arap and Yunam rivers there is, on the top of the hill, remarkable square rock, which has so much resemblance to a fort that it had received the name of *Lanka* from the shepherds and traders who frequent these parts. It is a well-known point, and it can be seen from the Bara Lacha pass as well as from the neighbourhood of the Gunam lake.".

From the Lanka peak to the eastward, the Commissioners, adhering to the principle which they had first laid down, determined that the whole of the Ts-arap valley and its tributaries belonged to the British Government; and that the snowy range on its right bank, which feeds all the northern affluents of the Ts-arap river, should be the boundary between Ladak and the British districts of Spiti. This same range extends towards the east, past the southern end of the Tsomoriri lake, where it forms the well-known boundary between Ladak and the Chinese territory. The Commissioners, therefore, determined that the boundary between Ladak and Spiti should continue from the head of the Ts-arap along this same range to the Chinese boundary, thus including within Spiti all the streams which water that district, and giving to Ladak all the streams which water it south-eastern district of Rupshu.

In 1872 the boundary line was drawn from the village of Narbu Sumdo (lat. 32^0 41', long.78^0 26') along a ridge to the Gya peak. At this point the boundary line of the Kashmir State adjoins Tibet.

Writing in 1875, Mr. Drew, who was for some time the Maharaja's governor of Ladak, stated that :

> "from the Kuenlun mountains southwards to the head of the Changehenmo valley, the boundary between Ladak and Tibet is quite doubtful. From the head of the Changchenmo valley to the south and south-west till Gya peak is reached, the boundary appeared to be fairly well understood as representing actual occupation,"

so'far that it divides pasture lands occupied by the subjects of the Maharaja from those occupied by subjects of Lhasa.

"In the neighbourhood of the Pangong lake,"Mr. Drew observes, "there have been boundary disputes, which may now be said to the latent."

Northern Boundary

At present it extends from the small State of Nagat on the west to the frontier of Tibet on the east. It had not yet been definitely determined. It includes the northern boundaries of Baltistan and Ladak.

Mr. Elias's account — Writing in 1878 about the trade routes to Central Asia, Mr. Elias, the British Joint Commissioner at Leh, said.

> "In the the above description the various loops of the road are followed up to the Yarkand frontier at Shahidula, but it would appear from the latest maps that the Maharaja's territory hardly extends so far as that post, but is limited by the Kuenlun water-parting,i.e., Karakoram."

Mr. Drew's account-Beginning from the north-western end of the line, Mr. Drew describes the boundary thus:

(a) "From Nagar for the most part, and from the upper part of the Hunza valley, the separation is effected by a great and almost impassable ridge of mountains.

(b) "As to the boundary with Yarkand territory, from the Mustgh pass to the Karakoram pass, there is no doubt whatever; a great watershed divides the two territories.

(c) "From the Karakoram pass eastwards to past the meridian of 80^0 there has been no authoritative demarcation, and as the country is quite uninhabited for more than 100 miles in every direction, the actual state of occupation is no guide."

North-Western Boundary

Commissioners were sent to demarcate this boundary, but do not appear to have arrived at definite results.

Colonel Tanner's account-Colonel Tanner of the Survey of India, who was for a time on duty at Gilgit, has described the boundary thus:

> "From the Kaghan boundary the frontier line follows the watershed of the Indus, the Kishan Ganga, and the Astor streams, till it dips into the Indus valley at a point nearly opposite Thalicha. It then follows the Indus for a short distance (say 2miles), after which it strikes up-hill to the watershed of the Gilgit river on one side, with Darel, Tangir, and Hndar on the other. This ridge is followed to a point where the Batras stream rises. It then leads down the Batras and Gakuch watersheds to Hupar on the Gilgit river, ascends the range opposite Hupar so as to take in the slopes above Hatun, circles round that place, descends, crosses the Ishkuman stream, and then strikes up the range, following the ridge to a point north of Bar. From this point ice-fields and glaciers occur, and the boundary is undefined; it eventually strikes a spur which leads south, down to the Hunza river midway between Budlas and Moyun, crosses the river and ascends the slope on the opposite side, after which it is taken along the east of the Himalayas over Rakaposhi to the Mustagh pass."

Western Boundary

Writing in August 1850, Major Abbott stated the western boundary to be complete, and described it in these words:

> "The Jhelum being here full of cultivated islands, boundary pillars are set up in the same, as the boundary ascends the river nearly to Manghuk, where the islands cease, and the deep, rapid, clearly-defined current of the Jhelum requires no columns to aid in exhibiting the boundary. At the confluence of the Nainsuk or Kunhar river with the Jhelum, the boundary quits the latter river and climbs the current of the Nainsuk to Berarkot British and Berarkot of

Jammu where, leaving the river, it strikes to the summit of the Dhab mountain, about 6 miles, and then follows the ridge of that very elevated mountain until lost in the snow, the water falling into the River Kishan Ganga belonging to Jammu, that received by the Nainsuk being British.

"Here also no boundary pillars are required, the mountain ridge being the best possible boundary. In the snow aforesaid terminates the boundary common to British India and Jammu-the British boundary afterwards meeting with lands inhabited by independent tribes."

The Hazara settlement report says that Kaghan, part of the Hazara district, is separated from these independent countries by the Kaghan range, and from Kashmir by the mountain range bordering the left bank of the Kunhar river. So, too, Mr. Drew (Jammu and Kashmir Territories, page 496) states that from the confluence of the Jhelum and Kaghan (or Kunhar) rivers "the boundary line, still fixed and undisputed, follows, the ridge which divides the drainage of Kaghan from that of Kishan Ganga."

Southern Boundary

(1) *From the Jhelum to the Ravi* — The only portion of the British Kashmir boundary which has been demarcated with boundaries is that which lies between the rivers Jhelum and Ravi from a point above Dulial to Madhopur, i.e., from lat. 32^0 58^0, long. 73^0 45', to lat. 32^0 22', long 75 39'.

(2) *From the Ravi to the Lahoul border* — The southward curve of the River Ravi is the boundary for most of the border between Madhopur and a point about 14 miles west-north-west of the town of Chamba. In regard to this portion the Boundary Commissioner explained the principles which he had followed thus:

"It was impossible in some cases to avoid the river boundaries. "When the river was a single clear stream, without cultivated islands, the main current was laid down as the boundary, and one boundary pillar of masonry was planted where the boundary from the east first entered the river, and another where it left the river, though the interval should be of many miles.

"When the boundary ran through the inhabited islands of a river, a in the Jhelum above the town so named, pillars were built all along the line dividing lands, and on either side of the subordinate arms of the river where these formed the boundary.

"Where the boundary line entered a river and ran up the main stream for miles, the boundary pillars were generally of greater size and stability than the ordinary pillars.

"As the rivers in India are constantly encroaching upon the land at their salient curves, and receding from it at their re-entering curves, and village lands become thus transferred from one State to the other, it was ruled that the proprietor of such village should remain, not withstanding, still proprietor, paying his dues to each State according to the extent and value of his lands in either."

The Chamba border was apparently demarcated with pillars by Captain Abbott in 1848-49. It reaches the westward limit of the Lahoul boundary defined by Captain Cunningham's Commission at a point 29 miles due north of the confluence of the Chandra Bhaga tributaries of the Chenab, and about the same distance west-north-west of the Bara Lacha pass. There is apparently no doubt about the boundary on the Chamba border.

Physical Geography

Natural Features

The form of the ground of the Maharaja's territories is thus generally described by Drew :

The lowest part is the strip of plain on the south-west, which is continuous with the great level plain of the Panjab; it is 900 to 1,000 feet above the sea. The mountains begin along a very definite line; the first ridge is a line of hills from 2,000 to 3,000 feet above the sea. Next comes a tract of rugged country which includes various ridges (3,000 to 4,000 feet) running nearly parallel to the first one, with long narrow valleys (2,000 feet) between them.

The foregoing is on the whole a rugged space, partly covered by a low forest or scrub, partly of bare sandstone rock.

Next within is a tract occupied by hills, commonly of 8,000 to 10,000 feet, covered with pasture, or else with forest. These hills are not like the last, in parallel lines, but in ramifications, divided by equally remifying valleys, some of the latter being as low as 2,500 feet.

More lofty mountains are then met with, which rise first to rocky heights, and then to the region of perpetual snow. A great chain of snowy mountains running south-east and north-west divides the drainage of the Chenab and Jhelum rivers form that of the higher branches of the Indus. The summits vary from 27,000 to 15,000 feet. Branches from this enclose the valley of Kashmir (5,000 to 6,000 feet) with hills, many of which are 14,000 to 15,000 feet high.

All beyond is a wide tract of mountainous country, the whole of which is at a high level with peaks from 17,000 to 22,000 feet and more; it is the north-west part of Tibet; and Ladak, Baltistan, and Gilgit are divisions of it. The valleys of this region vary very much in character; in the south-east part are high, level, flat valleys from 1 to 5 miles in width, at elevations of 14,000 and 15,000 feet; from that in a north-west direction their height descends (the space at the same time narrowing, lofty mountains always bounding them) ultimately to as low as 5,000 feet; at the lower levels also are sometimes widenings of the valley bottom.

In a few places are table-lands (too wide to be called valleys) surrounded by mountains. The most remarkable are the Deosai plateau (12,000 to 13,000 feet) and the Lingzithang and Kuenlun plains (16,000 to 17,000 feet).

Vigne remarks that the general character of the southern slopes of the Himalaya is, that they are comparatively bare of trees, although covered with long grass, and that the northern side of Kashmir, although so far from the plains and divided from them by four or five, intervening ranges, is, in accordance with this rule, nearly free from jungle, although covered with long grass and verdure, whilst the southern side on the contrary is nearly one mass of forest. He adds :

> "The reasons for this given to me by the Kashmiris were, in the first place, that no trees would grow where the bank was open to the hot winds from India, and further that no jungle will grow where the ground is not exposed to the rays of the morning sun."

It is certainly true that the fruits of the southern side of the valley are always the best. The reasons thus given are more plausible than satisfactory, but the fact of there being in many places so little forest on the southern abutments of the lower Himalaya, and still less on those of Kashmir, is simply owing to their receiving the rays of the sun more vertically than the long slopes on the opposite side of the valley.

Shaw gives the following graphic description of the difference in the aspect of the country on the two sides of the main Himalayan ridge :

> "The Bara Lacha pass is the boundary between two separate regions distinguished by their physical characters. On the southern side is what may be called the true Himalayan region. Here the gigantic ranges are covered with perpetual snow, furrowed by glaciers, and they rise from amidst dense forests which clothe their flanks up to a certain elevation.

"They are separated by deep gorges, whose sides are precipices, and through which large rivers flow. In fact the scenery is alpine.

"Once across the Bara Lacha pass, however (or any other pass on the same range), you enter a region where all gorges or valleys appear to have been filled up by an encroaching sea of gravel, which has risen to within a few hundred yards of the summits of the ranges. The space between the mountains no longer plunges down in a seemingly bottomless ravine whose sides narrow down till they barely leave room for the stream. Instead of that it is occupied by a broad, high level plain, out of which the summit ranges merely rise like undulations. We noticed the prevalence of the *horizontal* after the *vertical* lines to which the Himālaya has accustomed us. It is like leaving a *Gothic Cathedral* and approaching the *Parthenon.* At the same time, a kind of drought seems to have fallen over the face of the country.

"There are no vast fields of snow to supply streams of water, and no frequent showers to maintain verdure. It seems as if we had here a rough block from which nature intended hereafter to carve out the usual features of a mountain country by some change of climate which would bring snow and ice and water to sweep out the masses of earth or gravel by which the mountain ranges are now glued together. Crossing the Bara Lacha pass we are in barren or Tibetan region, where green spots are about as rare as islands in the ocean, and universal gravel is the rule.

"But there is one deep broad trench, which divides the region into two, lengthwise, that is (roughly) from south-east to north-west. This is the valley of the upper Indus or Ladak. This trench, however, does not descend below 10,000 or 11,000 feet of elevation.

"The round barren hills resemble nothing so much as a gigantic gravel-pit, unless it be a series of heaps of cinders, and have not a blade of verdure on them. There is hardly any snow even on the highest mountains around, for the outer ranges intercept every particle of moisture almost which could fall in the shape of snow.

"So that here at 15,000 feet they have no more snow in winter than on the Kangra range at 5,000 feet. But the dry cold and the bitter wind are in the inverse proportion."

Extent — The dominions of the Kashmir Maharaja extend approximately—

From south-east to north-west	400 miles.
From south-west to north-east	350 miles.
From south to north	240 miles.
From east to west	350 to 400 miles.

The area is estimated at 68,000 square miles.

Plains and Valley

Vigne estimates the plains in the valley of Kashmir, including the *wudars*, to contain, at a rough calculation, about 650 square miles, and that on the neighbouring mountains there is an extent of at least 150 square miles of pasturage. Mr. Vigne's estimate, however, is too low. Mr. Drew considers the area of the valley to be more probably between 1,800 and 1,900 square miles, and a calculation for the purposes of the land settlement in progress, based upon partial measurement compared with the total revenue, shows that the area within which culturable land lies cannot be less than 1,500 to 1,600 square miles, omitting the lakes. The pasture lands are very extensive and valuable; the Kashmir cattle grazing during the summer up to the confines of Ladak, while the higher altitudes are covered with thousands of sheep. But 150 square miles does not even adequately represent the grazing area of the valley itself. About one third of the valley may be said to afford grass, and the swamps and edges of the lakes produce very nourishing food for cows, besides which the slopes of the mountains, properly belonging to the villages below, can hardly be reckoned at less than a rim of two square miles along an edge of,say, 180 miles.-(*Wingate*).

The *margs* or mountain-downs, which are numerous on the tops of the range of hills immediately below the Pir Panjal, and also upon the northern slopes of those mountains which enclose the north-eastern side of the valley, are a peculiar feature of the country; covered with rich pasturage, they afford sustenance during the summer months to large herds of ponies, cattle, sheep, land goats. The principal of these *margs* frequented by Europeans are Gulmarg, above Baramula, to the eastward of Srinagar; Killan, about 1,000 feet above Gulmarg, Sonamarg in the Sind valley, and Tosha Maidan a few miles south of Gulmarg.

The most considerable of the minor valleys are the Lolab to the north, the Sind valley and Tilail to the north-east, the Nowbug and Maru Wardwan valleys to the south-east, and the Lidar valley also south-east.

Ladak is one of the most elevated regions of the earth, and very barren.

The lowest valleys have an elevation of about 9,000 or 10,000 feet.

The principal plains are the Deosai on the north-eastern boundary of Kashmir, the Dipsang, south of the Karakoram pass; the Hanle, the Kiang, the Lingti and the Linzithang or Aksai Chin. These plains are for the most part bare and unproductive, affording few means of subsistence to man or beast. The Hanle plain is very green during the summer months, and gives good feeding to large flocks of sheep.

Mountains

The great Himalaya, which bounds India on the north, in one continuous chain of gigantic peaks, from the southward bend of the Brahmaputra to the holy lake of Manasarowar, is extended to the westward from the sources of the Sutlej to the magnificent peaks of Nanga Parbat at the great bend of the Indus.

This western half forms the watershed parting between the Indus and its five affluents, and also divides the great Hindu family of India from the Bhots of Tibet; lastly, it divides the cold and dry climate of Tibet, with its dearth of trees, from the warm and humid climate of India, with its luxuriance of vegetables productions.

There is one marked difference between the eastern and western Himalayas: the inferior ranges of the eastern chain generally run at right angles to its axis, whereas those of the western chain are mostly disposed in subordinate parallel ranges. Thus we find no less than two distinct and independent ranges to the south of the western Himalaya, both stretching in the same general direction from south-east to north-west. These ranges may be called the middle Himalaya and the outer Himalaya.

Beyond the Himalaya the same system of parallel chains will be observed in at least three distinct ranges of mountains, which may be called the trans-Himalaya, the Kailas or Gangri range, and the Karakoram, beyond which latter is the Kuenlun range, forming the northern slope of the Great Tibetan plateau as the Himalaya form the southern.

The Himalaya divides the headwaters of the Sutlej from those of the Indus, and extends to the western limits of Astor and Rondu. The Kailas or Gangri range runs through the midst of western Tibet along the right bank of the Indus to the junction of the Shyok.

The main range (the western Himalaya) has already been noticed.

The mid-Himalaya divides the valleys of Spiti, Lahoul, Kishtwar,and Kashmir on the north, form those of Kulu, Chamba, and Punch on the south.

The outer Himalaya are those hills which occur between the mid-Himalaya and Siwaliks, or low hills which rise immediately out of the great plain of the Panjab.

These different ranges form the principal features, and consequently the natural boundaries of the Hill States. The whole mass of mountains from the Kuenlun range to the plains of the Panjab had an average breadth of nearly 300 miles. (*Cunningham.*)

Lakes

The lakes of the Kashmir valley are numerous, and may be divided into those in the valley itself, and those upon the mountains surrounding it; of the former the following are the principal : the Dal or"city lake," which is situated on the north-east of Srinagar, and connected with the Jhelum by a canal called the Tsont-i-kul, or "apple-tree canal," which enters it opposite the palace.

The Anchar is situated to the north of Srinagar; it is connected with the Dal by means of the Nali Mar, and it flows into the Sind river near Shadipur. It stretches as far south as the Idgah, where it is called the Kashal Sar; the portion midway near the village of Atsan is known as the Atsan Nambal; the Mar canal passes through it.

The Anchar can scarcely be called a lake; it is caused by the waters of the Sind overflowing the low ground to the north of the city.

The Manas Bal is situated near the right bank of the Jhelum, with which it is connected by a canal which enters it about 400 years below the village of Sumbal.

The Wular is the largest of all the lakes, and is situated to the east of Sopur; the Jhelum flows through it.

Among the mountain lakes the following are the most important:— the Konsa Nag, situated on the top of the Pir Panjal range, above the village of Sedau; the Shisha Nag, situated above the head of the Lidar valley, on the road to the cave of Amarnath; and Gangarbal Nag and Sarbal Nag, situated on the top of Haramuk, which overlooks the north-eastern shore of the Wular.

The city of Srinagar may be said to be surrounded with lakes and morasses, but only those to the north approach the actual limits of the city.

On the south, close of the left bank of the Jhelum, with which it communicates by a canal, the Vetnar stretches for some miles parallel with the belt of dry land which is traversed by the high road to Shupion; near to it is the Nagat Nambal, and, to the west of the road, on the left bank of the Dudh Ganga, lies the head of the Bimman, one of the series of morasses lying between the slopes on the south-west side of the valley and the Jhelum, which extend the entire distance to the Wular lake.

This lake extends from 5 to 6 miles from north to south, and is 2 to 3 miles from east to west at its broadest point. The mountains rise abruptly along its eastern edge.

The average depth of this lake is not more than 7 to 10 feet, though in one place it reaches 26 feet; the water being very clear, the bottom covered with weeds is almost constantly visible.

With a single exception, all the lakes in Ladak are land-locked, and, consequently, more or less salt. The principal are the Pangong lake, the Pangur Tso, the Tsomoriri lake, and the Tso-kar. There are besides some extensive salt lakes scattered about the Kuenlun plains.

The lakes in Ladak are all at a great height; they are moreover gradually drying up, as becomes apparent by the unmistakeable marks of larger surfaces remaining from former times. There are two small mountain lakes in the range of hills east of Jammu, Surninsar, and Mausar, situated respectively 14 and 20 miles distant form Jammu.

One of the principal rivers of Kashmir is the Jhelum, which in its course nearly intersects the valley. Formed by the junction of three streams, the Arpat, the Bring, and the Sandran, which rise at the south-east end of the valley, it receives in its course numerous tributaries; among those which join it by the right bank are the Lidar from the north-east near Islamabad, and the Sind from the east opposite Shadipur, and after emerging from the Wualr lake, the Pohru, which flows into it in the neighbourhood of Sopur. By its left bank it is joined by the combined waters of the Veshau and Rembiara near Murhama, by the Ramchu at Karkarpur, by the Dudh Ganga at Srinagar, and by the Suknag near Shadipur.

The Kishan Ganga, or river of Krishna, which has its sources on the edges of the Deosai plains and in the Tilail valley, is a very considerable stream; it flows in a north-north-westerly direction, and skirts the north-western extremity of Kashmir, joining the Jhelum just below the town of Mozafarabad, opposite the Domel dal bungalow.

The Maru Wardwan river drains the valley of that name; it takes its rise from the Saga glacier on the pass leading into Suru at the north-eastern extremity of the valley, and flows southward, joining the Chenab or Chandra Bhaga above Kishtwar. This latter river traverses Kishtwar, Badrawar, and Riasi, flowing into the plains at Aknur some miles to the west of Jammu.

Of these rivers the Jhelum is navigable from the neighbourhood of Islamabad to Baramula, a distance of about 60 miles. The boats used in Kashmir are of various kinds, *viz., the bahats, dunga, shikara, khuch, tsatawar, larinao, chakwari, parinda, and dinbahnao.*

The bahats is the largest description of boat, and is employed exclusively in the transport of grain and merchandise; some of these barges are of great size, and their draught is considerable, so much so that for about four months in winter there is not sufficient water in the river to float them. They have sloping mat-roofs running down the centre. For these boats a deep channel is maintained in the bed of the river, which enables them to traffic much longer than they otherwise could. The family live on board throughout the year. The smaller *bahats* is called *wahat*.

The *dunga* is the ordinary passenger boat of Kashmir; it is a long flat-bottomed craft, usually about 56 feet in length and 6 feet in width, drawing about 2 feet. It has reed-mat roof, and similar mats are rolled up along the sides; when they are dropped a fairly comfortable room is made. The boat people live in a compartment at the back. In winter the *dungas* engage in carrying *shali* (paddy) to Srinagar.

The *shikara* is of the same shape as the *dunga*, but much smaller, being usually only about 36 feet long, 3½ feet wide, and 1 foot deep. It is chiefly used in and about Srinagar, and answers the purpose of a carriage.

The *khuch* is a very large boat without a roof or awning, and is used for the carriage of goods. It is also called *khachu*.

The *tsatawar* is the smallest, lightest, and swiftest of all the boats used on the Kashmir lakes.

The *larinao* is a State barge, in which the boatmen are seated both before and behind the canopied portion occupied by the passenger. It is a sort of house-boat.

There are two other State boats, the *parinda* (a very light, long craft, with a small canopied space toward the fore part, propelled by 30 to 40 men, and possessing great speed) and the *chikwari*, a more substantial boat with a heavier canopy. All the boats on the Jhelum are propelled by heart-shaped paddles.

The *bahats*, or large grain-boats, are generally worked by poles, men on either side descending an inclined plane from the roof of the boat and chanting as they push.

The crew of the *dunga* are most useful, and on shore will act in almost any capacity. Lastly, there is the dinbahnao (or *dhemnao*), a little "dug-out", used for the cultivation of the melon-beds of the Dal lake, and for carrying vegetables, & c., to market. It is worked by a man or woman, squatted in the bow, with one paddle.

The Jhelum is spanned by thirteen bridges in its course through the valley of Kashmir; they are of peculiar construction and are called *kadals*.

In Ladak and Baltistan the principal river is the Indus, which flows in a general north-west direction through the whole length of these two provinces in a deep trough between the trans-Himalayan range on its left bank and the Kailas and Karakoram ranges on its right bank. Its chief tributaries on the left bank are the Hanle, Zanskar river, the Dras and Astor rivers, while on the right bank it receives the Shyok, the Shigar, and the Gilgit rivers. The Shyok receives the Nubra and the Changchenmo rivers; while the Shigar is formed by the junction of the Basha and Braldu rivers.

Both the Jhelum and the Chenab also join the Indus after it has entered the plains of the Panjab. The most remarkable feature about the Indus and its tributaries is the general parallelism of their courses, which has been determined by the direction of the principal mountain chains, and the same similarity may be observed in the peculiar knee-bends which are common to all the rivers of the Panjab. For the curious sweep southward, which occurs in the Sutlej below Bilaspur, is also found in all the other river, in the Beas below Hajipur; in the Ravi near Basaoli; in the Chenab below Kishtwar; in the Jhelum below Mozafarabad; and in the Indus at the junction of the Gilgit river.

Cunningham gives the following account of the passage of rivers in Ladak:

Passage of Rivers

The rivers are generally crossed by fording. *Gal* is the Tibetan term for a ford. In summer, the morning is the best time for fording, for after 10 or 11 a.m. the waters are much increased by the melting snows.

Ferry (grukha)

The common people are usually ferried over on a single inflated skin, but influential men are usually taken over on a raft, formed by placing a *charpai* on two inflated skins. The Shyok, opposite Satti, is crossed by boat in summer.

Bridges

There are two kinds of bridges met with in Ladak-

(1) The *zampa* or wooden bridge, made usually of large beams of poplars. Good specimens are to be seen at Lah and Khalsi.

(2) The *chug-zam*, or suspension bridge, is common on the Indus and Shyok, above their junction. It is formed of two stout ropes of twisted birch twigs, about the thickness of a man's arm.

The *chug-zam* is a very cheap and easy mode of bridging a stream, and is, when new and well constructed, quite safe. The passage of old bridges is, however, often both difficult and dangerous. In them the suspension ropes form a great curve; the sides are frequently unwattled and completely open, and the roadway sometimes reduced to a single rope. (*Cunningham.*)

Climate

Owing to the great variations of level, the climate must necessarily be different for every region.

The temperature ranges from more than the tropical heat of the Panjab summer, to such an intensity of cold as keeps perpetual snow on the mountains. In inhabited places even, the variation is such, that in the lower parts the people go about nearly unclad; in the higher, sheepskins are worn, and in some places the people are confined to their houses for seven months in the year by snow. The element of moisture also causes much variety in climate, and consequently in aspect of country.

Regions of four different degrees may be roughly distinguished as follow:

(1) Where the periodical rains prevail, as in the southern portions of British territory, including the outer hills and middle mountains.

(2) Where the rains do not reach, but there is rainfall enough for all crops, but rice, without irrigation. This area embraces Kashmir.

(3) Where irrigation is necessary for crops, and the hillsides are bare, with the exception of a little forest. This is a semi-Tibetan climate, and includes Astor, part of Gilgit and of Baltistan.

(4) A nearly rainless tract, where irrigation is necessary for crops, and the whole country is entirely bare. This has a Tibetan climate and includes the rest of Gilgit, the greater part of Baltistan, and all Ladak.

Communications

Roads

The cart-road now under construction up the Jhelum valley from Mari to Srinagar is the only road practicable for wheeled traffic. The remainder are only practicable for pack animals. Mr. Girdlestone says of the roads:

> "On land the means of communication in the towns are narrow, tortuous streets, whose uneven pavemnet is excruciating to the feet, and in the country the tracks worn by passengers and cattle, and following

the inequalities of the ground. In the side valleys, the footpath soon becomes difficult as the upper gorges are reached."

Mr. Wynne reported in 1873 that the Maharaja intended henceforth to devote to the improvement of roads an annual sum of half a lakh of *chilki* (ten-anna) rupees. Up to date little or nothing has been done towards the repairs of the roads.

To Srinagar the principal roads from India are:

(a) The Mari road, nearly finished, suitable for wheeled traffic, and with little alteration for a narrow-gauge line.

(b) The Pir Panjal route, which is very bad and much less used than formerly. Ponies go along it with difficulty.

(c) The Sialkot-Jammu-Srinagar route, a good deal used by natives, suitable for baggage animals.

From Srinagar the principal roads are :

(a) To Gilgit *via* the Kamri or Dorikun passes, Astor and Bunji. This road is continued to Chitral and then by the Dorah pass into Zebak. It is passable for baggage animals, but difficult in places.

(b) To Lah *via* the Zoji La and and thence on to Yarkand. A certain amount of money is being yearly spent by the Joint Commissioners on this road, and consequently it is generally very good going for baggage animals.

(c) To Skardu *via* the Zoji La and Indus valley. From where it leaves the Leh road this road is extremely bad and barely passable for baggage animals.

In the valley the best road is perhaps that leading from Srinagar to Shupion, and thence to the Pir Panjal pass. Other well-marked tracks are the roads from Baramula to Srinagar on the one side, and to Islamabad and Vernag and thence to the Banihal pass on the other side; the road to Leh up the Sind valley and thence over the Zoji La, and the road to Gilgit following the course of the Jhelum, and then skirting the east side of the Wular lake. All the roads appear to date from the time of the Delhi Emperors. Of the village paths, it may be said that from any large village there is usually a decent track leading to Srinagar. But communication between villages is very difficult owing to rivers, canals, unbridged irrigation cuttings, rice-lands, and swamps. On all main tracks the villagers maintain little crossings of logs covered with mud over irrigation canals and streams. Near Srinagar the roads generally begin with a mile or two of poplar avenue. The traffic is by ponies, mules, and coolies. (*Wingate*)

Bellew gives the following interesting account of the mode of tracking out a pass by the aid of yaks on the high passes of Ladak :

> "Before essaying the passage of the glacier, it is customary to drive a herd of ten or twelve yaks across to ascertain the route. These,in their way, sagacious animals, when urged up the side of the glacier, crowd together for a consultation on its edges, and after a good deal of grunting one of them takes the lead,the other following in single file. The leader, with his nose down on the snow, sniffs and grunts his way cautiously, and when tired, falls back for the next to take up the lead till land is reached on the other side. The Bhots follow the track of their brutes and erect little pillars of snow here and there along the route by way of guide in case of mists or snow obscuring the track."

Not unfrequently in the valley of the Indus, blocks of rocks are set in motion by the step of the wild sheep. These stone avalanches are of constant occurrence in these hills after rain and during the period the winter snows are melting away; and they are one of the most dreaded dangers, the traveller had to face. And, hence, it is that the Bhot never thinks of camping in the open in these valleys, but always take shelter in the cavern of some secure bank, or scoops out, or walls in, some ready hollow under the lee of any firm rock.

Sandals

In the Kashmir valley the better class of people wear *chaplis,* which consist of a soft-leather sock, laced, and over it a strong, think leather sole, bound to the foot by thngs, terminating in one buckle. Coolies, both in the valley and in the mountains, wear sandals made of rice-straw. *Chaplis* are useless in wet weathere, but the straw-shoe is good and safe, and worn over the European boot is comfortable, and safe for mountain climbing. (*Wingate.*)

The Tibetan sandals, or mocassins, will wear for a surprisingly long time, provided they do not get wet. They are made of ibex-skin, and on account of their roughness and pliability they are admirably adapted to walking over steep or dangerous paths.

Communications

Water

In the valley of Kashmir the Jhelum and the canals connected with it are much used as a means of communication, and have hitherto served all the purposes of traffic.

To avoid the necessity of crossing the dangerous Wular lake, through which flows the main stream of the Jhelum, a navigable canal was constructed in very early times to connect Sopur with Srinagar.

This canal, which is called the Naru, leaves the left bank of the river immediately below Shadipur and runs southward, dividing into two branches, the smaller of which continues straight on through the marshes to Patan and Palhallan, while the other turns to the right and finally enters the southern portion of the Wular lake.

When the water is high enough, this, which is the shorter route, is always selected by the boatmen when passing between Srinagar and Baramula.

Irrigation channels are numerous; of these the Shahkul canal in the Khourpara *pargana*, the Naindi and Ninnar canals, near Islamabad, are among the most important.

The construction of a canal connecting Aknur with Jammu was commenced, but proving a failure was abandoned; it is called the Shahnahar canal. Rafts and small boats are floated down the Chenab, but is cannot be called navigable above Aknur. There are falls and rapids, near where the river makes the knee-bend, which are dangerous. The Indus is too rapid to be navigated in any part of its course through the Kashmir State.

Postal

The earliest rules regarding postal communication with Kashmir were contained in Panjab Notification No. 673, dated 16th March 1867, and provided for the conveyance of a sealed bag to and from the British Officer on duty at Srinagar, by the Maharaja's agency. A fee equal to half the British postage was levied, on behalf of the Maharaja, on all letters to and from visitors in the valley, who used what was termed "the Resident's dak."

Changes in 1870-71

In 1870 the direct connection of the Srinagar post office with the office of the Officer on Special Duty was severed; but the Srinagar post office has always since been maintained by the Imperial post office during the Kashmir season of each year. At first sanction was experimentally given in 1870; but it was continued permanently in 1871. The establishment was as follows:

1 Deputy Postmaster	100 per mensem.
1 Clerk	30 per mensem.
1 Munshif	10 per mensem.
2 Peons	14 per mensem.
Stationery	6 per mensem.

From 1st January 1886 Srinagar was constituted a permanent head office, which is now open throughout the year. The time of transit between Sialkot and Srinagar averages about 63 hours. The present establishment consists of_

1 Postmaster	150 per mensem.
2 Clerks	30 per mensem.
1 clerk	20 per mensem.
2 Postmen	14 per mensem.
Stationery allowance	6 per mensem.

Gazetteer of Kashmir and Ladak, Superintendent of Government Printing Press, Calcutta, 1890.

2

Geography of Ladhak

By
Alexander Cunningham

1.—GENERAL DESCRIPTION

The most striking feature in the physical aspect of Ladak is the parallelism of its mountain-ranges, which stretch through the country from south-east to north-west. This general direction of the mountain-chains determines the courses of the rivers as well as the boundaries of the natural divisions of the country. The general aspect of Ladak is extreme barrenness. Seen from above, the country would appear a mere succession of yellow plains and barren mountains capped with snow, land the lakes of Pangkong and Tshomo Riri would seem like bright oases amidst a vast desert of rock and sand. No trace of man nor of human habitations would meet the eye: and even the large spots of cultivated land would be but small specks on the mighty waste of a deserted world. But a closer view would show many fertile tracts along the rivers, covered with luxuriant crops, land many picturesque monasteries, from which the chant of human voices ascends on high in daily prayer and praise. The yellow plains along the Indus would then be seen covered with flocks of the shawl-wool goat, and all the principal thoroughfares of the country dotted with numerous flocks of sheep laden with the merchandise of China and of India.

The territory of Ladak is one of the most elevated regions of the earth. Its different valleys lie along the head-waters of the Indus, the Sutluj, and the Chenab; and the joint effects of elevation and of isolation amidst snowy mountains produce perhaps the most singular climate in the known world. Burning heat by day is succeeded by piercing cold at night, and everything is parched by the extreme dryness of the air. The rarefied atmosphere offers but little impediment to the sun's rays, which during a short summer are sufficiently powerful to ripen barley at an elevation of 15,000 feet, although the temperature falls below the freezing point every night. This climate is equally favourable to animal life. The plains between 16,000 and 17,000 feet are covered with wild horses and hares and immense flocks of domestic goats and sheep; and the slopes of the hills up to 19,000 feet abound with marmots and Alpine hares. Such is the extreme dryness of the atmosphere, that no rain falls and but little snow, and both meats and fruits are cured by mere exposure to the air.

2.—BOUNDARIES AND EXTENT

Ladhak is the most westerly country occupied by the Tibetan race who profess the Buddhist faith. On the north it is divided by the Karakoram mountains from the Chinese district of Kotan. To the east and south-east are the Chinese districts of Rudok and Chumurti; and to the south are the districts of Lahul and Spiti, now attached to British India, but formerly belonging to Ladak. To the west lie Kashmir and Balti, the former separated by the western Himalaya, and the latter by an imaginary line drawn from the mouth of the Dras river to the sources of the Nubra river.

Its greatest extent is from north-west to south-east, from the head of the Dras river, in longitude 75° 30', to Chibra, on the Indus, in longitude 79° 10', a distance of 240 miles. Its greatest breadth is 290 miles, from the Karakoram Pass, in north latitude 35° 10', to the Rotang Pass in Lahul, in latitude 32° 25'. Its mean length is 200 miles, and its mean breadth 150 miles. Its whole extent is therefore only 30,000 square miles.

The natural divisions of the country are: 1st, Nubra on the Shayok: 2nd, Ladak Proper, on the Indus: 3rd, Zanskar, on the Zanskar river: 4th, Rukchu, around the lakes of Tshomo Riri and Tsho-Kar: 5th, Purik, Suru, and Dras, on the different branches of the Dras river: 6th, Spiti, on the Spiti river: and 7th, Lahul, on the Chandra and Bhaga, or head-waters of the Chenab. These also are the actual divisions of the country, for the natural boundaries of a mountainous district generally remain unaltered, in spite of the changes wrought by war and religion.

Ladak is divided politically between Maharaja Gulab Singh and the East-India Company. To the former belong all the northern districts, to the latter only the two southern districts of Lahul and Spiti.

3.—DIFFERENT NAMES OF LADAK.

Ladak, in Tibetan *La-tags*, is the most common name of the country; but it is also called *Mar-yul*, or Low-land or Red-land, and *Kha-chan-pa*, or Snow-land, both of which names are used by the old Chinese travellers; by Fa-Hian, A.D. 400, who calls the kingdom *Kie-chha*; and by Hwan Thsang, A.D. 640, who calls it *Ma-lo-pho*. The name of *Kha-chan-pa*, or Snowland, is also applied to the Lhasan kingdom of Great Tibet. The two central districts of Great Tibet are *dBus*, and *gTsang*, usually pronounced *U* and *Tsang*, or jointly *U-Tsang*. But the uncorrupted pronunciation is preserved by Ptolemy in *Dubase*, who must be the people of dBus; and in Turner's *Pue-koa-chin*, which is most probably *dBus-Kha-pa-chan*, or the "snowy land of *dBus*". Ladak was formerly subject to Lhasa, to which it paid a small tribute until A.D. 1834, when it was seized by Zorawar Singh, the enterprising general of Maharaja Gulab Singh, of Jammu; and it now forms a part of his new kingdom of Kashmir.

Ladak is inhabited by a peculiar race of people, who call themselves *Bot-pa*, who speak a peculiar language called Tibetan, and who profess the religion of Buddha, under a peculiar hierarchy of monks called Lamas. The name of Tibet is entirely unknown to the people as well as to the Indians, who call them Bhotiyas, and their country Bhutan. The use of the names of Bot and Bhutan is probably not older than the tenth or twelfth century, when the Buddhists, having been expelled from India, the hill country in which they settled naturally acquired the name of Bauddha-sthan or Bauddh-than, and Bod-tan or Bot.

According to Klaproth, Tibet is a Mogul word, which should more properly be written Tübet. But the name of Tibat is mentioned by Abu Zaid Al Hasan, in A.D. 915, by Ibn Haukal in about A.D.950, by Abu Rihan in 1030, land afterwards by Edrisi in A.D.1154, all long prior to the Mogul conquests of Changez Khan in the 13th century, before whose time it is highly improbable that any Mogul names could have been in use in Persia. Mir Izzet Ullah says that Tibet is a Turki word signifying shawl-wood: but I should think the shawlwool was called Tibeti because it came from Tibet. One might as well derive the name of India from indigo. There is no trace of the name of Tibet nor even of Bot in any of the classical authors: But the people are most probably described under the name of Seres, the inhabitants of Chinese Tartary, from whom the western merchants obtained their silks. According to Pausanias, "the Greeks called the silkworm *Ser*, but the people of Serika probably gave it another name." Now the Tibetans call a worm *Srin*, or *Srin-bu*, and the silkworm *Dar-kyi-Srin*; and Pausanias says that the silkworm was twice the size of a beetle. As the Greeks had not seen the silkworm when they first used the name of Ser, it seems to me more than probable that they would have adopted the native name rather than have invented one of their own.

4.—DISTRICTS OF LADAK

The different districts of Ladak have been partially named according to their relative geographical positions; as *Nub-ra*, the western district (or Wessex), and *Lho-yul*, the southern country (or Suffolk). To the south-east of Ladak, but to the north of *Ngari*, lies the extensive province of *Chang Thang*, or the "northern plains." Ladak itself is called Mar-yul or Low-land, perhaps from its inferior elevation to all the surrounding districts.

Nubra, or the north-western district of Ladak, includes all the country drained by the Nubra and Shayok rivers. It is by far the largest district in the country, being about 128 miles in length by 72 miles in breadth, with an area of 9,200 square miles. It is bounded on the north by the Karakoram mountains, and on the south by the Kailas range, which divides the Indus from the Shayok; and it extends from the frontier of Balti, in east longitude 77^0, to the Pangkong lake on the borders of Rudok. The mean elevation of the inhabited parts of the country, from an average of fourteen observations at different places, is 12,763 feet.

Ladak is the central and most populous district of the country, from which it is sometimes called *Mang-yul*, or the "district of many people." It stretches along the Indus in a north-westerly direction from Rukchu to the frontier of Balti, a length of 120 miles, with an average breadth of 33 miles. Its area is about 4,000 square miles, and the mean elevation of the inhabited portions, as deduced from observations along the Indus, is 11,500 feet.

Zanskar includes all the country lying along the two great branches of the Zanskar river, in a general direction from south-east to north-west. It is bounded by Ladak on the north, by Rukchu on the east, by Lahul on the south, and by the small districts of Purik and Wanla on the west. The southern boundary is formed by the great Himalaya itself, the western boundary by the transverse range of Singge La, and the northern boundary by the Trans-Himalayan chain. Its greatest length is 72 miles, but its mean length is not more than 56 miles, and its mean breadth is about the same, or 55 miles. It has an area of 3,000 square miles, and a mean elevation of 13,154 feet, as deduced from seven different observations along the course of the valley. The name of *Zangs-kar* means "white copper" or brass; but I have no idea why it is so named.

Rukchu is the most elevated district in Ladak, and one of the loftiest inhabited regions in the known world. The mean height of the plains, as determined from twenty-one different spots where I encamped in 1846 and 1847, is 15,634 feet. This is the mean height of the great plain of Kyang, which extends from the foot of the Thung-lung Pass to the fords of the Sum-Gal, a length of 35 miles. It is also the height of the plains around the *Tsho-kar*, or White Lake, and of the long sloping plains from the Lanak ridge to the Para river. Rukchu is bounded on the north by Ladak Proper, on the east by the Chinese district of Chumurti, on the south by Lahul and Spiti, and on the west by Zanskar. Its length from the Thung-lung Pass to the head of the Hanle river is 90 miles, and its mean breadth about 62 miles, which give an area of 5,500 square miles.

Purik, Suru, land *Dras* are three small districts to the west of Zanskar, on the high road between Kashmir and Le. To Purik belong the villages of the Waka and Phugal rivers, from their sources in the transverse range of Singge La to Kargyil, below their junction. The principal places in Purik are Mulbil, Paskyum, and Sod, each of which once had a petty chief of its own. *Suru* also owned a petty chief who lived at Lung Kartse, the principal place in the valley. The river is sometimes called by this name, but more generally by that of Suru. The Suru river joins the Waka-chu immediately below Kargyil. *Dras* is the most westerly of these small districts. Its Tibetan name of Hem-babs (snow-fed or snow descended) is descriptive of its most striking peculiarity, as the most snowy district of Ladak. It owes this peculiarity to the great depression in the Himalaya, at the head of the Dras river, which allows the constantly humid vapours of Kashmir to pass to the north of the mountains, where they become condensed by the cold, and are precipitated in rain or snow, according to the season of the year. These small districts extend in length from the frontier of Balti to Zanskar, a distance of 84 miles, land in breadth from the head of the Suru valley to the Photo-la, a distance of 50 miles. The area is 4,200 square miles, and the mean height of the inhabited parts, as determined by the elevation of thirteen camps, is 11,196 feet.

Spiti is bounded on the north by Rukchu, on the west by Lahul and Kullu, on the south by Kanawar, and on the east by the Chinese district of Chumurti. It comprises the whole valley of the Spiti river, from its source to the junction of the Para, a length of about 64 miles. Its mean length is not more than 52 miles, and its mean breadth only 36 miles, which give an area of about 1,900 square miles. The mean elevation of the inhabited parts, as determined by the heights of eight camps, is 12, 986 feet.

Lahul (or Lho-yul, the "southern district") is bounded on the north by Zanskar and Rukchu, on the west by Kashtwar, on the south by Chamba and Kullu, and on the east by Spiti. It comprises the valleys of the Chandra and Bhaga rivers, as well as that of the Chandra Bhaga or united stream as far as `Treloknath, below which the people are of Hindu race and religion, with but little admixture of Tibetan blood. With the single exception of the valley of the Indus, Lahul possesses more cultivable land, and a less rigorous climate than any of the other districts of Ladak. There the currant and the gooseberry are both found wild, and in the lower parts of the valley towards Treloknath the mountain slopes are covered with fir trees. Like Kanawar, Lahul partakes somewhat of the climate and productions of India as well as of those of Tibet. The people, their language, and their dwellings are mostly Tibetan, but with a strong mixture of Indian origin. Lahul is 68 miles in length by 34 in breadth, which give an area of 2,312 square miles. The mean elevation of its inhabited parts, as determined by the heights of nine camps, is 11,063 feet.

The following table of the extent and mean elevation of the different districts of Ladak is added for the sake of comparison.

		Extent in sq. miles.		Mean height.
British. M. Gulab Sing.	Nubra	9,216		12,763
	Ladak	3,960		11,500
	Zanskar	3,080		13,154
	Rukchu	5,580		15,634
	Purik-Suru-Dras	4,200		11,196
			26,036	
	Spiti	2,312		12,986
	Lahul	1,872		11,063
			4,184	
		Total sq. miles	30,220	
			Mean height	12,613

5. —NEIGHBOURING COUNTRIES

The countries to the north, the west, and the south of Ladak are inhabited by people who speak at least four languages quite distinct from Tibetan. To the north the people of Yarkand and Kotan speak Turki; to the west, beyond Balti, the people Astor, Gilget, and Hunza Nager speak different dialects of Dardu, while the Kashmiries have a language peculiar to themselves, and to the south the people of Chamba, Kullu, and Bisahar, speak a dialect of Hindi, which is chiefly derived from Sanskrit. To the east and south-west the people of Rudok, Chang-Thang, and Ngari speak Tibetan only.

To the north of the Karakoram range, lie the Chinese districts of Yarkand, Kotan and Kashgar, which, with the exception of the Chinese functionaries, and Tartar soldiers, are wholly peopled by Musulmans. As I found it difficult to obtain any truth-like information regarding the statistics of these countries, I confined my inquiries to their natural productions, in the hope of meeting with something that would tend to determine their approximate height above the sea. All my informants agreed in stating that the people of these countries usually drove two and three horses abreast in their carriages or wagons, and that even four horses were occasionally harnessed abreast. On hearing this, I asked the width of the streets, but I obtained no satisfactory reply. Some said ten yards, some twenty yards: but when asked to mark out the width on the ground, not one of them showed more than twenty-five feet.

Yarkand. Moorcroft was informed that the population of Yarkand was between 50,000 and 60,000, a number which would require about 10,000houses. Of these I was told that 500 houses belonged to Kashmiris alone, and thirty or thirty-two to Argons, or half-bloods. The productions were stated as follows.

Crops	*Vegetables*	*Fruits*	*Trees*
Rice	Cucumber	Grapes	Deoḍa
Jawar	Kadu	Apricots	Plane
Wheat	Tarohi	Peaches	Elaeaguns M.
Barley	Onions	Apples	
Pease	Radishes	Pears	
Alsi	Turnips	Plums	
Mung	Carrots	Mulberries	
Urd	Spinach	Melons	
Masur			

In the hill provinces of India we know that the deodar does not flourish under 5,000 feet, and that rise is seldom seen above 6,000 feet. We know, also, that both are found in Kashmir, which has a mean elevation of 5,300 feet. But as

Yarkand lies at least four degrees to the northward of Kashmir, the limits of the growth of deodars and of rice will of course of reduced. I do not, therefore, estimate the height of Yarkand at more than 4,000 feet above the sea.

At *Kotan* and *Aksu* the produce was said to be the same, with the sole additon of *gram* or pulse (Cicer arietinum), I should therefore estimate the height of these places at somewhat less, or between 3,500 and 4,000 feet.

The produce of *Kashgar* was said to be much the same as at Yarkand, with the single exception of rice, of which but very little is grown. As this indicates a somewhat higher elevation than Yarkand, I estimate the height of Kashgar at about 4,500 feet above the sea.

The districts lying along the Indus, to the westward of Ladak, are inhabited by two distinct races,the Tibetans, who have become Musulmans, and the Dards. They speak wholly different languages, and even the Dards themselves speak three distinct dialects, which have but few words common to all. The Tibetan districts are Khapolor, Chhorbad, land Keris, on the Shayok, Khartakshe, Totte, and Parguta, on the Singge-chu, Shigar, on the Shigar river, and Balti and Rongdo, on the Indus. The district of Astor, also, must once have belonged to the Tibetan race, as the chief even now bears the title of *Makpon*, and traces of descent from the same common ancestor as the Gyalpos of Balti, and several of the other states.

Chhorbad extends along the Shayok river, from Chulung, on the frontier of Ladak, to Daho, on the boundary of Khapolor, a distance of forty-two miles. Beyond this, Khapolor stretches twenty-five miles further down the Shayok, the whole length of the chiefship being sixty-seven miles. As the mean breadth is about thirty miles, the area will be 2,010 square miles. The mean height of the villages is about 9,000 feet. The chiefs of Khapolor have for several generations acknowledged the supremacy of the Gyalpos of Balti, but their ancestors most probably had possession of the country for several centuries before the rise of the Balti dynasty, whose very title of *Makpon*, or "General," betrays that they are the descendants of some military chief. The chiefs of Khapolor and Keris, who both trace their families up from Bewan-cho, declare that all the chiefs of these countries are descended from Bikam, the tenth generation from Bewan-cho. But Ahmed Shah of Balti, and the other chiefs of his family, traced their origin to a Fakir, who had married the daughter and only child of the reigning Gyalpo. The probability is, that the Makpons are descended from an adventurer named Bokha, who about A.D. 1500, established himself in the valley of the Indus, and obtained the title of *Makpon*, or General.

The following is the genealogy of the Gyalpos of Khapolor. It opens with Sultan Sikander, or Alexander the Great, whose successors were Abraham and Isaac. This part is evidently fabulous, but from Sultan Yagu, the 39th name, the list is perhaps tolerably correct, for the name of Yagu has descended to the present day as a title in the family, the present chief being styled Sultan Yagu Daolat Ali Khan. As there are sixty-seven princes in all, down to this time, the approximate date of Sultan Yagu's accession to power may be found by allowing a period of fifteen years for each reign. This estimates fixes the rise of Sultan Yagu in A.D. 1410, the very year in which Sikander Butshikan, the Idol-breaker of Kashmir, died. The coincidence of time is curious, and it is not improbable that Sultan Yagu may have been despatched by the bigoted Sikander to propagate the religion of Muhammed amongst the Tibetans on the Indus.

GYALPOS OF KHAPOLOR.

	Names	*Probable Date*
1	Sultan Sikandar	
2	" Ibrahim	
3	" Ishak	

Contd....

	Names	Probable Date
4	" Abdul Ralimad	
5	" Mir Barahir	
6	" Arman Samahir	
7	" Beshrab Nam	
8	" Tinlu Tung	
9	" Sultan Mahmud	
10	" Mehndi Ghazali	
11	" Ibrahim	
12	" Malik Haider Shah	
13	Sultan Malik Ghazali	
14	" Malik Shah	
15	" Juned Shah	
16	" Haider Shah	
17	" Haider Karar	
18	" Shah Ibrahim	
19	" Johar Fani	
20	" Najm Malik	
21	" Malik Rustam	
22	" Mehndi Mir	
23	" Malik Mir	
24	" Malik Jahar	
25	Saad Ulla Khan	
26	" Karun Beg	
27	" Jalil Khan	
28	" Rustam Beg	
29	" Atta Ulla Khan	
30	" Khalil Khan	
31	Saad Yakub Khan	

Contd....

		Names	Probable Date
32	Saad	Mir Ghazi	
33	"	Malik Purnur	
34	"	Babur Malik	
35	"	Mokhim Khan	
36	"	Shah Azim Beg	
37	"	Gohar Beg	
38	"	Malik Shah Shuja	A.D.
39	Sultan Yagu		1410
40	"	Yagu Latif Beg	1425
41	"	Yagu Sher Ghazi	1440
42	"	Yagu Ahmed Ghazi	1455
43	"	Nur Ghazi	1470
44	"	Alemgir Ghazi	1485
45	"	Biwan-Cho	1500
46	"	Hil Ghazi	1515
47	"	Sher Ghazi	1530
48	"	Beg Mantar	1545
49	"	Torab Khan	1560
50	"	Salmunde	1575
51	"	Brol De	1590
52	"	Malik Baz	1605
53	"	Arzona	1620
54	"	Tikam	1635
55	"	Bikam	1650
56	"	Kurkor	1665
57	"	Bairam	1680
58	"	Mir Khan	1695
59	"	Ibrahim	1710

Contd....

		Names	Probable Date	
60	"	Ghazi Mir Cho	1725	
61	"	Husen Khan	1740	
62	"	Rahim Khan	1755	
63	"	Hatim Khan	1770	
64	"	Daolut Khan	1785	
65	"	Mahmud Ali Khan	1800	
66	"	Yahia Khan	1815	
67	"	Daolut Ali Khan has a son, Md. Ali Khan.	1830	now reigning.

Keris. The small district of Keris is situated along the lower course of the Shayok, just above its junction with the Indus. It is above sixteen miles in length, and ten miies in mean breadth. Its area is not more than 160 square miles, and the mean height of its villages above the sea is about 8,000 feet. The present chief, Kuram Ali Khan, claims descent from Biwan-cho, one of the Gyalpos of Khapolor, and he gives the following genealogy of that family.

	Names	Probable Date	
1	Biwan-cho	1500	
2	Leo	1540	
3	Raja Ali Mir Sher	1575	
4	Ahmed Mir	1610	
5	Amir	1645	
6	Ali Khan	1680	reigning
7	Mir-Beg	1715	in A.D.
8	Mirza-Beg	1750	1685.
9	Zulfikar Khan	1785	
10	Kuram Ali Khan	1820	

Parguta. The present chiefship of Parguta extends from Sarmik ten miles above the confluence of the Shayok and Indus, to Goltari, near the junction of the Dras river, thus including both Khartakshe (or Khar-Mang) and Tolti. Its length is about forty-three miles; its mean breadth thirty-two miles; and its area 1,548 square miles. The mean height of its villages above the sea is about 7,800 feet.

The Gyalpo of Parguta claims to be the eleventh in descent from the Makpon Bokka, who is perhaps the same as the fakir whom Vigne mentions as thé progenitor of all the Makpon families. The following is the genealogy, with the probable dates of accession.

	Names	*Probable Date*
1	Makpon Bokha	1500
2	" Sher	1530
3	" Ghazi	1560
4	" Ali Sher Khan	1590
5	" Ahmed Khan	1620
6	" Sher Shah	1650
7	" Azizcho	1680
8	" Azim Khan	1710
9	" Sahadat Khan	1740
10	" Abdul Rahim	1770
11	Mahomed Ali	1800
12	Ali Sher Khan	1830
	Son, Jafar Ali Khan.	

Ali Sher Khan, the fourth in descent from Bokha, conquered Ladak and Khapolor, and bequeathed them to his son, Ahmed Khan, who was the last of the supreme Makpons. On his death the country was divided amongst his sons: but the former chief of Khapolor soon declared his independence, and ejected the new ruler, Sultan Khan. The Gyalpos of Balti always selected their wives from this family, as the most exalted of their neighbours.

Shigar. The little chiefship of Shigar is confined entirely to the valley of the Shigar river, a large feeder of the Indus, to the north of Balti. Its length, from south-east to north-west, is seventy-two miles, and its breadth thirty-six miles. Its area is 2,592 square miles; and the probable mean height of its villages above the sea is not less than 8,000 feet. Shigar possesses a Gyalpo of its own, but he has generally been subject to the chiefs of Balti. The following genealogy was obtained from Suliman Khan, the present chief of Shigar. It is curious, for two reasons-first, because the title of *Tham*, or King, borne by the earlier princes, proves that the family must be connected with the Dards of Hunza-Nager, whose chiefs bear the same title at present; and second, because the approximate date obtained for the first chief's accession, agrees very nearly with that of Sultan Yagu, of Khapolor. It is probable, therefore, that the Khapolor and Shigar families both owe their rise to some common cause, perhaps connected with the extension of the Muhammedan religion.

	Names	*Probable Date*
1	Amachah	1440
2	Chah-tham	1455
3	Chama-tham	1470
4	Yaksir Gao-tham	1485
5	Khomulgo tham	1500
6	Gobulgo tham	1515
7	Khan	1530
8	Makhan	1545
9	Ram	1560
10	Rahmum	1575

Contd.....

	Names	Probable Date
11	Daolat Shah	1590
12	Haripal Marchak	1605
13	Ambarot	1620
14	Ghazi Mir	1635
15	Ali Mir	1650
16	Ama Chan De	1665
17	Ghir-ze	1680
18	Haidar Khan	1695
19	Husan Khan	1710
20	Imam Kuli Khan	1725
21	Kuli Khan	1740
22	Azem Khan	1755
23	Ali Khan	1770
24	Husen Khan	1785
25	Mohammed Khan	1800
26	Kuli Khan	1815
27	Suliman Khan	1830

Balti, or *Balti-yul*, is called Palolo, or Balor, by the Dards, and *Nang-kod* by the Tibetans. Balti is the most common name, and perhaps the oldest, as it is preserved by Ptolemy in Byltae. The country is also frequently called Skardo, from the name of its well-known fort and capital. This name means either the "inclosed place," or more probably the "starry place," as the Lamas of Ladak write the name, *Skar-ma-mDo*. Vigne states that the Botis of Ladak call it Sagar-khoad, which is only a variety of the same; for Skar-kod means simply the "starry building." The Dogra soldiers always call the place Kardo; but the true name, as written by the Tibetans, is Skardo.

Balti proper is a small district bounded by Shigar on the north, by Keris and Parguta on the east, by Gures on the south, and by Astor and Rongdo on the west. Including the table-land of Deotsu, it is about sixty miles long and thirty-six miles broad. Its area is about 2,160 square miles, and the mean height of its villages above the sea is about 7,000 feet.

The Gyalpos of Balti trace their descent from a Fakir who married the daughter and only child of the ruling sovereign. As the chiefs of Parguta, who are of the same family, trace their descent from Makpon Bokha, it is probable that the Fakir and Bokha are the same person. The story, as related to Vigne by Ahmed Shah himself, is as follows: The last Gyalpo had an only daughter, whose hand was sought by twelve petty chiefs. Before any choice was made, a fakir was found siting on a large stone in the village of Shikari. He remained seated day and night, and in a short time acquired a reputation for sanctity; after which the young lady was given to him by the consent of all parties. In proof of this story, the people still show the holy stone called *Burdonas*, or the "smooth stone cushion", on which the holy man was wont to rest, and on which the heir apparent was always inaugurated on his reaching manhood.

The following is the genealogy of the Gyalpos of Balti with the probable dates of their accession.

	Name	Probable Date	
1	Ali Sher	1590	conquered Ladak.
2	Ahmed	1620	
3	Shah Murad	1650	
4	Rafi Khan	1680	
5	Sultan Murad Khan	1710	
6	Zafar Khan	1740	
7	Ali Sher Khan	1770	
8	Ahmed Shah	1800	deposed by Zorawar Sing
9	Mahomed Shah	1840	

Ali Sher, descendant of the Fakir, is the first chief of whom anything is mentioned. He built the fort of Skardo, and conquered Ladak in the reign of Jehangir, or about A.D. 1610. His son Ahmed Shah lost Ladak. Shah Murad, the third prince, is said to have taken possession of Gilgit, Hunza-Nager, and Chitral, and to have reconquered Ladak. His reign extended from about 1720 to 1750 A.D., and his conquest of Ladak was probably only a plundering excursion into the western districts, which the plunderers dignified with the name of a conquest. The last independent chief was Ahmed Shah. In 1840 his country was invaded by Zorawar Sing, and after a short siege, the fort of Skardo surrendered for want of water. In the winter of 1841, Ahmed Shah accompanied the unfortunate expedition against Lhasa; and on Zorawar Singh's death, was taken prisoner and confined in Balwalte near Lhasa, where he soon after died. Balti is now held in jaghir by Muhammad Shah, the disinherited son of Ahmed Shah, who pays an annual tribute of Rs. 7,000 to Maharaja Gulab Sing, of Kashmir.

Rongdo is the last Tibetan district on the Indus to the westward of Balti. On the north lie Shigar and Hunza-Nager, and to the west and south are Gilgit and Astor. The name means the "district of defiles," and is descriptive of the bed of the Indus, which throughout Rongdo is a deep rocky gorge. The district extends from Gurbidas to a tree at Makpon-i-Shang-Rong, a distance of forty-five miles, with a mean breadth of thirty-two miles. Its area is about 1,440 square miles, and the mean height of its villages about 6,200 feet.

The chief of Rongdo claims descent from the Makpons of Balti, to whom the district has always been subject.

The following list gives the genealogy of the chiefs, with the probable dates of accession.

	Name	Probable Date	
1	Ali Sher	1590	
2	Ahmed Khan	1620	
3	Ali Shah	1650	
4	Daolat Sher	1680	
5	Assad Ulla Khan	1710	
6	Mahomed Ali Khan	1740	
7	Murad Khan	1770	
8	Abbas Beg	1800	
9	Ali Khan	1830	now reigning.
	Husen Khan (son)		
	Abdullah Khan (grandson)		

DARDU DISTRICTS ON THE INDUS

Of the country inhabited by the Dards, my information is scanty but interesting. When I was in Kashmir I found the Vazirs of Gilgit and Nager in attendance upon the Maharaja Gulab Sing, by whose permission they came twice to visit me. As they both spoke Persian and a little Hindustani, I obtained from them tolerably complete vocabularies of the dialects of their own districts, and a less perfect vocabulary of the dialect of Chitral. The words in these vocabularies are correctly written according to the spelling in the Persian character, which all the Dards make use of in writing their own language of which there are three distinct dialects, the Shina, the Khajunah, and the Arniya.

The *Shina* dialect is spoken by the people of Astor, Gilgit, Chelas, Darel, Kohli, and Palas.

The *Khajunah* dialect is spoken by the people of Hunza and Nager.

The *Arniya* is spoken in Yasan and Chitral.

These dialects have little in common with each other, and are widely different from those of the surrounding people.

Astor is situated on the left bank of the Indus, below Makpon-i-Shang-Rong. It has an area of about 1,600 square miles. Its chief claims descent from Ali Sher of Balti, and takes the title of Makpon.

Gilgit is situated on the right bank of the Indus, along the lower course of the Gilgit river. It is about 100 miles long from north to south, with a mean breadth of twenty-six miles. Its area is therefore about 2,500 square miles. The chief takes the title of Trakhna, from an ancestor.

The districts of Chelas, Darel, Kohli, and Palas, lie along both banks of the Indus below Gilgit and Astor.

Hunza Nager is a small tract of country on the upper course of a large feeder of the Gilgit river. It is named from two towns situated close to each other, on opposite banks of the river. The two districts have an area of 1,672 square miles. The chief of Hunza is called Girkhis, and the chief of Nager is called Magalato. The former name is no doubt the same as the Kirghis,who inhabit the steppes of Pamer to the north of Hunza-Nager beyond the Karakoram. I presume that this district was formerly inhabited by the Dards, and that they were displaced by the Kirghis nomads. The chiefs of Shigar who take the Khajunak title of Tham, must also be Kirghis.

Yasan is a large district on the upper course of the Gilgit river. It is seventy miles long from south-east to north-west, with a mean breadth of sixty miles. Its area is therefore about 4,200 square miles. The chief places are Yasan and Chatorkun. The chief takes the title, of Bakhto, which is the name of his tribe.

When Mahmud Ghaznavi invaded India in A.D. 1030, the people of Gilgit, Astor, and Chelas were Turks, who spoke the Turki language. These Turks, were of the *Bhatawari* tribe, and their king took the title of Bhata Shah, or king of the

Bhata tribe. I presume that these are the same as the Bakhto of the present day; but their language has become mixed with that of all the surrounding people, and no longer bears any affinity to Turki.

Chitral is a large district on the upper course of the Kunar river. The king takes the title of Shah Kator, which has been held for nearly 2,000 years, and the story of their descent from Alexander may be traced to the fact that they were the successors of the Indo-Grecian kings in the Kabul valley.

The large and interesting country of Kashmir, and the small principalities of the Alpine Panjab to the south of Ladak, are too numerous to be treated of in this place.

To the east and south-east of Ladak lie the Chinese districts of Rudok, Chang-Thang, and Ngari.

Rudok lies immediately to the east of Ladak and Rukchu, but its climate is like that of the latter district. The principal feature of Rudok is the great Pang kong lake, which stretches through the whole length of the country from east to west, a distance of about eighty miles. As the mean breadth is about sixty miles, the area of this district will be 4,800 square miles. The mean height is probably not under 14,500 feet, as the lake has an elevation of 14,200 feet above the sea.

Chang-Thang comprises the two districts of Chumurti and Garo on the Indus, but its extent to the eastward is unknown. The monastery of Tashigong is the chief place in those districts; but the government of the country is in the hands of the Gar-pon or Deputy Governor of Garo.

Ngari embraces the whole of the upper valley of the Sutluj, from the Manasarovara lake to the crest of the Porgyal mountain. It is subdivided into three smaller districts, Guge, Gangri, and Purang. Guge is the largest of the three, and contains the well-known towns of Tholing and Tsaprang. Gangri is the country around the holy lakes, and Purang is the upper valley of the Gogra or Karnali river.

(From *Ladak - Physical, Statistical and Historical, 1853*)

3

Ladhak : The Higher Valleys

By
Drew F.

We now come to that lofty part of Ladakh where the lowest ground touched is as much as 13,500 feet above the sea, where there are long flat valleys at 15,000 feet, while the mountains that include these keep to the same height of 20,000 and 21,000 feet, which we have seen to be so general over a great part of the country.

RUPSHU

The first that shall be described of these high tracts is that called Rupshu or Rukshu. It is a district at the south-east end of Ladakh, lying between the Watershed Range and the Indus. From the side of Leh it is approached by leaving the Indus at Upshi and following up the narrow ravine which there joins in from the south. In this, for many miles, the road continues gradually rising; it is a good road for this country, having now been made fit for the passage of camels in case the owners of any from Yarkand should bring them this way towards the Panjab. The ravine is narrow; it is immediately bounded by no lofty mountains, but by bare slopes of earth and rock, composed of shale and sandstone. After 13 or 14 miles we come to Gya, the last village in this direction, a place elevated 13,500 feet above the sea; it is a village of some forty houses, with a proportionately wide area of cultivation; both at Gya and at an outlying hamlet, which is some 300 feet higher still, naked barley ripens and nothing else; peas are grown, but only for green food. It is one of the most, but not quite the most, elevated of all the villages in the country. At this place we leave houses behind, for at the next inhabited parts we shall come to, tents are the only dwellings.

But to reach those parts we have to cross the Toglung Pass, of 17,500 feet elevation, which we approach by continuing up, the same valley for some 14 miles more; it gradually increases in slope, but even at the end is not steep; a smooth neck of ground makes the Pass, and the hills near are themselves rounded. From the summit we obtain a view which gives us some insight into Rupshu. There is a pretty steep slope beneath us of near 1500 feet, and then a flat valley extending long to the south-east and widening, thus showing us far off, 18 miles distant, the blue waters of one of the lakes which we shall visit-the Salt Lake. The flat bottom of the valley is bounded by smooth naked hills. It is such valleys as this, varying from a mile to (rarely) six miles in width, and enclosed by mountains rising sometimes 2,000 feet and sometimes as much as 5,000 feet above them, that make what are called the uplands, or sometimes the table-lands, of Rupshu.

Before detailing the many interesting phenomena in physical geography which are presented to us in the various portions of this district, we will look at those circumstances which affect the peopling of it; which cause it in a certain degree to be fit as a dwelling-place for man, yet limit narrowly the number of people it can support.

RUPSHU AS INHABITED

With an elevation of 14,000 and 15,000 feet for the valleys, the climate is necessarily extremely severe in point of temperature; it is at the same time of an extreme dryness. The character of the summer climate of Rupshu is warmth of sun and constant coolness of the air. At midday the son's rays are exceedingly powerful; on the decline one experiences cold, which is intensified by the biting wind that commonly springs up in the afternoon. At night, even in the height of summer, except when the sky may be overcast, water freezes; in the beginning of August I have seen ice caking the pools. The snow limit is about 20,000 feet; this great height of it is due to the dryness of the air, to the small amount of snowfall of each year, an amount so small that below that level, it all becomes melted during summer. Mountains that rise above 20,000 feet originate glaciers; there are small ones in the hollows of several such peaks; but there is no great snowy area. The surface of the hills is chiefly disintegrated rock, and the surface of the valleys is earth or gravel. Vegetation is extremely scant; here and there is some green by a spring or along the moistened bank of a stream, and on some hill-sides is a thin herbage. It is this herbage that is the support of the flocks and herds which sustain the small population of Rupshu. Cultivation is carried on in two places only, and to a very small extent; it is on their flocks that the people depend.

In the whole area of the district, which is about 4,000 square miles in extent, there are but 500 souls. These, as will have been understood, are Champas; they are dwellers in tents, or, as the Persian Phrase has it, "wearers of tents." This small tribe, the Rupshu Champas, have about 100 tents, one to a family; they are divided into two camps,which separate in summer, and frequent distinct pastures, but reunite in winter. They make about four moves during the year, with, I think, much regularity, though the time of these must vary if the season be unusually late or early; thus their stay at each encamping ground is nearly three months on the average. The tents are of a black hair-cloth, made from either yaks or goats'hair. They are of a peculiar form; they are constructed in two pieces, which are not closely united, but put together so as to leave an opening of six inches all along the top; this allows the exist of smoke, while the fall of rain or snow is so small as to cause little inconvenience, or the space may be temporarily covered with a piece of carpeting. The space within the tents is enlarged by the hair-cloth being pulled out here and there by extra ropes, which are led over a forked stick and then pegged down. The tent is ornamented with little flags and with yaks tails fastened to the poles. I have no measurement, but from memory should say that the tents are about 14 feet long, 10 feet wide, and nearly 6 feet high; in one of these lives a whole family. The sheep and goats are very numerous. At evening time one sees the flocks and the herds coming down the hill-side and collecting at the encampment by hundreds, land even thousands. The sheep is of a large kind; it is here made use of for carrying loads; the salt from the lake is carried out of and grain is brought into the country on the backs of sheep; a small pack or double bag is made to hang over the back, filled to an average weight of 24 lbs.; the stronger animals will be loaded up to 32 lbs. The larger of the two kinds of goat kept here is made use of in just the same way. The more general is the shawl-wool goat, a small long-haired species; the kids of this sort are beautiful little animals. The wool that goes to make the soft fabrics of Kashmir is an undergrowth at the root of the long hair of these smaller goats. It comes in winter time, not only to the goats but to the yaks, dogs, and other animals, domestic and wild both, as a protection against the severe cold. At the beginning of summer the wool grows out or lossens; it is then combed out from the goats and sent to Leh, where it is picked free from hairs and either worked up or sent on to Kashmir. It must not be supposed that the greater part of the shawl-wool used in Kashmir comes from Rupshu; the greater quantity and that of better quality comes either from the Chinese districts beyond the boundary of Ladakh, or from the Amir of Kashgar's country. The horned cattle are all of the yak species. In Rupshu, as far as I know, there is neither the cow nor any of the hybrids of yak and cow. The yak is a half-wild, not easily tractable, beast; his numbers are not very large in Rupshu; there maybe 400 or 500 head. The yak's duty is that of a load carrier. The Rupshu people do not carry loads on their backs like the Ladakhis, they depend entirely on their cattle, on their sheep and goats for merchandise that is easily divisible, on their yaks for that of larger bulk. In this way the Rupshu people are great carriers. Between Central Ladakh on the one hand and Gar in Chinese Tibet or Lahol in the British country on the other, they are kept well employed in helping forward merchants goods. For this service they get good payment; sometimes it is in cash sometimes in grain; with one or two slight exceptions, all the farinaceous food they consume is imported, Kulu and Lahol supplying the greater part of it.

The intermediate position of Rupshu is such that many travelling merchants come through the country. The tea-merchants of Lhasa-a shrewd and eager set of men-yearly come this way with their venture of brick tea for Leh; their merchandise is carried free by the Rupshu people, according to an old arrangement between the authorities of Lhasa and of Leh, but for their riding and light baggage they have with them a number of fine mules of rare pace. From Kunawar in the Sutlej Valley come the Kunus, a people of mixed Tibetan and Indian breed; from Lahol and Kulu come others of pure and of mixed Tibetan blood; these have in many cases their own sheep to carry their merchandise. Of late years there has been a greater through traffic from the Panjab to Leh, land even Yarkand, by the road that goes through Rupshu. Panjabi, Pathan, and Yarkandi merchants have all passed this way, which, indeed, as far as the road is concerned, is now the best by far between Eastern Turkistan and the Panjab. The objection to the route is that the Pass over the Snowy Range may close before the circumstances of the trade allow the merchant to get away from Leh for the downward journey.

Although, then, Rupshu possesses so inhospitable a climate, though it is at one and the same time both parched and bleak, though its hills are barren and its valleys desolate, yet a busy life exists at times in certain portions of it. After travelling for some days without seeing a trace of man, one may come on an encampment of traders with some hundreds of sheep to carry their merchandise, their loads carefully piled up and protected by white tent-cloths; or one may meet on the road the merchants on their ponies, jingling with bells, accompanying their heavy-laden and somewhat unmanageable flock.

For people who are natives of temperate climes, the air of Rupshu in summer, though somewhat trying, is not too severe when the constitution is strong and the system in good order. The extreme cold of winter also could probably by endured if one had the appliances one is used to where it is much less intense. But the Champas weather it in their tents. The hardiness of these people, the way in which they enjoy rather than endure their climate, is an instance somewhat remarkable of the power of adaptation that the human race possesses. These men consider Leh as a place that should only be approached in winter, and Kashmir as a country hot and unhealthy, much in the same way as we, on better grounds, look on the Gold Coast.

RARITY OF THE AIR

There is one characteristic of Rupshu that is always making itself felt by those who use to dwell at lower altitudes. This is the rarity of the air.

In the valleys water boils at about the temperature of 187^0, which corresponds to a barometer-height of 17.8 inches; hence the amount of air-and of oxygen-taken into the lungs with an ordinary inhalation is only 7/12ths of what would enter them were one at the level of the sea. How this is compensated in the case of the Champas I do not know for certain; I think, for one thing, that there is less waste of tissue in their bodies, as compared with those living in lower and warmer regions ; they do not use such an amount of muscular exertion as the people of some of the neighbouring countries; walking it is true they are good at, but they are not always practising it, and loads they will not carry. The tending of flocks and herds is not an occupation that brings the muscles into powerful use. Still this will not account for all; there must be some compensating habit which enables them to take in a large volume of the thin air; probably they have an unconscious way of inhaling deeply.

With us the system tries in the simplest and most direct way to make up its wanted supply of oxygen; the breathing becomes both quicker and more powerful, that is to say there is an effort to increase both the number of inhalations and the volume of each. The intensity of this effect increases with every rise when once above the altitude where one's ordinary breathing-or an increase in it which is not enough to produce a consciousness of change-suffices. At the greater heights, besides the feeling of oppression and shortness of breath, there comes on a headache and feeling of sickness such as one often has at the beginning of fever or sea-sickness, but this is not accompanied by either increased heat or cold of the body. With some, at the higher levels, vomiting comes on, but serious results do not seem to follow, and relief is felt almost at once on descending to a lower level.

The height at which these effects are observed varies much, and it is not always easy to trace the cause of the irregularities. A great deal depends on habit of body; a man in good condition will hold out much higher than one who is unused to exercise. One first notices sit when using some more than ordinary exertion, as when running or when walking up hill; in this way, for people who live below 6,000 feet, the effects generally come on between 11,000 and 12,000 feet. At 14,000 and 15,000 feet one is liable, at times, to have an attack, as it were, of shortness of breath even when in repose. When I first visited Rupshu (15,000 feet), this came upon me when lying down at night and lasted for half an hour or so; but after a week I got over that liability, and never afterwards, when at rest, felt a want of breath, even when the camp was 2,000 or 3,000 feet higher still. Again, I have known a native of the Panjab-one it is true little used to physical exertion-have a like attack at 11,000 feet. But though one may get so far used to the rarity of the air as not to feel it thus, yet any but the most ordinary exertion will surely remind one of it. At 15,000 feet the least slope upward in the path will make one as much out of breath as if one were, at a lower altitude, pressing up a steep mountain side. Talking when walking,even on a level, soon brings sit own conclusion from want of breath. And when one comes to the greater heights for here every thousand feet distinctly tells-ascending a slope becomes a painful labour. I have crossed a pass at 19,500 feet (one that lower down would have been an easy walk) where, on the ascent, at every fifty or sixty steps, one ws absolutely obliged to halt and pant to recover breath; then, however, I felt neither headache nor other bad effect; the usage of a month or two at high levels had done something to harden one to the circumstances.

The natives whose lot occasionally leads them into the highlands, very commonly attribute these results of rarefied air to some plant, which, for the purposes of their argument, they invest with the power of poisoning the air. Some of the herbs at high elevations give out a smell when rubbed, and these are brought in to account for the sickness. The much-abused onion, which grows wild in some parts at a good height up, often has these things laid to it. Of course an easy answer to this hypothesis is that the effect is greatest at those heights whence all these plants, and even all vegetation, are absent.

THE SALT LAKE VALLEY

We will now begin to examine in detail various portions of Rupshu and some of the physical phenomena which it presents, commencing with the Salt Lake Valley. This is the widest opening in the whole of Rupshu; the length, in a direction north-north-west and south-south-east, is 13 miles, and along a considerable part of that length the valley is five miles wide; the level of it is 14,900 feet. It is a flat surrounded by hills, occupied partly by land and partly by water. The original outlet-an opening between the hills on the north-west-is now filled up to some 70 feet above the plain, so that there is no passage for the waters that collect in the valley, which, therefore, with its enclosing hills, forms a separate drainage-basin. The hills are for the most part low in comparison with the mountains we have met with, all are bare of visible vegetation; as a rule they are not rugged, but have smooth surfaces of loosened stones. The surface of the plain is varied; in parts there is sand and gravel; in other parts an expanse of white clay; this again is sometimes caked with a thin covering, still whiter, of salts, various in composition; lastly, a not inconsiderable portion is occupied by two lakes-about a square mile by the one of them which has fresh water, and seven square miles by the Salt Lake.

The history of all lake-basins and of the deposits in them is a subject of so much interest to geologists and geographers, that a statement of the facts that bear upon the origin of this one is sure to interest some readers. I shall therefore in this place not withhold the details of the results of such an examination of this valley as I was able to make.

What first catches the eye of any observer is the *margin-marks* at various levels above the present plain and lake, which show to what height the waters formerly filled this basin. These are sometimes lines of shingle upon, and sometimes indentations in, the hill-side. The indentations are either in the superficial debris or in the rock, where the waters had eaten their way in and formed not quite a cliff, but the beginning of one-a notch so to say. Looking from a distance one can sometimes count ten or twelve lines, of one sort or another, at different levels; they are most distinctly shown on the surface of some of the southern bounding hills; but all round, at intervals, they can be traced, the highest seeming to be the most continuous. Cunningham gives the height of these above the present lake-level as 150 feet; some of the marks, however, are at a considerably greater height than that. The second time I visited this plain I measured, as carefully as I could by levelling with a clinometer, their height at the spur of gneiss at the head of the small lake. Here the highest mark was very distinct; it is an indentation worn in the mountain-side, and it can be traced by the eye (which catches it at some distance even where a near look will hardly detect a mark at a particular spot) nearly all round, but it is here and there broken by taluses of more recent formation. This highest mark I found to be 320 feet above the fresh-water lake, which is three or four feet above the salt lake; this measurement cannot be more than a few feet from the truth. To this height, then, at all events, the basin once was filled with water.

The lake of that time must have had an area of something between 60 and 70 square miles, reckoning to the beginning of the narrow outlet. We shall presently come to this outlet or gorge to look at it closely, but here it may be said that the level of the bottom of it, of the highest part of the bottom, though above the present level of the lakes, and above that of the great expanse of flat, *is not so high as the margin-marks.* We do not therefore find the cause of the lake, as it was, in the gorge at that spot.

We now will look at the deposits left by the lake when it was of greater extent than at present deposits which lie between the level of the highest margin and the present level of the water. At the south-east corner of the plain a narrow valley leads down to it from Folokonka Pass, a Pass which is more than 1,200 feet above the plain. Between the mouth of that narrow valley and the fresh-water lake, there is a deposit of sand and pebbly gravel ridged in beautiful curves continuous for miles; these concentric ridges of fine shingle are mostly low and flat, not steep like the shingle-fulls of a sea beach on a tidal coast; this shingle is found thus for 100 feet and more above the plain; it was a littoral deposit of the lake, and it seems to have been ridged at these intervals on the receding of the waters. Some of the material of this deposit was very likely supplied by a stream from Folokonka Pass, so that in part it may be of the nature of a delta deposit; but it was both acted on by the deeper wave-movements of the waters of the lake and modified by the surface-movements at the time of their receding. The composition of the central part of the plan is various. In some parts it is sandy and even shingly; in others it is of a whitish laminated clay. To the east of the northern end of the fresh lake is an expanse of this clay. Between the fresh lake and the salt lake is a plain some four miles across of sand and shingle with flat thin stones of mica-schist scattered over it, some of them as much as a foot across; this plan has very slight undulations. On the north of the salt lake, again, is a plain or plateau of white clay about 20 feet above the level of that lake; at the edge we see a section to that depth in a little cliff; it shows laminated whitish clay, with layers in it of a flattened tape-like water-plant; there are also strata of yellow clay and of fine sand; below is coarse sand with pebbles, mostly flat, varying in size up to that of a shilling; the coarser beds are false-bedded in the cases I observed the false bedding was from north to south; in some of the clay there were shells of *Lymnea auricularia*, and Cunningham mentions a *cyclas*. Beyond, to the north of this dry clay plain, the flat again becomes sandy, with small stones strewn over it; this shingly plain slopes upwards towards the gorge; near the beginning of this gorge or outlet I see a section exposing 20 feet in thickness of sandy beds of various degrees of fineness, from an ordinary sand down to an extremely fine, slightly micaceous, sand. Thus we see that by the southern and northern edges of the old lake, and for some distance in, are sandy and shingly deposits; while at other places, including the centre of the area, is laminated clay, with some fine sand. These latter were deposited where, from depth, or from distance from the shore, or from the absence of currents, the waters were most still. The coarser sand and the shingle were more marginal or else were accumulated in shallower water.

For the sake of trying to understand the geological causes of the lake, we will, before looking more closely at the wider space, follow the outlet and examine the phenomena shown along that comparatively narrow valley. In this there are similar lacustrine beds of laminated clay, with the same *lymnea*; and here these deposits are at a level about 100 feet higher than the present Salt Lake; but above them the margin-marks still are visible, in continuation of those we measured. So that here we are where there was a narrow continuation of the great lake; the dam which caused it must be looked for farther on. But in going on we find a complication of the question to be solved. While the valley continues, about level, to the north-west, another valley, also level, opens on the south (which is that in which Rukchin and Kyangehu are situated) and since each of these has an outlet to the general drainage of the country, we find that we shall have to discover the position of *two* dams in order to account for our ancient lake. After travelling along the valley that leads to the north-west, as far as three miles beyond the opening of the new one, we come to where two low sloped fans from opposite sides have met; the height of the rise or neck made by their meeting would, as near as I could judge without levelling, account for the whole depth of the lake. Still we will look somewhat beyond them. The flat valley continues with a width of about a mile, turning southwards to Zarra; here, at the joining in of a small valley from the north-west, is a great high bank of stony ground, which I consider to be an old moraine, though it is more regular and level topped than most moraines; it juts out from that side ravine and comes across the valley, except that a narrow channel exists between the end of it and the mountain on the south-east. This embankment of loose stones must altogether have supported a glacier that came down the side ravine from the north-west, since, when traced back, it is found to take up the whole width of that ravine. This glacier and moraine very likely had to do with the damming of the lake, in conjunction with the two fans before described; that is to say one or other, at various times, was the cause of the damming in this direction according to their respective heights. For up to this very moraine extends the lacustrine clay in the hitherto level valley-flat. The lake therefore, once, or sometimes, extended an arm to the moraine and glacier dam, and sometimes was intercepted by the fans. Thus far we have dealt with one only of the outlet valleys. Let us now turn to that which led out to the south, to Rukchin and beyond. We see the margin-marks extending into it, not much above the valley-bottom; this is almost a complete level; some of the drainage water it receives flows towards the Salt Lake, but becomes absorbed before reaching it, while some flows south-westward, and loses itself in a periodically-forming lake seven or eight miles from Rukchin, which lake is made by the meeting of two side fans. So here, too,is a damming, though perhaps not one that would account for all the depth of the old lake. The truth is that without careful levelling one cannot ascertain the exact spot to which in this direction the lake may have extended, but we cannot here be far from its extremity, as will now be seen. Going on southwards we continue on a similar flat plain, and then come suddenly to the edge of a steep cliff, which ends it off and forms the side of a ravine. This cliff shows the composition of the ground below to be, for several hundred feet in depth, beds of rounded pebbles. From here for this valley, and from Zarra in the case of the other, the two are in connection with the drainage of the Zanskar River. I have elsewhere tried to prove that such accumulations as these last were made during some part of the glacial period, by the rivers themselves, on account of there being a greater supply of material disintegrated from the mountains than could be carried off by the water. Starting from this we can understand how that the two valleys, of Rukchin and Zarra, were first gradually filled with alluvial gravel. I have little doubt that there was at one time a neck separating the areas drained by these two valleys; we cannot tell exactly where it was, nor can we tell near enough to say into which of the two valleys the area of the Salt Lake at first drained; it is now obliterated, covered in, by the alluvial and the lacustrine deposits. Then, at some stage of this filling in, the damming must have occurred either by the meeting of fans, or by the glacier and moraine, or by both. Until the time when the level of the plain had been raised as high as the neck, a dam in *one* of the two valleys might have produced a lake; as the filling up went on there came a time when the waters flowed over where the neck itself had been; then, for the lacustrine beds to have extended into both outlet valleys, and covered the neck, required the two dams, and this extension is evidenced by the margin-marks being found along both valleys.

Now returning to the Salt plain we will look more than we did before at the present state of it. Originally belonging, as we have seen, to the basin of the Zanskar River, it is now a completely separated drainage-basin. Its waters not only do not visibly flow out but do not even filter out through the sands and gravel. On the contrary, it is likely that some from outside oozes through to the plain, for a spring of water comes out of the lacustrine sands near the mouth. A few other springs are to the found in the area; these; with the surface-drainage of the yearly snow and of occasional rain, constitute the supply to the lakes. The fresh-water lake is partly, or chiefly, supplied from springs; its waters, though commonly called fresh, are slightly brackish, but only very slightly, not so much so but that they can be drunk by cattle and by men; I think this brackishness to be due not to evaporation but to the original impurity of the water. The greatest depth I could find in this lake was 10 1/2 feet in the very middle. Its water flows into and makes the chief supply of the Salt Lake.

The shrinking of the lake from the height and area to which we have shown that it formerly reached was, or may have been, due to two causes. First, it is probable that on the waters reaching the maximum height and overflowing their dams they began to wear away those dams and so to lower their own level. To what extent this action went on we cannot be sure, only it cannot have brought down the level lower than to 60 or 70 feet above the present Salt Lake, because the ground at the gorge is as high as that now. The further lowering, and the consequent great diminution of water-area within the wide valley, can be due only to a change of climate, a change to one drier and probably warmer than before. Such a change would have acted in two ways-it diminished the supply of water to the lake and increased evaporation from it. The consequences is that the lake shrinks into the lowest hollows of the basin, reducing the evaporating surface, until, by this reduction, a balance between supply and loss is attained. This balance is at present held by the waters, which once extended (without counting in the outlet valleys) over 60 or 70 square miles, having diminished their area to about eight square miles, so that the humidity of the climate must have been reduced to *one-eighth* of what it was formerly; that is to say, one-eighth of what is was when the lake first became a lake without effluence; how much diminution of humidity occurred before that it is impossible to say. Another natural results has followed. The salts held in solution-which occur more or less in every source of water from the earth, and, as we saw by the supply of water not pure to the fresh-water lake; are here present in quantity- have become concentrated, and a Salt Lake is the result. The salts in this lake are indeed very much concentrated, and are ever being deposited from their solution. Some details about this must now be given.

The Salt Lake is shallow; at the eastern end I have heard that there is about 30 feet of water, in other parts I have not found more than six feet, while over a great space towards the western end there was but one foot of water; at that part the water was of a dirty yellow-brown colour; at the bottom of it was a quarter-inch cake of some alkaline salt, probably chiefly carbonate of soda; of this cake some was in a half-crystallized state, which was flexible like leather. There is an inlet in the northern shore of the lake, or rather there is a series of small lagoons separated from the main water by a bank of shingle and clay. Here the water, drying, deposits common salt, not indeed pure, but nearly enough so for it to be used for food. The salt is removed from this place by the Champas, and fresh salt forms; the deposit is best and most plentiful when a good dry season succeeds the snow-melting. I saw four such pools separated from the lake and from each other. The water must ooze into them either from underneath or through the bar. As far as I know it is only in this part that common salt is deposited; the different salts in solution are thrown down in different parts, according to the degree of concentration; this last must depend on the shallowness and on currents; these again may be caused by the wind, which is apt to be regular at certain times of the day. The salt thus obtained has an admixture of magnesian salts; it is bitter to the taste, and is not liked by those who have been used to the pure salt of the Salt Range of the Panjab; it is indeed apt to produce an itchiness on the skin. Still it is consumed all over Ladakh, and is carried as far as Kashmir. Over part of the plain, especially when it is composed of white clay, there is an efflorescence of some saline compound. Most generally it is carbonate of soda, which is called by the Rupshu people *patsa*. Again, one sometimes sees a layer, over an area of a few square yards, of a hard colourless translucent substance, which seems to be a mixture of sulphate of magnesia with a compound of soda; of this the native name is gurm. There are certain curious inequalities in parts of the plain which should be mentioned and if possible accounted for. That part which lies on the north of the Salt Lake, as before said, is of white clay; the level of it is from 10 to 20 feet above the lake; on this plain we see many hollows, commonly from 10 to 40 yards across, and 10 to 15 feet deep, with, usually, gently-sloping sides; at the bottom is generally a crust or deposit of some salt, as of the *gurm*. One of these hollows was as much as 180 yards across; in this there was a little water. A somewhat different phenomenon is seen on the east of the fresh lake; there is a plain of similar white clay, from which rise small mounds of the same material to the height of about four feet; they seem to be bulgings up of the clay, for the laminal curve over from the centre of each. Of these two phenomena I have not a clear explanation to offer, but I think there must be connected with them a certain sloping of the layers of the lacustrine deposit which I observed at two or three places. Towards the gorge the beds of fine sand before described are slightly waved, and dip on the whole to the north-north-east, at an angle of 8^0. At the place where the salt is scraped up a cliff section shows the beds to be waving and sloping. These things are not due to any deep seated ground-movements such as produce the dip of strata in general, but must be caused by some local settling, brought about perhaps by a dissolving out of salt that had been deposited. However these deceptive dips were caused, no doubt the explanation of them must apply to the surface inequalities as well.

TSOMORIRI

Rupshu includes not only tracts which are drained to the Indus, and lake-tracts whose drainage originally connected itself with the Indus, but also portions of the basin of the Sutlej River, whose arms thus reach to the back of some of the Himalayan ranges. Rupshu is indeed a space where the valleys of certain tributary streams of the Indus and Sutlej, near their sources, have become so filled with alluvial land lacustrine deposits that their levels approach in places to that of the watershed between the two rivers. This watershed is altogether irregular in its course; it follows now a ridge and now a low neck; varying much in altitude as well as in direction. I crossed it by a way that leads from the wide valley of Rukchin towards the south end of the lake called Tsomoriri. That high-level Rukchin Valley is, as before was said, ended off by a ravine; this cuts down for 500 feet between the plateau of alluvial beds on the north and the limestone mountains on the south. Following up the ravine from the that lower level, the base of it very gradually rose, and at the head of it was a low neck of rather soft shale, which lay between the limestone rock on the south-west and the shaly or the schistose rock of the mountains on the north-east. This neck, which may be 15,600 feet high, is a point on the Indus and Sutlej watershed. Beyond it a valley leads down to the south-east, through which flows the stream called the Phirsa; the mountains round are from 3,000 to 5,000 feet above the valley. More than 30 miles down, this valley (which had become narrowed) opens into a wider one, running north and south, which is that of which part is occupied by Tsomoriri. At the debouchment there is a wide, rather sloping, plain, the fan made by the Phirsa stream; this is bounded, at a distance of three or four miles from the mouth of the gorge, by the low ridge, of smooth rounded form and brown earthy surface, which these makes the eastern side of the larger valley. The mountains here are much varied; soon on the north of that low ridge they rise, first with undulations and then in bolder slopes, to heights of perpetual snow. Between these eastern hills and nearly equally lofty ones on the west lies the blue lake.

Tsomoriri (the name contains in itself the Tibetan word for lake,tso) is a fine mountain-bounded expanse of water; it extends 15 miles in length, land from three to nearly five miles in breadth, at a height of 14,900 feet above the sea. At a little distance from the shores the water is clear and blue; it is slightly brackish, enough so to be unwholesome for man to drink of, but not for horses and yaks. In winter time it freezes, and cattle can pass over it. The saltness is caused by its being a lake without effluence; several streams flow into it, but there is no outlet; the water supplied is evaporated from the wide surface of the lake. Here the balance of inflow and evaporation is maintained by the lake occupying the whole of the flat of the valley, to the very hill sides-unlike the last lake-basin we examined, where the area of water had dwindled to a hollow in that flat.

The first thing one considers in coming to a lake is the *cause of the confinement of its waters*. In this instance the observer need not for long be at a loss to account for the formation of the basin. Col. H. Strachey has well described how the Phirsa stream, debouching into the wide valley which is the southern continuation of the hollow occupied by the lake, has spread out a large fan-shaped delta across the breadth of that valley, and how the Phirsa waters wander over that deposit, sometimes finding their way to the lake and sometimes to the Para River. Col. Strachey does not himself draw the conclusion (though probably it was present in his mind) that the formation of this alluvial fan by the Phirsa stream was the cause of the lake being formed. I myself am convinced that it is the true and sufficient cause. The fan which, like others that have been described, is part of a low cone, has a slope in all directions from its apex of about 1½° and a radius of about two miles, so that there is a fall of 250 or 300 feet from the apex or centre to the circumference; the material of the fan is a gravel of shale and limestone. If we go from the debouchure along a radius nearly due east across the valley, we reach to where the fan abuts against a spur of the opposite low ridge. Now that portion of the water of the Phirsa which comes down north of this sport flows into the lake; any which should come down to the south of it would flow into the Para River and so join the Sutlej. At the time I was there no stream was flowing from the Phirsa Valley mouth to the Para, but there were water channels leading in that direction, which I could see would be filled on the rise of the waters in spring-time, and indeed there was water coming out of the gravel lower down-Phirsa water-which was finding its way to the Para. Col. Strachey states that the Phirsa sends its waters in the two directions, sometimes at once and sometimes alternately in different years; no doubt the action is very varying, a very slight change in the disposition of the gravel brought down by the stream, near the mouth, would make all the difference in the destination of the water.

The sufficiency of the explanation I have given of the origin of this lake, as it is and was, must depend on whether it satisfies the conditions, first, of its depth, secondly, of the height to which formerly it may have risen. The fan will be enough to account for a lake of moderate depth, but if it be like the deep Alpine lakes other causes must be looked for. Col. Strachey had no means of ascertaining the depth of Tsomoriri, but he infers (of this and other lakes) that "with reference to the general formation of the valleys in which they are embedded, it may be conjectured to range within 200 to 300 feet." I was at the pains to take an india-rubber boat to Tsomoriri, for the purpose of sounding it, and my observations curiously coincide with the estimate which Col, Strachey founded on inference alone. The results of the soundings I will give in some detail.

From Kyangdum (south-west corner of lake), course 25° north of east, towards first promontory on eastern shore:

		Depth in Feet
At 100 yards from shore		36
At 200 " "		75
At 1¾ miles "	(middle of the lake)	198
At 2½ "	(three-quarters of the way across)	242
In the bay between the two promontories on the eastern side		248

Around the little island (which is perhaps half a mile from the western shore):

Half-way between the island and the western shore	98
70 yards north of the island	22
¼ mile north of the island	178

From Karzok, course east:

At 20 yards from shore		12
At 40 " "		21
At 100 " "		93
At 200 " "		105
At ¼ mile "		122
At ½ " "		139
At 1¼ " "		166
At 1½ " "	(this was the middle of the lake)	180

Thus the depth (at all events in the southern part) was most, not in the middle, but towards the eastern shore, and the greatest depth found was 248 feet. We have, then, no reason to think that the basin of this lake is other than an ordinary valley dammed by the alluvial fan of a side stream, for the thickness to which such fans are known to accumulate will account for all the depth observed.

Next we must consider the evidence, if there be any, of a former greater height of the water, and the relation of that to the fan considered as a dam. The greater part of the shore of the lake is edged with shingle; it is a shingle of, for the most part, flattish, not thoroughly rounded, stones. Such shingle also, at higher levels, I found in several places. Landing in the bay at the eastern side-a deep inlet, bounded by promontories of rounded hills of a light-brown earthy surface-I observed that in this sheltered place had been formed and preserved shingle ridges at levels which clearly told of the water having once been higher; there were several ridges, at different heights, the highest of them must have been formed when the lake was 36 feet above its present level. Again, if we go from Kyangdum (at the south-west corner) along the western side of the lake to Karzok, we shall pass over shingle which lies in sweeping curves at different levels up to 40 feet above the water. Just south of Karzok is a bay with shingle banks curving round it; here I measured the height of the highest ridges, and found them to be in one case 34 feet and in another 44 feet above the water. The still level of the water need not have been so much as this last by a little, because waves throw up shingle a few feet higher; there would not, however, be so much difference from that cause in a land locked lake like this as where long waves roll in from the sea. We may take 40 feet above the present as the level to which the lake once reached. Now as to the height of the dam. I think that it would take a rise of somewhere between 50 and 100 feet to carry the waters over it,at the point where, as was described, the fan abuts against the eastern hills. The fan therefore accounts for all we know of the lake.

The question remains, what change of climate does the lowering of the lake from that 40 feet higher level evidence?

In the recession, the area of the lake necessarily contracted; not, however, to a great extent; probably the contraction has not been more than one-fifth, the area of the present lake being about four-fifths of that which ws occupied by the lake at its maximum. The supply of water being lessened, and the rate of evaporation being increased, an area of evaporation lessened by one-fifth is enough to balance the supply from streams and springs. This, then, is the measure of the increase of dryness from the time when the lake was first cut off from any outflow. But, as pointed out in the case of the Salt Lake, any amount of change in this direction may have occurred *before* the lake because an isolated drainage basin. It may be remarked that on a large evaporating area being formed the water may begin in some degree to get saline even before the outflow has ceased; wherever there is less outflow than inflow there must be concentration of salts, and there will be less outflow than inflow for any lake of large area even if it have an outlet.

A few facts must be given about the lacustrine deposits that have been formed and are now forming. At the south end of the lake there is a flat plain about 20 feet above the water level; this lies between the shore of the lake and the Phirsa fan, extending for about two miles; the surface is clayey, and sections show interstratifications of finely laminated brown clay and very fine sand; the laminae are sometimes curved about on a small scale, making as it were pot-holes in the clay filled with sand. This is clearly a lacustrine deposit: it was made when the lake was about at its highest. There are traces of the same deposit along the eastern bank of the lake, for a mile and a half or so north of the north-east corner of it. To a great extent the material must have been supplied by the branching streams of the Phirsa River; but some of it may have been derived from the waste of the lake-side rocks by wave-action. This supply of material to form lacustrine beds *close to the outlet*, brought down by the stream that formed the fan that makes the dam, is a circumstance that I have never seen noticed in any account of a lake, but it is one that must often have occurred. Where the Karzok stream comes down is a very similar deposit. A flat 15 feet above the water extends out for half a mile from the hills; it is composed of beds of clay and sand, some of the latter very fine, and on the surface a fine shingle is strewn; this was the subaqueous delta of the Karzok stream, formed when the lake was higher than now; it ends off in a low cliff to the lake. At the north end of the lake, where another stream comes in, is a flat partly of shingle partly of sand; the sand from it has been blown by into small hillocks.

The *island* is about half a mile from the shore, near midway in the length of the western side; it may be 100 yards from corner to corner in one direction and 60 yards in another; it is of gneiss rock, rising only nine or ten feet above the water; the soundings before given show that there is about 100 feet of water between the island and the near shore. This little place, being ordinarily undisturbed by man, is a great resort of the gull, which in Ladakhi is called *Chagharatse*; the surface was nearly all covered with its droppings, and there were hundreds of the young about; most of these must have been hatched near the beginning of July. Having heard that it was a matter of interest with some ornithologists to learn about the nidification of the wild goose, I was on the look out for information concerning it, and I found that this island is one of the places where it lays its eggs. I was told by the Champas that they find the eggs there just before the ice breaks up-say the beginning of May, after that they have no means of reaching the island; I myself found there a broken egg, but at the time I was on the island (the last week in July) the young had all been hatched. A few days later I followed the same inquiry in the valley of the Salt Lake, land on an earthy island in the fresh-water lake called Panbuk I found a nest where the mother was sitting with some goslings and two eggs, one just breaking with the chick; the other egg I measured and found to be 3¼ inches by 2¼, and very nearly elliptical in form. The nest was a slight hollow, lined with, first, a few bits of a soft herb, then with feathers; I was told that these goose eggs are found also at the edge of the Salt Lake itself.

For man and his followings the banks of Tsomoriri are inhospitable. The bare rocky or earthy mountains and the stony plains afford little pasture for the flocks. Still the traveller finds patches of grazing ground just near enough for one to go from one to another in a day's march. Karzok, which is the head-quarters of Rupshu, is situated near the shore of the lake. Here is a house and a monastery. The houses belongs to the chief man of the district and of the tribe. The monastery is for about thirty-five Lamas; the building of this under the difficult circumstances of the place, whither every bit of wood had to be carried from far, and the keeping up of it, is creditable to the Rupshu people. There are, besides, eight or ten small houses-mere hovels-where some old and sick remain when the camp has gone to the Indus Valley. The summer encampment is not close to Karzok, but it is made two or three miles up the side valley; at that distance up the ravine widens out, and on a stony expanse, through which a stream flowed watering a narrow green strip, were about fifty black tents of the Champas, and a few white ones of merchants from Kulu, who had come to trade with them; this was the encampment of that half of the Rupshu tribe which keeps to the south-eastern pastures. The flocks were spread over the hills, seeking for the scarce herbage.

Karzok is one of the two or three places in Rupshu where there is cultivation; here some 12 acres are sown with naked barley. Close upon 15,000 feet, it is the highest cultivation the I know of. When I was there the crop was thriving, but in some years it fails of ripening. The land is irrigated from the stream of the side valley, that which made the delta before spoken of, which is one of the chief affluents to the lake.

The climate of this part is thoroughly Tibetan. Snow falls in winter, but not to a great depth. In summer the air is usually clear and cloudless. The year I was at Tsomoriri, however, 1871, was an exceptional one all over Ladakh, and rain fell in showers such as had seldom been seen, accompanied by thunder. In these storms we saw the mountains in colours different from those native ones which the glaring sun had brought out so strongly. Before, the lofty hills, except where whitened by a capping of snow, had shown nothing but rocks and stony or earthy slopes of brown and grey, the distant ones seeming close from the rarity and clearness of the air. But now, with the clouds overhead and the storms filling the valley, the recesses of the purpled mountains seemed more distant; yet we saw deeper and deeper into them as the various shades showed out the successive spurs and ridges, and the water of the lake formed a bright belt in front of the richly tinted hills.

TSO KYAGHAR

North of Karzok a high ridge of mountains edges Tsomoriri on the west, having high cliffs in its upper part and sloping more gently below. At the very head of that lake there is first a sandy flat and then a narrow grassy strip watered by a stream which ranks with the Karzok stream as one of the larger feeders of the lake. After a few miles this stream turns to the west, and another fifteen miles up would bring one to its source, which is at the old water-shed of the Sutlej and Indus. A path up this valley leads to the Salt Lake plain; this direction I did not follow, but I took a way to the north-east, and in doing so came across a problem in physical geography which was quite unexpected.

At the bend of the stream, by its left bank, there is a terraced plateau of old alluvium. On this I rose to a height of a couple of hundred feet, and reaching the top found that this alluvium constituted a barrier to a side valley from the north-east, which now, on account of this barrier, is a completely isolated hollow, holding a lake about two miles long and one mile wide, land about 150 feet below the alluvial plateau. The lake is called by the *Champas Tso Kyaghar*. The question is, how could that alluvium have been formed so as to have the hollow on its farther side? For this is not a fan of alluvial gravel sloping down at the angle of its formation to the lake it dams; sections of it show nearly horizontal beds of clay and sand, with rounded gravel fine and coarse, interstratified. The lake is bounded on the south, east, north, and partly on the west, by low ridges of gneiss rocks, from 150 to 300 feet high. In the middle of the north-west side the alluvium fits on to the gneiss ridge, and completes the circuit. On this lake also I launched my boat for soundings, and found the greatest depth to be 67 feet; this was about 300 yards from the southern end; in the very centre of the lake the depth was 48 feet. The water is brackish as in Tsomoriri, being fit for animals to drink and not for men; the colour, even at the deepest, is green, not blue. A spring of water rises on the west side. There are signs of the lake having been some feet higher than it is now. Immediately on the north of the lake is a ridge of gneiss about 1000 feet high, which is part of the old Sutlej watershed.

I have not been able to solve satisfactorily to myself the question of the origin of this lake, but I have turned over in my mind two or three hypotheses. The alluvium might at one time have filled the basin, which doubtless was originally but part of a valley tributary to that down which flows the stream; then, during some part of the glacial period, a glacier from the north-east may have scooped the hollow out of the gneiss and of the alluvium; thus the hollow would be a rock basin, counting the alluvium as part of the rock. Another theory is that at the time this tributary valley opened out to the larger one it was occupied by a glacier, land then the alluvium of the larger valley was deposited *against that glacier*; then, later, the ice disappearing left the hollow. The difficulty in the way of this is to know why no outlet was kept open by the water that must have flowed from the glacier. Altogether this little lake is about the most puzzling one I have met with.

INDUS VALLEY

East of Tsomoriri there is a part of Rupshu which I have

never visited-the valley of Hanle. It seems from the accounts to be another of these flat, high level, alluvium filled valleys, bounded by mountains which soon rise up to a height of 4,000 or 5,000 feet or more above it. At Hanle, which is 14,276 feet high, is a monastery built on a rocky spur some hundred feet above the plain. Passing to this tract, of which I have no personal knowledge, let us go to the Indus valley, which, in the highest part of it included in the Maharaja's dominions, forms a portion of Rupshu, and is periodically visited by the Rupshu tribe with their flocks.

From the south-east corner of the Salt Lake plain there leads a valley, which, followed up, brings one to an easy Pass, by name Folokonka, about 16,500 feet high, and beyond that one comes into the valley of Puga, a place where borax and sulphur are dug. The road from Tsomoriri, by the little lake Tso Kyaghar, also leads over a saddle of rock down into the Puga Valley, which, farther followed down, brings us in a few miles to the Indus River. The former of these two paths is the way taken by the Rupshu Champas in the course of their migrations. The portion of the Indus valley thus reached is just above the narrow defile or gorge called *Rong*, which, as mentioned in the last chapter, confines the river above Upshi. Where we have now come to (where Maiya is marked on the map) the valley is again upon; the Indus flows in a wide smooth stream, between banks of alluvial gravel, with a depth that makes it just fordable; the hills rise, in some parts smooth and with a gentle slope, in others bold and steep, on both sides reaching, within a few miles, to a height of 5,000 feet above the river. From Maiya I marched for four days up the valley, to the place marked Dora; what was see in the 50 miles then passed over may be described in the same order as it was met with.

Maiya is one of those places often met with in wild countries about which one wonders that they should ever have had a name. There is no house or shelter of any sort, only a little sandy flat by the edge of the river, with no wood and no grass. Still it is a common halting place, and for that reason it bears a name. The yaks (which through all Rupshu have been our carriers) were bidden by voice alone to swim the river, by doing which they reached a bit of pasture on the right bank. From Maiya the way lies along the left bank over ground stony and sandy, but with a little grass here and there. The Indus was flowing by in a gentle stream, with a speed that seemed between 1 1/2 and 2 1/2 miles an hour; the alluvial flat it flowed through widened to a breadth of perhaps three-quarters of a mile, this being confined either by the spurs of the hills or by higher alluvial deposits, as of the fans of side streams. As is usual one could not see well the hills on the side one was passing along; the hills on the north were a series of irregular spurs connected with the great range which is a continuation of that behind Leh; they were made of stratified rock-shale and sandstone-sometimes showing the outcrop of beds, sometimes only a surface of earth and loose stones, of various tints of brown, grey, and purple, all, to the eye, perfectly bare of vegetation.

Now after passing over several miles of these stony tracts we come to where there are two or three small villages, which are the highest in the Indus Valley. This bit of the valley is properly out of Rupshu, still it is traversed by the Champas in going from one part of their district to another. The villages are three. On the left bank is Nidar, in a ravine that comes down from the south; it has three houses only. On the right bank are Nimu, of twelve houses, and Mad, of ten. Nimu is about 14,000 feet above the sea; it shows a tract of bright green at the edge of a great stony expanse; naked barley and peas are sown here, but only the former ripens. Of trees there are a few large willows of great age. I have two three times noticed that in the villages near the upper limit of trees, where few grow, there are some of more than usual size; this probably is from more respect being paid to, more care taken of them; there is also a newly-made plantation of willows. At Nimu little snow falls, and what comes does not stay long on the plain; in winter the cattle and the flocks graze on the plain by the river, but are brought under cover at night. The people of Nimu are not Champas, but are nearer the Ladakhis both in look and language; they are, however, to some extent nomadic, since some of them take their flocks to other pastures in winter and live in tents while tending them. The village of Mad is in the next ravine to the east.

Leaving these last villages we follow up the valley of the Indus. It has widened to a plain, some four miles across, sandy at the outer portions, but covered with pasture about where the river flows through it. There are some small isolated rocky hills projecting up in the plain. This extends to where the river makes a sudden bend to the north-east.

Here we must pause to look more widely at the physical geography of the neighbourhood.

Cunningham, in his book on Ladakh, speaks of the "Kailas Range" as extending in one unbroken chain from the source of the Indus to the junction of the Shayok, the name being taken from a peak on it near Mansarowar Lake (which is far to the south-east of the country we are dealing with), and he calls the great ridge behind Leh, between the Indus and the Shayok, by the same name, "Kailas or Gangri Range." It will be seen that I have not used this name is my map nor elsewhere; in this I follow Col. H. Strachey, who does not connect by its name this last ridge (which I have called "Leh Range," though on the maps I have put no name to it) with any of the chains to the east or south-east of the part we have now reached. As I have before remarked, the question whether two certain lines of mountain should or should not be counted to belong to the same chain or range must depend on the definition you give to the words "chain" and "range." It is conceivable that the definition might be different in the mouths of the biologist, the meteorologist, the geologist, and the pure geographer. In any case it would only be a difference of terms. I myself have been and am using the words in the most restricted sense, as merely descriptive of the most patent facts. Let us look at some of these facts in connection with the

Leh Range. We are now where the unbroken continuation of the Leh Range ceases. That long line of granite mountain, which began at the Indus and Shayok junction, and has, up to here, extended from north-west to south-east for 220 miles, in that direction ends, and the Indus Valley occurs. Immediately beyond the river, between the Indus and the Hanle stream, occur again granite mountains, which, geologically, are a continuation of the others, and indeed lie in the same line with them. So that it would not be alien to the methods of geological description to say, that the Indus here cuts through the granite range; the range being taken to extend from the Indus and Shayok junction to the neighbourhood of Hanle at all events how much farther to the south-east I know not. Now to the north-east of all this is a distinct line of mountain, of which Sajum Station,20,021 feet, is one of the summits; this, according to Cunningham, would be part of the Kailas Range; here this range also is of granite, though farther east its composition changes; the line of it runs north-westward, overlapping the line of the Leh Range; the granite of the two ranges is in part continuous and in part separated, as regards the surface, by some shale and limestone; in the line of the occurrence of these last rocks is the depression separating the two ridges; the highest part of this depression is the Tsaka Pass, about 1,200 feet above the Indus Valley, but nearly 5,000 feet below the hill summits, on either side; the rise to this is a gentle ascent of 3^0; the Pass divides the Upper Indus Valley from the Pangkong drainage-basin. According to General Cunningham's nomenclature this Pass is a depression in the Kailas Range. According to the plan of description just followed by me the Tsaka Pass is a neck connecting two ridges, the Leh Range on the south-west and this other on the north-east. The difference seems to me unimportant in itself.

To return now to the valley of the Indus. On coming to the second bend-the one with its salient angle to the north-we find ourselves in a level plain, of an average width of two miles, that stretches far to the south-east. Near where flows the river is a thin growth of grass, which makes this plain by far the most important pasture ground in Rupshu. Farther from the water the flat is sandy, dotted in places with clumps of Tibetan furze. The plain is so even as well as so straight that the horizon of the curvature of the earth can be distinctly seen in both directions, hiding the bases of the distant hills. The mountains which bound on both sides the valley rise, uncapped by snow, to 19,000 and 20,000 feet; that is to say, they are about 6,000 feet above the flat. On the north-east the crest of the ridge is about eight miles distant; a succession of spurs come down from it; between them are hollows from which come out, at their base, wide spreading fans. The hill-sides are completely bare of vegetation. On the slopes of the northern ridge, up to 2,000 feet, blown sand has accumulated, sand blown up from the river plain; this sometimes lies in masses in the hollows, sometimes is spread on the hill-sides in varying thicknesses, in places it has been washed down again into the valleys on to the other debris. The different colour of this sand from that of the rock gives a strange look to the hills; it often reverses the usual light and shade, making the hollows bright and leaving the projections dark.

I went about 20 miles farther, south-eastwards up the valley, along the alluvial plain between the mountains. After that, as I could see, the space between the mountains narrowed; in the line of the valley there seemed to be an opening like a gateway; it is through this that goes the road into the Chinese territory; the river is deflected to the north-east, flowing in a narrow space, but after another 20 miles up the two valleys or hollows reunite.

Our farthest camp was at a place called Dora. This is where the Champas of Rupshu spend the winter. Here are built some low walled spaces for sheltering cattle at night; there were many small hollows dug two feet deep in the ground with a course or two of sun-dried brick above, these are made for the tents to be pitched is them; at one end is a rude house built for the headman-low walls washed over with a glittering micaceous mud and roofed in with sticks covered with turf. When I was there, in August, there was not a soul in the settlement. At Dora falls hardly any snow. This is why the place is chosen for winter quarters, the sheep and the cattle being thus able to graze on the extensive though thin pasture found on the flat. Close by is a small shallow lake in the alluvium; it is about three-quarters of a mile long and a furlong wide, of clear fresh water. Two or three miles off are some little salt ponds in the alluvium, the water of these tastes both salt and bitter. About north-north-east from Dora the northern mountain-ridge changes in point of composition from granite to a more or less altered shale; the line of it is continued more to the east than before, while in the line of its original direction are some more hills which are joined to the other ridge by a neck called on the Survey Map "Chang Pass" this Pass is practically the boundary of Chinese Tibet in that direction; in the Indus Valley the boundary will be a day of two's march beyond Dora.

It is natural that the more favourable circumstances of this part of the Indus Valley should encourage animal life to a greater extent than is common in Rupshu. I saw here some small herds of the Tibetan antelope, and the Tibetan hare is common here as well as lower down towards Nimu and again towards Chushal; it is a large hare, with much white, the back of a brownish gray. But the animal one sees most of in these parts is the Kyang or wild ass-wild horse it has sometimes been called-an animal which is met with singly or in twos and threes in many parts of Rupshu (as, for instance, the Salt Lake plain) but here is in far greater number than anywhere else. In a day's march I saw some 300 kyang, as many as 100 at one view. There were several different herds; they all let us come to about 250 yards from them and then trotted off, or if frightened by noise galloped away, often leaving the low ground and taking to the stony slopes. This animal is decidedly nearer the ass than the horse, but in outward appearance is much more like a mule than either. He is like a good mule such as one gets in the upper part of the Panjab, about Rawal Pindi. The colour is brown, but white under the belly; there is a dark stripe down the back, but no cross on the shoulder. Of a full-grown male, a fine handsome animal, that I shot in order to make closer observations, the following are some measurements:

Height	54 inches (13 hands 2 in.)	
Length of head (from point of muzzle to root of ear)	21½	"
Length of ear	9½	"
Fore hoof, length	5	"
" width	4	"
Hind hoof, length	$4\frac{7}{8}$	"
" width	3½	"

On getting as near as we could to one of the herds and dispersing it, we separated and at last with some difficulty caught a colt of fifteen days or a little more. He was 35 inches high, his head was 13 inches long, his ear 6 inches; his coat was thick but soft, the same short and curly, the tail short and bushy. His voice, as well as the voice of full grown ones that we got pretty near to, was almost exactly like that of a mule -a subdued grunt or abortive bray. This little fellow soon lost his shyness and would let anyone come near him without fear. we tried hard to rear him, but he died in two or three days. Several attempts have been made to tame the kyang, but little success has attended them. I have eaten the flesh of kyang in the form of steak, and found it very like beefsteak, but rather coarser, the Champas are glad to eat it when they get a chance.

PANGKONG LAKE

In entering another of the high-level valleys of Ladakh we leave the area draining directly into the Indus, and come to where the drainage either communicates or has communicated with the river Shayok. We saw that the neck of the Tsaka Pass is a point on the watershed between the two basins. From its summit there is an easy descent into a very gradually sloping valley, which, is less than 30 miles, leads us past the village of Chushal to the shores of the Pangkong Lake.

The series of lakes in one and the same line of valley, but just separated from each other, the lowest of which bears the name of Pangkong or Pangkong, occupy a length of valley of 90 miles, or it may be more; the eastern end is unexplored, but the people about speak of its being an eight day's journey from end to end of the lakes. The upper part of Pangkong itself and the lake next above are known to us only through the explorations (make in 1863) of Major H.H. Godwin-Austen, of the G.T. Survey, whose journal gives an admirable account of it, and whose typographical work on the Survey Map is a most valuable guide to anyone who may follow his footsteps as I did to some extent. Co. H. Strachey also gives some valuable general information on the subject.

The uppermost lakes of the chain Major Godwin-Austen himself was unable to reach, as they lay too far within the Chinese territory; below these there is a somewhat narrow winding lake over 40 miles in length; next (within the same valley) is a plain, three or four miles long, through which is a channel of still water; next to that is Pangkong itself, the only one of the lakes that I myself have seen. Pangkong is 40 miles in length and from two to nearly four miles in width, its height above the sea is 13,930 feet. The valley leading down from the Tsaka Pass and Chushal debouches into that occupied by the lake at about the centre of this 40 miles, at such a point that, in spite of the great bend in its direction, a great length, up and down, is visible. What strikes the eye in coming first in view of this lake is the lovely colour of its waters; especially towards evening is it of the richest deep blue, over the whole expanse; at morning time it is of a lighter but a very brilliant colour; close to the shore, indeed, the water is both so limpid that the bottom can be seen far down and colourless, but here too, if it is at all disturbed by the wind, at the rolling over of the waves before breaking, a beautiful sapphire tint is seen in it. In the eastern part, on both sides, high mountains bound the lake, whose bold spurs jut out in succession and, at last meeting, close in the view. These hills, like all those we have so long been amongst, are bare, showing naught but rock and loose stones; they are of shades of brown and yellow, only in the far distance is this earthy look modified by the tone which the atmosphere gives. It is but this absence of vegetation, this want of varied hues which are one great charm of the best scenery, that prevents Pangkong from being ranked for beauty with Lucena or Killarney. Assuredly for grandeur of aspect, for combination of fine-formed mountains with the stretch of waters, and for the colour of the clear blue sky contrasting with the mountains, neither surpasses it, and indeed, under some aspects, it is difficult to persuade oneself that it is not as beautiful as can be. The western part of the lake has, on its north-east side, hills like those we have been looking on; we see long projecting spurs, sharpedged, with sloping sides in places broken with rocky prominences; at some times of the day, the sun, glaring on them, is reflected from the stone-surfaces in such a way as to give a peculiar shiny, almost metallic, look; these spurs enclose regular slopes, of alluvial deposit confined fans of gravel. Opposite, to the west, there is a great ridge a little retired from the shore, a great ridge rising to bold rocky and snowy peaks, with snowbeds on the higher slopes and small glaciers in the hollows, the lower part a mass of stony debris. Between the foot of this and the lake extends a strip of ground stony and sandy.

The water of the lake is salt, with a slightly bitter taste; I had counted it, reckoning by the taste, to the something less than half as salt as sea-water, and this estimate is nearly verified by an analysis of it by Dr. Frankland given in Dr. Henderson's book 'Lahore to Yarkand', by which close on 1.3 per cent of salts is shown to exist in it, nearly half of which is common salt, and the rest mostly sulphates of soda and magnesia, and chloride of potassium. This sample of water was taken from the western end; as one goes eastward it becomes more fresh; the water of the far end is, I believe, drinkable. This saltness denotes that the lake is without a present outlet for its waters; where the outlet might have been or has been we shall examine later, at present it will suffice us to know that all the supply of water evaporates, and we will now look to see what that supply is. The amount of rain falling on the area drained must be very small; the greater part of the water that reaches to the lake is due to streams flowing in, most or all of which rise in glaciers. The Chushal stream winds through the sandy flat of Takkung and falls into the lake, much diminished in volume from what it was above. Of the numerous small glaciers contained in the south-western mountains each sends down a rill, and many of these reach the lake, not perhaps continuously, but intermittingly, according to the melting of the snows, but whether changing diurnally or as sunny weather comes and goes I do not know. The Lukung stream, which comes in at the far north-west corner, is an important one, it flows into the lake in a channel cut through a spread of sand. A few springs, too, rise near the edge and add a small amount, and some supply. I know not how much, must flow from the upper lakes through the channel at Ot.

Here and there at the edge of the lake, particularly in shallow places, there is a little vegetation; a flat seaweed-like plant, in form like narrow tape, grows apparently attached to the sand, that is with the end or root of it an inch or two deep in the sand; one sees small accumulations of this thrown up in company with shells of lymnea and planorbis. The lake, I am told, is frozen over for three months in winter, and can then be traversed. At places along the beach, a little above the level of the water, there are *ice-margin* marks, that is lines which denote the position of the frozen edge of the lake; these have been described fully by Major Godwin-Austen; I did not see such large examples of the effect of frost as he did, but I saw as it were turned furrows of the shore deposits lying parallel to the water's edge; these were from six inches to a foot high, and to two forms, first, elongated mounds of loose earth or stones, secondly where a layer of some cohesion had been bodily lifted or tilted up. I take these to be due to the expansion laterally of the ice on its formation over the surface of the lake. These marks I noticed at the following levels: 1½ feet above the present surface of the water, 3 feet above, and 7 feet above, with perhaps intermediate ones; these, of course, mark former higher levels of the lake. As to annual variation I have no very precise information, but I hear that the level varies some 3 feet from early summer, when it is highest, to autumn or winter. A former general greater height of the waters is shown by such evidences as proved to us the same condition for the Salt Lake. These we will now examine in some detail.

There is almost everywhere a beach at the margin, either sandy or pebbly. The bays are adorned by the regular curving of the beach-lines. The promontories have been cut into by the waves of the lake, which thus evince no inconsiderable power of denudation, for at one point a spur of hard rock has been cut back so as to form a cliff of 200 feet or more in height, and several other points that I went to on the south side had a cliff-face to the lake of at least 100 feet. Thus far the effects might have been produced by the action of the waves at the present level of the water; let us now seek for beaches and other marks at higher levels. My examination was confined to the southern side of the lake, and was especially directed to places but a few miles from the great bend. In many places there were beaches at levels of from 40 to 50 feet above the present level of the water; they are very distinct in the bays south-east of Takkung. In a sheltered nook of the first bay were a succession of beaches which I carefully measured, and have represented in the annexed figure, drawn to scale. The shingle was composed of well rounded pebbles of limestone, calcareous sandstone, and shale, mostly from one to three inches in diameter; the two ridges in the space marked a were of loose shingle; beyond, beneath b, the shingle was consolidated by carbonate of lime into a moderately hard conglomerate, it had been cut into a cliff by later denudation; below this was a slope of sand to the water; a little way beyond the edge the lake became suddenly deep. The topmost shingle-ridge here was 45 or 50 feet above the lake. The material of the beaches is not always well-rounded shingle; angular and half-angular stones often make up part of it. Besides the beaches there are other traces of a former high-water level, and these mark a level higher than that to which the beaches themselves rise. These are margin-marks similar to what we saw round the Salt Lake plain, impressions made in the hill-side by the action of the waves. Those at the highest levels are slight, and there is no accumulation of beach beneath them; indeed in some cases they cannot be traced on approaching near, but, when seen from a distance, their continuation at one level for a considerable length renders them distinct. The margin-marks occur at various levels above that of the highest beach up to about 120 feet (or perhaps only 100 feet) from the lake, several lines being sometimes seen in one cliff. These may be observed on the hills behind Takkung, and on the promontories between Mirak and Man.

All that has hitherto been described was formed by the waves at or about the surface-level of the water, at the different heights to which it reached. We will now look for deposits formed on the lake-bottom below the surface. At Takkung is a plain from 12 to 18 feet above the lake, occupying two or three square miles; it is chiefly composed of white clay, with a sub angular granite-gravel of stones the size of a pea strewn over it. The Chushal stream flows through it in a little ravine; sections cut by this show inter stratifications of the clay with plant beds, each layer being from a quarter to half an inch thick; sometimes sand also is inter stratified; the plant is the same tape-like weed that we saw growing in the water. These beds must have been formed in the still waters of the lake when they were higher than now; the material was no doubt in part, perhaps almost entirely, brought down by the Chushal stream. By Mirak are beds of clay, sandy clay, and sand; this doubtless, as Major Godwin-Austen has described it,is a delta of the stream that there falls in, deposited when the lake was at a higher level than now; it extends into the lake and there is being added to; the shallow made by the deposit ends off suddenly and at a short distance from the shore, the end of it being clearly marked by the change to blue water. Between Mirak and Man is a repetition of the phenomenon, and at the north-west end of the lake, towards Lukung, is a sandy flat of like origin.

If now we begin to reason as to the origin of the lake, the investigation is hindered by our having no information as to its depth. It had not, when visiting Pangkong, procured my boat, and there was no means ot taking soundings. I shall proceed on the supposition that the lake is not materially deeper than Tsomoriri, ready to alter any conclusion as to its origin which we may come ot if measurements are taken which show this supposition to be wrong. The hollow in which Pangkong Lake is situated is continued, though much narrowed up, from the north-west end of it, past Tanktse, to the valley of the Shayok. Major Godwin-Austen examined the old outlet in detail, and showed the true cause of the lake to be the damming of its waters by side alluvial deposits near to this spot. The sand and shingle at the north-west end, curving round, separate the waters of the lake at their present level from the outlet valley or gorge; they themselves, however, are evidence of the former extension of the lake water towards that opening. Again, tracing on in this direction the highest margin-marks (those 100 or 120 feet above the lake) we find them to end against a fan, composed of gneiss, that comes out of a steep valley on the south-west, and abuts against the opposite (north-eastern) hill-boundary of our gorge, the width of which gorge is here about a quarter of a mile. This then is what dammed the waters at the highest level to which we have traced them; it is the fan described by Major Godwin-Austen; the place is called Surtokh. At each side of this are other fans, which extend across the outlet valley at somewhat lower levels; it is quite possible that they too at different times dammed the waters, and so made the lake; which of them was the active agent must have depended on the different rates of formation of each fan. We have now the material from which to recount the history of the lake. The hollow in which it lies, a valley cut through the mountains, not different from many parts of the valleys of other tributaries to the Indus, and to be referred to the same origin as they, had its drainage flow out by Tanktse to the Shayok. Then came the damming of the waters of that valley by one or other of the fans which have been pointed out. The water rose in the valley and made a lake gradually increasing in height probably equally with the increase of the fan, which by no means was made all at once. Doubtless the water flowed over between the end of the fan and the mountain opposite. This overflow of the water very likely wore down the channel to some extent, and so the lake may have been partly drained again. Then, later, came a change of climate to a state drier than before, and a sinking and receding of the lake-waters to their present position, where they are enclosed by deposits which were laid down in the lake during its greater extension. It was at this stage that the water got salt. This drying up went on until the diminished area of evaporation was only just enough to balance the supply of water. It will be remembered that the margin-marks, at the higher levels, were but slight impressions on the mountains, while below 50 feet from the water were shingle beaches, which must have taken a great length of time in forming. I infer that the lake did not stay long at the 100-foot level, but was lowered from that down to 50 feet by the *wearing down of the dam,* while from 50 feet downwards the change of level was due to increased evaporation (or the increased ratio of evaporation to the supply of water) consequent on *change of climate,* this change being so gradual as to allow, at every level, of the fashioning by the waves of the stones which form the beaches.

The explanation here given will, I believe, account for at all events the two great stretches of the lake, or the two lower lakes if they be called so; for there seems to be hardly any difference of level between the two, a deep channel of almost still water connects them; it will be the delta of the Ot. Valley that makes the plain that lies between them. As to the higher lakes, it would be rash with our present knowledge to say much about them, but I will venture the supposition that each has been formed by an alluvial fan coming out from a ravine on one side or another of the main valley.

The great ridge of mountains on the south-west side of the lake is one that deserves closer attention than we have yet given to it. This may be called the Pangkong Ridge. It extends unbroken from Chushal to near Tanktse, a distance of 40 miles; beyond are mountains closely connected with it in structure, which, in combination with this, may be said to form a range parallel to the Leh Range. From Chushal to Tanktse the ridge is very lofty; there are peaks in it over 21,000 feet, and these are not isolated ones high above the rest, but the general level of all approaches to that. The crest is a sharp, irregular, rocky line. On those parts of the highest slopes which are not too steep, snow lies on it which never melts, and small glaciers lie in the hollows below. As we look at the range from the Mirak we get a clearer view of its form, which is somewhat analogous to that of the mountains that we looked at on the left bank of the Nubra River. There is one outer line of peaks, the gate-posts, so to say, of the hollows through which, at a high level, protrude the glaciers that mostly end off when still 3,000 feet above the valley. From these near peaks there is a face of slope towards the lake, a descent of 5,000 feet, interrupted in its lateral extension by the intervals of the glacier valleys. Back from these peaks run ridges, increasing in height to join the central ridge, on which are the highest peaks of all. The small glaciers occupy the comparatively flat bottoms of hollows which are surrounded by steep cliffs; they are, indeed, in the arena of cirques or amphitheatres; they come out of this space by a narrower mouth, and there they rest on the terminal moraine; beneath these are still larger accumulations of debris matter, the brown, weathered, colour of which often is enough to distinguish it from the greyer glacier stuff lately accumulated, though the two are sometimes so mixed up as to be indistinguishable. West of Man the central ridge comes more into view from below; the outer gate-post peaks do not exist; this I connect with the fact of softer, schistose, beds here forming the outer part of the mountain, flanking the granite and granitic gneiss which south of this had formed the whole mass of the range. The outlet valley, which at first runs parallel to this ridge, at a distance of 13 miles from the lake suddenly bends at right angles to the south-west and crosses the line of the ridge, making a great gorge through the gneiss rock. The gorge here is very narrow; on the left bank is a great height of rocky mountain, part of the slope of which is worn and broken into pinnacles; on the right is a huge cliff of gneiss curiously marked on a very large scale by waving streaks of lighter-coloured layers and veins. Four or five miles of this and the valley bends again to the north-west, and leads down to the village of Tanktse. This is where a ravine from the south joins the valley we have traced; this ravine drains another valley which lies, parallel to that of Pangkong Lake, between the Pangkong Ridge and the Leh Range; at the head of it is a neck joining the two ranges.

Let me now say a few words about the manner in which this country near Pangkong is inhabited. Considered as a dwelling place for man, Pangkong is a grade or two better than Tsomoriri. Along its western shore are small villages, whose inhabitants cultivate the few crops-such as naked barley and peas-that will grow at this height of 14,000 feet. From Takkung, going north-westward, the inhabited places met with are *Karkfe,* with three houses; *Mirak,* a fair village; *Man,* with six houses, *Spanmik,* with one or two houses, and *Lukung,* two or three miles from the north-west corner, with perhaps five houses. On the northern shore of the two long lakes are no houses, but the tent-dwellers, chiefly those who belong to the Chinese territory, frequent certain spots in small numbers. *Tanktse* is a larger village than any of these. There is an open space at the junction of the valleys, part covered by masses of rock either fallen or transported; from out of the space rises a long, isolated, steep-faced rock, crowned with the ruined walls of a fort and monastery. Until the Dogras came to Ladakh the villagers, houses also were built on the rock; but when the place was restored from the ruin that the wars had brought upon it, they were rebuilt on the plain. There is another village or two below in the same valley; then the Tanktse stream bends round to east of north to join the Shayok, passing through a narrow gorge, which is not only uninhabited, but in summer time is quite impassable.

CHANGCHENMO

Changehenmo is the name of a long valley, tributary to the Shayok, which extends nearly east and west for more than 70 miles as the crow flies. The height of its junction with that river must be about 12,000 feet; at the middle of its length it is 15,000 feet high, and from there it rises gradually to a Pass which makes the boundary of the Rudokh district.

It is only in winter that the valley is accessible from the Shayok. In summer time the approach from Central Ladakh say-is by Tanktse and Lukung, the little village at the north-west corner of Pangkong Lake. This is the course of the road to Yarkand that of late years has been planned and to some extent followed. Between Lukung and Changehenmo a Pass (called Masimik Pass) of over 18,000 feet has to be crossed. In going up the Lukung stream towards it one almost immediately comes to a tract three miles long and one mile wide (about 2 1/2 square miles in area), covered with irregular mounds of detritus, except where two streams have worn out channels and made narrow flat spaces for themselves; it is a complete instance of an old terminal moraine; it is composed of blocks, some angular, some half-rounded, and stones, many of them rounded, chiefly of granite and gneiss, but also of white crystalline limestone, sandstone, and shale; there are many very large blocks, one (of gneiss) measured 27 feet by 20 by 9 as seen above the ground, probably there was more than as much again beneath, and there were several others of about the same dimensions. The height of the mounds is often 250 feet above the low parts of the flat where two streams are flowing, and very likely this is the thickness of the moraine-stuff at those places, but the average thickness over the area may be less. This moraine is evidently the deposit of a glacier that occupied not only that valley which still, as the map shows, holds a glacier of a considerable size, but also those branches which extend to the north-east; it very probably rose over the low spur behind Lukung; this is about 250 feet high, and nearly to the summit, quite up to 200 feet above the valley, *on the south side of it*, I observed transported blocks of granite, and the glacier may have entered, and even crossed, the valley of the Pangkong Lake.

The last hamlet in this valley, the last in Ladakh in this direction, is Phobrang, some five miles above Lukung; it is 14,500 feet above the sea, there are one or two houses, occupied in summer for the sake of the cultivation of some naked barley on the alluvial flat, and deserted in winter for Lukung itself. A little higher up is Chagra, 15,000 feet, a place of encampment, at some seasons, of a few families of Champas. From Chagra the road takes to an easterly branch of the valley and rises gradually, with hills on either side rounded in form and stony in surface. Thus we get to the Pass which is a little below the level of the hills on each side, though at some distance they rise nearly 2,000 feet higher; they are of a dark-brown colour, in form for the most part rounded; their whole surface is covered with loose stones, either taluses or else rock disintegrated into angular blocks, remaining as yet unmoved. On the farther side comes a stony valley similar to the one we have just left; down this we continue for a day and a half's march, going sometimes across taluses, sometimes along alluvial terraces, over stony ground, gradually descending till we reach the Changchenmo River itself. Here is a valley stretching straight east and west for far, the bottom of it a stony tract with the river flowing through it in many channels. In front of us, on the north side, is a bold line of mountains 5,000 or 6,000 feet above us, rocky in face, rising to a rugged ridge.

Below this spot where we first reach it (called both Pamzal and Tsolu) I have not followed the Changchenmo Valley; I believe it in that part to be a rapid stream flowing between narrowing rocky mountains. Above, the valley is partly occupied by the wide gravelly river-bed and partly by alluvial terraces, all stony and bare; the hills that bound this very much in height and steepness, some are smooth-sided and comparatively low, others both lofty and steep. A branch from the main valley leads to the north, up to the plateaus that will be described in the next chapter; it contains a stream of as great volume as the other. Gogra is a place where a rest-house has been built a few miles up that valley, soon above which it divides into Kugrang, the westerly branch, and Chonglung, the north-easterly.

The places where the three requisites for travellers in these regions occur together, namely, water, grass, and fuel, are found several miles apart. One is Pamzal, already mentioned; here is some pasture, and, close by, a great supply of fuel in the bushy growth of myricaria (umbu) and of tamarisk on the alluvium. Then there is a stretch of over 12 miles before any more vegetation is met with. Then at Kyam, where some hot springs come out, there is a spread of grass extending some way up the valley, and there is brushwood also, and farther up, to the very head, there is grass to be found in places. Again, at Gogra, in the side valley, there is fuel and a little pasture. Thus scattered and scant is the vegetation; excepting these far-between patches the whole surface is a waste of rock or stone. Still the vegetation, scarce though it be, is enough to help on the traveller, and even to support the following of one or two families of tent-dwellers who pass a portion of the year in Changchenmo.

(From *Landmarks in Indian Anthropology - Jammu and Kashmir Territories , 1875*)

4

Journey from Kangra to Ladhak

By
Robert Shaw

The Valley of Kooloo—A Yarkandee Orphan taken in charge—The Bara 'Lacha Pass—Change of Physical Aspect—Characteristics of a Rainless Region — Trench-like Valley of the Indus — Detour east of Ladak in search of new Route — Extracts from Journal-Letters — Hajjis on return to Central Asia — Their view of Christians — The Plateau of Roopshoo — Chinese Aspect of People — The Pangong Lake — Dr. Cayley's exploration — Author joins him and goes to Leh — Interview with Envoy from Yarkand — Arrangement to despatch the Moonshee with the Envoy — Mr. Douglas Forsyth at Leh — Troubles of Preparation — The Argoons of Half-bloods, and their rascalities — Mr. Thorp's proposal to join the Author — Departure from Ladak.

On the 6th of May, 1868, I started to retrace my steps of the previous year up to Ladak. But my progress at first was not very rapid. It was necessary to make arrangements for the transport of the goods, and this entailed going a-head of them and providing change of carriage (mules or coolies) at the end of every seven or eight days' march, to be in readiness to bring them on. Besides, our old enemy, the Bara Lacha Pass was not even open yet, so there was plenty of time for shooting, and that at the best time of the year.

I travelled up to Kooloo, a lovely valley some seven days' march from Kangra, with the English official who was put in charge of it for that year. This charming appointment generally falls to the lot of some young civilian, who is sent up to reign for six months in solitary grandeur over a district as large as a Swiss canton. On reaching the headquarters of this little sovereignty, almost the first person who presented himself was the native doctor (maintained there by Government), who carne to report that an orphan boy, a Yarkandee, had been left on his hands by the death of the child's mother in the hospital there, a short time before. The father and mother, with two children, an elder daughter and this boy, had left Toorkistan two or three years before to go on a pilgrimage to Mecca. The fate of this party is only a sample of what is happening yearly to hundreds of ill-provisioned and unacclimatised Toorkee pilgrims who venture into India. The father and daughter had died first; the mother has reached Kooloo, on her way back to her home, only to die there, almost on its threshold. Some money had been left too, which the boy was too young to have the charge of. We sent for him, and he soon appeared, quite self-possessed and happy apparently, a rosy fat-cheeked boy, with high cheekbones and narrow eyes, very Mongolian in type, dressed in a curious combination of the garments of Mecca, India, and Toorkistan. He wore a red skull-cap from the first place, a white cotton frock of the second, finished off by a stout pair of Yarkandee riding-boots reaching to the knee. I asked him whether he would start off with me for his home, and he at once said "Yes." All was soon arranged with my friend, the Assistant-Commissioner of Kooloo, who, as representative of Government, stood *in loco parentis* to this orphan. I cannot claim any great amount of merit for thus taking charge of the boy. Doubtless I preserved his property from the plunder to which it would have been exposed on the way up; but I confess the thought that had chief possession of my mind was, how much this would help my plans. Even with barbarians, it could not but be a good introduction for a stranger, to bring back an orphan of their race, found abandoned in a distant land. They could scarcely cut one's throat arriving in their country on such an errand! So Rozee was made over to the charge of my Moonshee, with orders to feed him well, and to keep him out of mischief as much as was consistent with his nature.

We did not cross the Bara Lacha Pass till the 2nd of July, the interval having been occupied by the arrangements for bringing on my caravan, and by shooting in the mountains while waiting for the opening of the pass.

The Bara Lacha is the boundary between two separate regions distinguished by their physical characters. That which we have already passed through may be called the true Himalayan region. Here the gigantic ranges are covered with perpetual snow, furrowed by glaciers, and they rise from amidst dense forests which clothe their flanks up to certain elevation. They are separated by deep gorges, whose sides are precipices, and through which large rivers flow. In fact the scenery is Alpine. Once across the Bara Lacha Pass, however (or any other pass on the same range), you enter a region where all gorges or valleys appear to have been filled up by an encroaching sea of gravel, which has risen to within a few hundred feet of the summits of the ranges. The space between the mountains no longer plunges down into a seemingly bottomless ravine, whose sides narrow down till they barely leave room for the stream. Instead of that it is occupied by a broad high-level plain, out of which the summit ranges merely rise like undulations. We notice the prevalence of the *horizontal*, after the *vertical* lines to which the Himalaya has accustomed us. It is like leaving a *Gothic cathedral*, and approaching the *Parthenon*. At the same time, a kind of drought seems to have fallen over the face of the country. There are no vast fields of snow to supply streams of water, and no frequent showers to maintain verdure. Such must be the aspect of a landscape in the moon

It seems as if we had here a rough block, from which Nature intended hereafter to carve out the usual features of a mountain country by some change of climate, which should bring snow ice and water to sweep out the masses of earth or gravel by which the mountain ranges are now glued together. The almost entire absence of rainfall suggests a speculation as to whether its presence might not (after Geologic ages) bring the country into resemblance to its neighbour region, where copious rain and deep-cut ravines exist together.

Henceforward, however, we must bear in mind that we are in the barren or Tibetan region, where green spots are about as rare as islands in the ocean, and universal gravel is the rule.

But there is one deep broad trench, which divides this region into two, lengthwise, that is (roughly) from south-east to north-west. This is the valley of the Upper Indus or Ladak, as I mentioned when speaking of my previous visit there. This trench, however, does not descend below 10,000 or 11,000 feet of elevation.

Before proceeding to Leh, the capital of this district, and the place where I had stayed so long the previous year, I determined to make a *detour* to the eastward of Ladak, skirting the border of Chinese Tibet, in order to find some short cut which should avoid the town by crossing the Indus higher up its course, and strike into a new route which was supposed to lead more directly into Toorkistan. Of this new route I shall have much more to say by-and-by. The following extracts from letters written at the time will form the best description of this portion of the journey.

The first is dated "*Camp Rookshin, July 9th*, 1868". This was the point at which I diverged from the main route to Ladak in order to make the *detour* mentioned above.

"Having arrived at a kind of oasis of travel, viz. a temporary camp of Tartars the first inhabited spot after nine days' desert, before I plunge again into the wilderness, I write you a report of my progress. I am now preparing to send off my Mussulman agent to Yarkand to try and arrange for my own visit there. We are travelling with a lot of hajjees (pilgrims) returning from Mecca to their home in Central Asia. It is interesting to see their ceremonious prayers, which as hajjees they are particular to observe. Five times a day they wash head, face and arms; and then you hear sonorous cries of 'La Illahi ill' Allah, Mahammad ar' Rasool Ulla-a-a-ah!' (very much prolonged). At a given signal a whole row of them prostrate themselves with forehead to the ground; then rising on to their knees, they sit back with their hands folded, praying in silence. All together they stroke their beards, and, following their Prayer-leader, turn their heads simultaneously first right and then left, addressing an invisible angel at each shoulder.

"I think I told you of my small *protege*, an orphan boy whose parents died on their return from Mecca. I am taking him back as far as I can towards Yarkand. He is very sharp, and, in broken Hindoostanee, tells us about his country. He declares he will send me down a lot of gold as a present from his home at Khoten, where there are mines of it. Sitting over the camp-fire the other night, my shepherd-boy, who has struck up a friendship with him, asked whether he would take him back to Yarkand with him. 'No,' said Rozee, 'you are a Hindoo, and they would kill first you, and then me for associating with a "Kafir" (heathen)!'

"I have had many talks with the Mussulmans about religion and the Koran. Christians (or as they call them, 'Nasaree.' '*Nazarenes!*') are looked upon as little inferior to Mussulmans, being 'men of the Book' to whom the scriptures of Moses, David, and Jesus have been sent; and whose special prophet is only next to Mahammad in rank. Hindoos, and other idolaters, they look upon very differently. There is a large assembly of Tartars round my tent from their neighbouring encampment of low black tents, dirty and smoky, and I can hardly write; so will say good-bye."

Letter dated "Camp Siool, July 12th, 1868."

"This is the first village I have seen for twelve days, and even this contains only one house. So I am rather out of the world, as you may imagine, and fell myself fast growing a

Tartar. For the last ten days I have been on the high plateau of Roopshoo, averaging 15,000 feet above the sea, exclusive of the peaks which rise to 18,000 and 20,000. I have now begun to descend from this high plateau by the gorge of a feeder of the Upper Indus running eastward, and am encamped at an elevation of only about 14,000 feet, which seems quite reasonable. The round barren hills on each side, which resemble nothing so much as a gigantic gravel-pit, unless it be a series of cinder-heaps, have not a blade of verdure on them. They are scored near the village with diverging marks like the scratchings of a comb. These are the tracks of the sheep, who travel far and wide to pick up their subsistence in occasional hollows where a few widely divided blades of grass push through the sandy grit. An ancient *moraine,* some 100 feet high, appears to close the valley below, and at one time must have really done so, damming up the stream into a little lake, as is evident by remains of stratified clay 40 feet high which have been left in places plastered against the sides of the valley when a general *debacle* swept away the bed of the lake, and made room for the present village. This is the history of many of the Tibetan valleys. A cave in one of these fragments of stratified cliff has been built up in front by a whitewashed wall,and forms the only habitation here. This is the usual style of Tibetan 'gompa,' or monastery, and sometimes of the villagers' houses, as in the present case. Near this is a long row of 'chortens,' monuments that look like a lot of pepper-castors white-washed and set in a line, while one or two bigger ones attain to the dignity of a reversed tea-pot.

"We are here only a couple of marches from the Chinese borders, and the people are very Chinese-looking, with mandarin caps and pig-tails. One of my *yak*-drivers (all our things are carried on *yaks,* a kind of long-haired cattle) reminds me exactly of the pictures of Chang, the Chinese giant lately exhibited in England. They are a grinning, good-natured set of beings. The names too are very Chinese. Our next pass in the 'Chang-la,' leading to the 'Pangong' Lake, and to the

'Chang-chenmo' Valley. There is hardly any snow even on the highest mountains around, for five outer ranges here intercept every particle of moisture almost which could fall in the shape of snow. So that here at 15,000 feet they have no more snow in winter than on the Kangra range at 5,000 feet. But they dry cold and the bitter wind are in the inverse proportion.

"I hope you will take an interest in my attempt to get to Yarkand. The attraction consists in the fact that this region (known indifferently as Chinese Tartary or Eastern Toorkistan) is almost utterly unknown to Europe. It has just thrown off the yoke of China, and started in life afresh as a Mussulman kingdom. It is divided from Bokhara or Western Toorkistan (which is the part of Central Asia explored by Vambery and others) by the Pamir mountains and steppes (called the 'Bam-i-doonya,' or 'Upper Floor of the World'), the former being a range running from north to south, and resembling in most respects, as far as one can learn, this very country of Tibet. Most of the rivers on either side of the Pamir range are absorbed by the cultivation of Western and Eastern Toorkistan respectively, leaving deserts beyond. The latter must be a magnificent country. Even an official report of the Russians says that their recent acquisitions must be valued, not by the limited market of 70,00,000 of people in Western Toorkistan, but by the market of Eastern Toorkistan and Western China of 350,00,000 to which they have thus obtained indirect access. In fact, Yarkand is a kind of Eldorado hitherto closed to Europeans. Schlagintweit went there during a rebellion, and was murdered .... Now that the exclusive Chinese are expelled, I believe that intercourse is possible, and would be welcomed. The envoy from Yarkand to Cashmeer told me so last winter, and others confirm the impression. Anyhow, I mean to try whether the obstacle lies with the Yarkandees. I am sending presents and a letter to Yakoob Beg, the king of that country, asking his permission to come. I believe the thing has only to be tried to succeed. Hundreds of Yarkandees come to India every year. Why should this not be reciprocated?"

"*July 20th, Camp Pangong Lake.*—Your letter being still with me (for want of opportunities of sending it off), I must tell you of my further progress. Imagine yourself on the Lake of Geneva going from Lausanne to Vevay, with a view of a high snowy range beyond the head of the lake added to its present features. So you will party realise our view *ahead* during to-day's march. Imagine yourself on board a Lucerne steamer just turning into the Bay of Uri, and you will have our view eastward or to our *right*. But that view eastward is into China, for the Pangong Lake comes down from the north-west, and opposite our camp of last night turns off eastward, where it continues many days' march into the Chinese dominions. It is altogether about eighty miles long, but only four or five miles wide. The colour of its water, the shape of its mountains, the climate (at this moment), everything almost, reminds me of the Lake of Geneva. But there is one great exception to be made: there is not one blade of green! For the distant mountain view this does not make much difference. The purples and blues remain the same. But, for the nearer view the alteration is most striking. Instead of the green vineyards and trees of Lausanne and Vevay you have a great sloping plain of gravelly white sand, with less grass than on a well-trodden gravel walk. This slopes down on the left from a little snowy range (little only because it rises from such a prodigious altitude) whose glaciers come down to within a few hundred feet of this plain. Some of them are bright and sugary like the Glacier des Bossons (a rare sight in the Himalaya). One of them runs down between its dark *moraine* sides, like an old gentleman's white shirt-frill. Three times to-day we have seen grass, and our camp is actually at a village where a glacier stream is made with great trouble to fertilise a few acres of ground. The lake being brackish, although beautifully clear and deep blue, does not produce any grass on its banks.

"Four or five days ago we crossed the Upper Indus (north-eastward). With great difficulty, I saved all my things from a wetting; for the men were up to their necks in water crossing, and the current strong. I lashed my loads on the top of two parallel tent-poles which four men carried on their shoulders; four other men assisted these at each crossing, and so in the course of four or five hours we managed the job. I had to wade and swim across, sending my clothes on the top of the loads. The stream was only fifty yards across, rather a contrast with the same river as it passes through the Punjab and Sinde, where during the floods it is ten miles wide! Have you noticed what a curious course it has? It rises in the mysterious and scared Lake of Mansarowar, near the source of the great Brahmapootra. It runs north-west for many hundred miles before its course becomes known. It continues in the same direction through Ladak Baltistan, after which it again enters a mysterious and unexplored country, where it entirely changes its direction, emerging at Attock with a south-westerly course through the Punjab and Sinde. It is very curious knowing little bits of a river, while the rest is altogether unknown.

"*July 30th.*—The day before yesterday I joined Dr. Cayley (the British Resident at Ladak). He has been exploring towards Yarkand by the proposed new route. He got as far as the Karakash River. We are returning together to Ladak, where I have to go to start off my emissary to Yarkand."

Letter dated "Leh, August 6th, 1868."

"Yesterday I had the delight of receiving a large batch of letters. You have no idea of the pleasure of getting a post in, and finding a lot of home letters in it, to carry one into a different scene, and blot out for the moment pig-tails and Tartars, turbans and Mussulmans.

"I seem to have made a stride in advance towards my object. About ten days ago I jointed Dr. Cayley on his return from an exploration of the high desert plateau between this and Toorkistan. I came back with him to Leh, where I have had several interviews with the Yarkand envoy who is on his return from Cashmeer. I mentioned that I intended to go as far as the Karakash River, where Dr. Cayley had just been. He said, 'If you come as far as that, you must come on to Yarkand; for how could I report to my King that I had left an Englishman so near his country?' I said that I heard a great report of the justice and greatness of his King, so that I was devoured by a desire to go and witness his virtues for myself, and that I should be very happy to join him (the envoy) in his journey if he were willing. He said, 'Certainly he would take me.' Afterwards, I had another private talk with him. I said that perhaps my best plan would be to ask permission of his King first, and, for that purpose, to send my agent with him. He replied, 'Khoob ast' ('It is good'); and promised that an answer should reach me at Leh in forty days. After giving him and his suite some tea to drink, I again said, 'Then I will consider it settled that my servant goes with you, if that be your pleasure.' He turned round, and clapped my man on the back in a hearty way, saying, 'Of course, it is my pleasure-he is my brother.' Since then he has desired my man, Diwan Bakhsh, to be in readiness to a accompany him; so I trust that is settled. I intend to send with him some presents for the King and other chiefs there, in order to procure permission for myself to follow. The envoy, I hear, has just sent of a letter to his master, saying that an Englishman (myself) whom he had met at Lahore when he went down to visit the Lord Sahib (the Governor of the Punjab) had now come to Ladak, and asked to be allowed to go with him to Yarkand; but that he had refused permission until his Highness's pleasure was known! Rather a perversion of facts, for it was I that suggested my waiting for the King's permission! But they have a fearful dread of taking on themselves any responsibility.

"I am preparing some presents for the envoy (Mahammad Nazzar is his name) — some English cloth, &c., and a Cashmeer 'Choga' or robe of red shawl-stuff with embroidery, & c."

Letter dated "Ladak, August 30th, 1868."

"Here I am still at Leh, although several steps have been gained since I wrote to you. Mr. Forsyth has arrived, and been received in great state—the fort firing a salute, and the Governor going out several marches to meet him. Mr. Forsyth, you know, is the originator of the present movement in, favour of intercourse with Central Asia. In his capacity of Commissioner of the Trans-Sutlej States (a little principality about the size of Wales, and containing about two millions and a half of inhabitants), he has tried to attract the Yarkand merchants by establishing an annual fair at Palampoor, in the Kangra Valley, where the traders from the plains of India can go up and meet those from Central Asia. His enthusiasm for the cause is unbounded; and my own was first lit at its flame, I believe. Now, however, he is trying to dissuade me from my expedition on account of its possible dangers. But men very often fear perils for others which they would not in their own case, and I believe Mr. Forsyth would be more than ready to go to Yarkand himself, did Government allow him.

"Yesterday the Yarkand envoy started on his return journey. My agent, Diwan Bakhsh, has started to-day. He will join the envoy's party this evening. He bears a letter and presents from me to the King. If things succeed, I shall have the honour of opening up Central Asia.

"My two Goorka sepoys (men or furlough from one of our native regiments, whom I had engaged for the journey) have been fraternising with an Afghan here (men of all countries meet at Leh). It appears that in the last frontier war this Afghan fought against the English at Umbeyla, while these Goorkas were engaged on our side. They have taken to one another immensely, comparing notes, and finding that they had been present on opposite sides in the very same actions. The Goorkas are jolly little fellows, as plucky as possible—regular soldiers. You will have heard that another small war has just broken out on the Hazarah frontier. News of it reached Leh with the addition that these men's regiment had been ordered to the front. Immediately they took leave of me, and, without waiting for orders, started off at once by double marches across Cashmeer for the scene of action. They told me that their arms and accoutrements were at Kangra; but that did not matter, as plenty of men would have been knocked over by the time they should reach the regiment, and their arms would be disposable! So off they went as happy as possible in the prospect of a good row, with a chance of loot and promotion; or at any rate, what they like nearly as well, plenty of hard knocks to be given and received.

"I am learning to vaccinate, so that I may be able to introduce the practice in Yarkand. I have already been practising on the youthful population of several villages near here with Dr. Cayley."

I will not here inflict on the reader a history of the troubles I underwent in arranging for a start. Ladak is infested with a set of ruffians called Argoons. half-bred between Toorkistan fathers and Ladak mothers. Like most half-castes, they possess all the evil qualities of both races without any of their virtues. They also in Ladak possess a monopoly of the carrying traffic. They own a few miserable ponies, and as soon as they have made a bargain with a merchant for the carriage of his goods, and received a large advance, they go and buy a few more from some brother Argoon, who has just arrived with his cattle half-dead from a journey. These ghosts of horses are then fed up for a few days till their sores begin to heal, when they are started again under loads that would break down a London dray-horse in such country. This is a favourable specimen of an Argoon's conduct. You are happy if he does not insist on getting the whole money in advance, and then get himself taken up by some convenient creditor, who will only let him go on receipt of a further sum of good money which you have to throw after the bad. With me the case was even worse. For, in addition to their natural cupidity, there was the fear of being punished for introducing a possibly unwelcome visitor into Yarkand. Having a home, and a wife or two at each end of their journey—both at Yarkand and at

Leh—they are equally in dread of the rulers of both places. The very thought of the vexation I endured with these men makes my flesh creep even now. How impossible it began to seem at last that I should ever start: as the men who had good horses, after making me accept exorbitant terms of their own asking, finally started away without a word of explanation with some other employer, leaving me *Plante;* while those who had skeletons of horses, or no horses at all, were profuse in their promises to come, but, by tissues of the most involved falsehoods, avoided producing their entire team at one time, the only real proof I could have of its existence. How I envied the Yarkand merchants travelling with their own horses, strong and fit for work! How I tried to buy some for myself, but left off when the first one died under the hands of an Argoon who was officiously giving him some medicine!

All these troubles I will leave to the imagination, merely saying that I did not start till the 20th of September from Ladak, being compelled to trust the greater part of the goods to the tender mercies of an Argoon named "Momin" (=the faithful one), who promised to start after me in eight or ten days when his horses should be ready. The native Governor of Ladak promised to give the man guides to take him by the new route which I was going to try. The Governor also gave me an order on several villages near the Pangong Lake for ponies, which according to the custom of the country the villagers are bound to hire out to travellers at fixed rates. This determination I had come to when I found I could not get enough horses from the Argoons to carry both the goods and also my own camp and baggage. I thought I could shift for myself, and secure ponies from the villagers better than the servant in charge of the goods could do.

Just before starting a companion offered himself for the journey. Mr. Thorp, who had formerly been in the 98th Regiment, and had recently been travelling about in Tibet, hearing that I was starting for Yarkand, volunteered to go with me. For the moment I accepted the offer, but afterwards, on consulting with friends who had the best means of judging, I was advised that it would be over rash to take a companion. I had spoken to the envoy only about myself; I had written to the King only in my own name; and now, if a second Englishman were to appear with me on the frontier, the suspicion of these Asiatics would be deeply aroused. Mr. Thorp, with great good-nature, gave in to these reasons, and consented to abandon his intention of accompanying me-preferring to do that rather than risk the failure of my expedition.

I may here mention incidentally that on my return to India I was much shocked to hear that Mr. Thorp had suddenly died of heart-complaint during my absence.

At this time I also heard a report that another Englishman, of the name of Hayward, was on his way up with intention of attempting to reach Yarkand. I wrote him a letter on the chance of its catching him in Cashmeer, urging the same reasons against his coming which had already prevailed with Mr. Thorp.

Finally, on the 20th of September, I said good-bye to Dr. Cayley, and started from Ladak.

(From *Visit to High Tartary Yarkand und Kashgar, 1871)*

5

Climate of Ladhak

By
Alexander Cunningham

I.—GENERAL REMARKS

The various meteorological processes which combine to form a climate, are all generated by the sun. Thunder and lightning, snow and rain, the pleasant breeze and the mighty whirlwind, all alike own their origin to the sun. Through the changes produced the varying diffusion of solar heat through the atmosphere, the still air is put in motion, and become a gentle breeze, a high wind, or a mighty hurricane. By the sun's beams the multitudinous waters of the ocean and its tributary rivers are vapourized and formed into clouds, which, rising with the ascending and heated air, and borne upon the wings of the wind to loftier or more northerly regions, where, as they become condensed by the cold, they sink with their burthen towards the earth, and fall down in the shape of rain, hail, or snow. The rain washes over the surface, or permeates through the ground, the snow melts as it falls, and percolates through the fissures of the rocks; both to appear again in countless rills, which join and form mighty rivers, that bear back again to the sea all the water formerly abstracted by evaporation.

II.—WINDS

The constancy of the prevailing winds in different. quarters of the globe is one of the most interesting phenomena of nature. In the Trans-Himalayan districts of Ladak, the dry wind is nearly always southerly and westerly, both in summer and in winter. This fact was partially observed by Alexander Gerard, who remarks that "on peaks upwards of 20,000 (feet) and at heights of 16,000 (feet) the winds were always W. or S. W." The same fact was also noticed by my brother, Captain Joseph Cunningham, who resided for nearly a whole year, including one entire winter season of 1841-42, in the districts of Upper Kanawar, Spiti, and Chumurti. He observed that "the winds blew almost constantly from the south or south-west, as noticed by the Gerards. A northerly wind was of rare occurrence."

When I first observed the steadiness of the day-breeze in these regions, I was under the impression that the wind blew constantly in the same direction from the south-south west and west, but after a few days, observation I found that the morning wind blew generally from the north-Cast. It then struck me that the prevailing winds alternated day and night, like the land and sea breezes on the coast of India. I was confirmed in this opinion by finding occasion a due northerly wind blowing about midnight, and when I afterwards began to observe the magnetical instruments, I always found a light northerly breeze from two to five in the morning, which as the day broke, gradually took a north-easterly direction. I then observed the course and strength of the wind at half-hour intervals, and my first day's observations at once convinced me that my opinion was right. I continued my observations at different places during August, September, and October, and always with the same results. Since then my opinion has been most completely substantiated by my brother's observations for one whole year in Spiti.

The generality of travellers get too much fatigued with their exertions by day to be able to make any observations at night; and thus the south-westerly wind, which was found to prevail during the day, was supposed to last through the night, and to be a mere continuation of the south-westerly monsoon, which blows up the valleys of the Chenab, the Byas, and the Sutluj. But as the day-and-night wind of Ladak blow throughout the entire year, it is clear that it must be due to some other cause; for in the intertropical regions the course of the wind is dependent upon the sun's declination, which when northerly attracts the ascending current of heated equatorial air in its own direction, thus producing a south wind. But as this stream of air, when it reaches the higher northerly latitudes, where the surface motion of the earth is less rapid, still retains its superior equatorial velocity, it gains daily more and more upon the easterly motion of the earth, until at length, when it descends to the surface, it becomes a south-westerly breeze, which blows steadily during the six months of the sun's northern declination. But when the declination become southerly, just the reverse of this process takes place; for the ascending current of heated air follows the sun towards the south, thus producing a northerly breeze, which, owing to the difference of rotatory velocities before mentioned, gradually becomes a north-westerly breeze, which blows steadily during the six months of the sun's southern declination. These are the monsoons or seasonal winds, which depend entirely upon sun's position in the ecliptic; the south-westerly monsoon being the summer wind, and the north-easterly monsoon the winter wind. But the alternation of the day-and-night wind throughout Ladak is constant throughout the year; and as the subject is one of some interest, I will here attempt to explain what appears to me to be the cause that generates it, and that afterwards carries it round all the points of the compass.

This cause is, I believe, the great mid-day radiation of heat from the bare surface of the vastly elevated plains of Ladak and the neighbouring districts, which have a mean height of 13,000 feet above the sea. The following table shows the extent and mean elevation of these great masses of table-land.

EXTENT AND MEAN HEIGHT OF THE TIBETAN TABLE-LAND

	Extent.		Height	
Districts	Sq. miles	Total	Sq. miles	Mean.
Rukchu	5,580		15,634	
Garo	6,500		15,500	
Rudok	4,800		14,500	
		16,880		15,211
Zanskar	3,080		13,154	
Spiti	2,312		12,986	
Nubra	9,216		12,763	
Ngari	9,000		12,500	
		23,608		12,851
Ladak	3,960		11,500	
Purik	4,200		11,196	
Lahul	1,872		10,535	
		10,032		11,077
	Sq. miles	50,520	Mn. height	13,026

Now as nearly one-half of our terrestrial atmosphere lies beneath the level of these elevated regions, the highly rarefied air offers but little cheek to the direct transmission of the solar rays, which are more powerful in Ladàk, at a height of 15,000 feet, than in the low-lying plains of India. At Gwalior the greatest heat of the sun's rays in the hot winds of 1850 was 133^0; at Simla, 7,500 feet, it was 134^0; but in Rukchu, 15,500 feet, Trebeck observed a solar heat of 144^0, and in the same district Gerard measured the incredible rise of 158^0, which is only 27^0 below the boiling point of water in that district.

Toward mid-day the lower strata of the atmosphere become rapidly heated, and the rarefied air begins streaming towards the north pole, as a light southerly breeze. As the day advances, the current of air quickly increases in strength until it becomes a high winds, which blows steadily during the afternoon, with occasional gusts of great violence. In the evening it becomes fainter. The progress of this wind is well shown in the following observations made by myself with Lind's wind-gauge.

DIRECTION AND PRESSURE OF THE WIND

Time			Direction	Pressure
10h.	30m. A. M.		N. E.	faint
11	00	"	E	very faint
11	30	"	S.	light puffs
	Noon.		S. W.	0.2
12.	30	P. M	W. S. W.	0.4
1	00	"	W. S. W.	0.5
1	30	"	W.	0.8
2	00	"	W.	1.0
2	30	"	N. W.	1.2
3	00	"	W. N. W.	0.8
3	30	"	N. W.	0.8
4	00	"	N. N. W.	1.0
4	30	"	N.N.W.	0.4

The greatest pressure was at 2h, 30m. P. M., when the wind exerted force of 6.25 Ibs. per square foot. This is a single example of what I observed daily. The day-breeze or southerly wind always began to blow before mid-day, and continued rising and veering towards the west with frequent strong gusts until three or four o'clock in the afternoon, when it reached its greatest force, and remained steady for some time. Towards sunset it changed to the west-north-west, and gradually lessened, until at 9 P. M. it was only a gentle breeze from the north-west. At midnight there was always a light northerly wind, which become fainter towards the morning, when if often freshened into a north-easterly breeze.

The following extracts in support of my opinion are taken from my brother's journal.

1842

Jan. 3 *from noon* to 4 P. M. a strong *southerly* wind.

5 *southerly wind after* 2 P. M.

10 *afternoon*, winds *southerly*, blowing is violent gusts.

11 after 9 A. M. wind southerly in strong gusts.

18 after 5 P. M. light snow with north wind.

19 *night a light northerly wind.*

20 *morning, a light northerly wind.*
afternoon, south wind blowing in gusts

21, 22 } *afternoon*, strong south wind chiefly in gusts.

23 strong wind from south and south-west.

24 a light *northerly* wind *until noon.*

28 wind in gusts from *south after* 10 A. M.

30 *northerly* wind *until* 10 A. M.

Feb. 4 *early morning, wind northerly*, afterwards, gusts from south.

6 *until* 10 A. M. *northerly wind.*

7, 8 } *ditto ditto.*

25 *afternoon*, wind *southerly.*

March 22 afternoon, wind in gusts from south.

	29	ditto ditto.
1842		
April	8	puffs of wind from south.
	12-18	ditto ditto.
		A very cloudy month.
May	14	mid-day, strong south wind.
	16, 17	noon to evening, light south wind.
	18, 19	after 9 A. M. strong southerly wind.
	21	after 10 A. M. strong southerly wind chiefly in gusts.
	24	after 11 A. M. light southerly wind chiefly in prolonged puffs.
	26 to 31	afternoon, moderate south wind.
June	1to 4	afternoon, ditto.
	5	from 9 A. M. high southerly wind to 7 P. M.
	6 to 9	ditto ditto until dusk.
	10-12	after 10 A. M. strong south wind.
	14	after 2 P. M. light south wind.
	15	after 11 A. M. south wind.
		The same for the rest of the month.
July	1 to 31	south wind for 28 days.
August	1 to 31	south wind every day.
Sept.	1 to 30	south wind ditto.
October		no observations.
November		strong south wind.

In these observations it will be observed that whenever the morning wind is recorded it is always northerly, and that the southerly wind never rises until 9 A. M., and usually later. The constancy of the southerly wind here recorded is simply accounted for the fact, that the valleys of the Le and Para rivers, where my brother's observations were made, run almost, due north and south. The course of the wind was therefore influenced by the direction of the valleys. This is proved by the change of the wind at Sumra, on the Spiti river, where the direction of the valley being from east to west, my brother found the afternoon wind blowing from the east. I found the same in the Spiti valley during August and September, when the wind was always up the valley or easterly during the heat of the day. On the Parang river, on the contrary, the wind was south-westerly during the afternoon, but north-easterly before mid-day, both the up and down currents taking the direction of the valley. At the foot of the Lanak Pass the wind was north- easterly and unsettled until noon, after which it blew steadily from the south-west up the valley.

I have already stated that the cause of the southerly or day breeze is the intense solar heat and greatly increased radiation, which are due to the vast elevation of the mass of the table-land of Ladak and the neighbouring districts. The air, rarefied by the heat radiated from the soil, streams towards the north pole in a southerly current. As it advances, it is gradually deflected to the south-west and west by the greater rotatory velocity which it possesses; and as the evening approaches, it unities with the north wind, and becomes a north-westerly breeze. The northern or night breeze is due to the intense cold generated by the great nocturnal radiation, and which begins in the loftier snowy regions at 3 P. M. The condensed air finds an outlet to the south towards the low plains of India, and becomes a northerly current of air. At first it is deflected into a north-westerly current by its meeting with the westerly breeze of the afternoon, but as the evening grows colder, the nocturnal breeze prevails, and streams gently southward towards the plains. As it advances towards the equator, its inferior rotatory velocity causes it to be deflected gradually towards the north-east and east until the sun has again raised the southern wind, and then the gentle breeze of night becomes fainter and fainter, and dies gradually away.

This explanation seems to me sufficient to account for the constancy of the day and night breezes of the table-land of Ladak; but the violent gusts which my brother mentions, and which I have myself experienced, are due to another cause. The lighter gusts in a single valley are most probably caused by the small eddies of wind meeting the onward current at every turn ; but the violent gusts which I have felt at the Thung-Lung Pass, can only be attributed to the meeting of two strong currents of the same southerly breeze, which have been deflected during their courses into almost opposite winds. Thus, the day wind, which blows up the plain of Kyang towards the Thung-Lung Pass, in a south-westerly current, while that which blows up the Puga rivulet and over the plain of Tsho-kar towards the same point, is an easterly current. The meeting of these two strong currents blowing from opposite directions, would produce small whirlwinds and most violent gusts.

III.-RAIN AND SNOW

The quantity of rain and snow that falls in Ladak is exceedingly small. In the more elevated districts of Rukchu, Nubra, Zanskar, and Ladak Proper, it rains, or rather drizzles, for an hour or two about three times a year. Snow falls much oftener, but not in any quantity, and in Ladak and Rudok it is never more than six inches deep. In Rukchu, as a Lama of the Korzo Gonpa on the Tshomo-Riri Lake told me, the winter snow is never more than knee-deep, and the people reside at the monastery during the whole year. Light falls of snow occur at night, even in the middle of summer, as the nocturnal temperature is generally below freezing. In the end of September, 1846, I was encamped on the bank of Tshomo-Riri Lake, in a snow-storm which lasted for twenty-two hours, but the snow was not more than six inches-deep, and it disappeared during the following day. In Dras the fall of snow is so great, that by the end of November the Seoji-la Pass into Kashmir is always closed, from which the district takes its Tibetan name of Hem-babs, or "snow-fed." In Lahul and Spiti, the snow falls to a very great depth, and in many places is doubled by accumulations of drift. The suspension-bridge at Koksar, in Lahul, is annually carried away by a mass of drift-snow, which buries it during the winter. In both these districts whole villages are occasionally snowed up for three weeks at a time ; but so long as the houses stand, the people suffer but little inconvenience. In 1838, however, the village of Tunda, near Treloknath, was overwhelmed by a mass of snow, when several houses were thrown down, and sixteen people perished. The temple of Treloknath was half-buried, and the bed of the river was filled with snow.

Heavy showers of rain fall along the Chandra river in Lahul during July and August; but after the end of September the snow begins to fall, at first in small quantities which soon disappear; but the fall gradually increases until November, when the snow ceases to melt, and the passes are finally closed.

In Spiti the fall of snow in much less than in Lahul, its greatest depth, where not drifted, being only two feet and a half. During my brother's residence in Spiti the snow "commenced regularly on the 27th November, and from that date until the end of February, 1842, it snowed more or less heavily, and nearly all day and night, for thirty-nine days. It was cloudy or hazy and snowing on the heights for thirty-four days, leaving twenty-one fine clear days out of ninety-four." During July and August, light showers of rain were frequent, but only one heavy fall occurred during the whole year.

IV.—TEMPERATURE

The climate of Ladak is characterized by great extremes of heat and cold and by excessive dryness. It the earth did not possess an atmosphere, the extremes of burning heat by day and of freezing cold by night would be unbearable. It follows, therefore, that the rarer the atmosphere becomes as one ascends above the general surface-level of the earth, so much greater will be the extremes of temperature between the day and the night. This is a general rule when the atmospheric changes are not otherwise affected by peculiar circumstances. It is thus in Ladhak, and more particularly in Rukchu, where the dry and highly evaporative day breeze, exhausts the little moisture held in the atmosphere, and the clear dry air becomes intensely cold by the great terrestrial radiation under a cloudless sky. In the elevated district of Rukchu it freezes almost every night during summer; but the highly rarefied atmosphere offers so slight a check to the transmission of the sun's rays, that the noon-day sun is sometimes 25^0 hotter than it is any part of India. In the less lofty districts in Spiti, both the cold and the heat decrease; but in Spiti the noon-day sun is still 15^0 hotter than in India, while in Ladhak it is about the same. The extremes of cold are equally great, and in the more elevated districts the winters are particularly severe. In Rukchu the thermometer falls as low as +9^0 of Fahrenheit, even in September, and the minimum temperature of the mouth is only 23.5^0, while the mean temperature is 42^0 93'. In Spiti, during the same month, the minimum temperature is only 37^{0}2', and I have seen the themometer as low as 22^0, the mean temperature being 55^{0}5'. Most of the travellers who have visited Rukchu have been there is September. Trebeck, it is true, traversed it alone in June, yet both Moorcroft and Dr. Gerard passed through it in September, and I have twice visited it in that month. We have, therefore, good observations for the temperature of September, while that of the rest of the year is almost unknown. But as the climate of Spiti approaches nearest to that of Rukchu, both in its extremes of temperature and in its excessive dryness, we may obtain a tolerably accurate approximation to the annual mean temperature of the latter district by a comparison with that of the other. The following table gives the result of all my brother's observations for one whole year in Spiti, with the addition of my own for the months of August and September.

TEMPERATURE OF SPITI

	Temperature			Extremes		Moisture			
	-	+	Max.	-	+	Dry Bulb.	Wet.	Diff.	Sum.
January	11.7	31.0	19.18	-11	35				50
February	7.3	35.0	18.68	-6	40				56
March	10.8	40.0	24.46	-4	45				71
April	31.5	50.0	40.89	+26	65				84
May	38.0	60.0	49.00	34	75				95
June	45.0	74.0	59.50	44	85				120
July	48.0	80.0	63.60	46	90.0				148
August	43.0	74.3	58.60	41	83.5	78.25	53.25	25	98
September	37.2	75.3	55.50	22	84.5	70	45	25	97 6
October	28.0	56.0	40.12	20	65				80
November	17.0	35.0	22.85	+16	50				60.5
December	2.5	35.7	14.35	-13	42				50.7
Mean annual temperature				38.39					

By this table it will be seen that the mean annual temperature in Spiti is just one-third less than the mean temperature of September. On applying the same rule to the September mean temperature of Rukchu, 43.08⁰, we obtain 28.72⁰ for the mean annual temperature. The extreme of cold is probably between twenty and thirty degrees below zero, and the mean temperature of the winter months cannot be more than a few degrees above zero.

For Ladak Proper, I possess observations for the months of September and October which, when compared with the Spiti observations, would give a mean annual temperature of 39^0 for the valley of the Indus. The following are the observations.

—	Min.	Max.	Mean.	Extremes	
				—	+
September	44.93	70.00	57.01	24.0	82.0
October	22.22	60.87	38.95	0	65.5

By deducting one-third from the September mean, are get 38.01^0 for the annual mean temperature, and by deducting one-twentieth from the October mean, we get 37.00^0. The mean of these two gives 37.5^0 as the mean annual temperature of the valley of the Indus in Ladak.

The climate of Zanskar is like that of Spiti, and that of Nubra like that of the valley of the Indus. The climate of Lahul is similar to that of Kanawar, but somewhat colder, as Lahul is more elevated. The mean height of Lahul is 10,535 feet, while that of Kanam, in Kanawar, is only 9,296 feet. The following results are calculated from the observations made for two successive years by the celebrated Tibetan scholar Csoma de Koros, while he was studying with a Lama in the monastery of Kanam.

TEMPERATURE OR KANAWAR

—	Min.	Max.	Mean.	Extremes	
				—	—
January	24.87	40.00	34.00	14	
February	28.82	46.00	36.00	21	
March	30.04	52.37	40.49	18	
April	44.23	59.23	49.88	26	68
May	50.30	68.80	59.77	40	78

Contd....

	Min.	Max.	Mean.	Extremes	
June	57.60	74.94	66.28	48	82
July	61.26	77.59	69.22	56	80
August	59.91	75.40	67.65	56	79
September	54.78	73.71	63.90	49	78
October	47.27	67.82	56.16	40	74
November	36.46	55.43	43.68	32	67
December	30.71	49.05	37.25	26	

Mean Annual temperature 52.02

Lahul is subject to greater extremes both of heat and cold than Kanawar. The greatest temperature observed by Csoma de Koros was only 82^0, whereas I have seen the thermometer at 84^0 on the 2nd september in Lahul. The lowest temperature of Kanawar in August was only 56^0, but in Lahul the minimum temperature is always under 50^0, and the lowest that I observed was 42^0. The temperature of Lahul for several days in August was

Min.	Max.	Mean.	Extremes	
			—	+
46.00	78.2	62.1	42	84

From the similarity of climate and of geographical position, the mean annual temperature of Lahul may be deduced from its September temperature by taking the same proportion as we find in the Kanawar observations. This proportion will give a mean annual temperature of 47^0 30' for the inhabited parts of Lahul. The uninhabited portions of the district on the upper courses of the Chandra and Bhaga rivers partake more of climate of Spiti.

The mean annual temperature for the whole of Ladak may be obtained approximately from the details before given.

TABLE OF ANNUAL MEAN TEMPERATURE

Districts.	Height	Annual Temperature in°
Rukchu	15,634	28°.72
Garo	15,500	28.62
Rudok	14,500	30.00
Zanskar	13,154	39.00
Spiti	12,986	38.89
Nubra	12,763	39.00
Ngari	12,500	38.00
Ladhak	11,500	37.00
Purik	11,196	42.00
Lahul	10,535	47.30
Mean	13,026	36.85

The following table shows the mean daily range of the thermometer; by which it will be seen that the difference between the temperature of day and night increases with the elevation.

DAILY RANGE OF TEMPERATURE

Districts	Height	Daily Range in°	Extreme Range in°
Rukchu	15,634	40.28	57.00
Spiti	12,986	36.00	43.00
Ladak	11,500	33.00	39.75
Purik	11,196	32.50	39.50
Lahul	10,535	31.14	34.00

V.—MOISTURE

The excessive dryness of the climate of Ladak is due chiefly to elevation, by which the air is so rarefied as to be incapable of holding much moisture is suspension. It is also partly due to the great radiation of heat from the bare soil, by which any moisture is rapidly evaporated. The dryness ot the climate increases with the height, and the temperature of the dew-point is so very low, that the deposition of dew is quite unknown in the more elevated districts. The depression of the wet-blub thermometer in different districts of Ladak is shown in the following table, to which I have added for comparison the mean of one week's observations at Gwalior during the hot winds in the end of May 1850, and the mean of another week in the end of March and beginning of April, which is the more correct time for comparison.

TABLE OF MOISTURE

Month	Districts	Height	Moisture				
			Dry in°	Wet in°	Dep^n in°	Dew point in°	Greatest Dep^n in°
September	Rukchu	15,634	67.5	40.5	27.0	18.9	31.0
September	Spiti	12,986	70.0	45.0	25.0	25.0	30.0
September	Ladak	11,500	65.7	42.9	22.8	24.6	23.5
October	Purik	11,196	55.8	37.2	18.6	20.5	19.7
August	Lahul	10,535	74.3	52.9	21.4	38.0	28.0
May-June	Gwalior		110.12	33.80	33.80	35.32	38.5
Mar-Apr.	Ditto		91.75	25.83	25.83	42.68	28.75

The hottest time in India is the end of May and the beginning of June, and the hottest month in Ladak is July. The fairest comparison therefore that can be made between the dryness of the two climates is that of September in Ladak, and of the end of March and the beginning of April in India. By this comparison it will be seen, that the plains of India are less arid than the lofty table-land of Rukchu, and that their dryness is about equal to that of the Spiti valley. The most convincing proof which I can give of the excessive dryness of the climate of Rukchu is the fact, that the stock of my gun, which had been exposed to fourteen hot season in India, shrank at least one-eighth of an inch during a single-month's residence in Rukchu.

VI.—RADIATION

I have already observed that the noon-day radiation of heat from the elevated table-lands of Ladak is one of the principal causes of the great dryness of the climate. The following table exhibits the maximum radiation of solar heat at about 1 P. M. in different districts of Ladak during the months of September and October, and in the plains of India in May and June, and in March and April. The observations were taken with a black-blub thermometer, by Newman, the instrument being invariably placed at a height of three inches above the ground, and fully exposed to the sun.

TABLE OF SOLAR RADIATION

Month	District	Height	Air in°	Black Bulb in°	Diff in°	Greatest Diff in°
September	Rukchu	15,634	65.75	86.75	23.00	23.5
September	Spiti	12,986	70.00	91.31	21.31	28.5
October	Ladak	11,500	58.54	85.33	26.79	39.5
October	Purik	11,196	55.83	73.16	17.33	25.5
May-June	Gwalior		109.87	129.66	19.46	23.75
Mar.April	Ditto		88.37	111.40	23.37	26.25

As the climate of India during March and April is just two months removed from the hottest season of the year, a fair comparison can be made between it and the climate of Ladak during the month of September. The comparison shows that the mean noon-day radiation of solar heat throughout Ladak is about the same as it is in the plains of India.

My observations for the terrestrial radiation of Ladak were all taken during the day, as I was afraid to leave the instrument exposed on a dark night amongst loose cattle. The instrument was one of Newman's register spirit thermometers, with the bulb fixed in the focus of a parabolic metallic mirror exposed to the clear northern sky. Compared with the observations taken on the plains of India for march and April, the terrestrial radiation of Ladak is extremely great. The lowest temperature observed at Gwalior was 10^0 below the external air, and the mean of the minima was only 6^0 below it. The minimum generally occurred about sunrise.

TABLE OF TERRESTRIAL RADIATION

	Hours	VII	VIII	IX	X	XI	Noon	I	II	III	IV	V	Mean daily dep
Puga	Air	18	25	38.5	45.7	54	56	58	61.75	59.75	56	50.5	
	Rad.Th.	9	18	27.5	35.0	43	45	49	55	52.5	48	44	
	Diff	9	7	11	10.7	11	11	9	6.75	7.25	8	6.5	8.84
Gya	Air			39	40	40.75	45.5	45.75	45	47			
	Rad.				31	32	36	36.5	36.5	38			
	Diff				9	8.75	9.5	9.25	8.5	9			9.00
Le	Air		38	46	48.5	55	56.5	58.5		60.5	57	58	
	Rad.		33	37	42	48	49	49		55	51	47	
	Diff.		5	9	6.5	7	7.5	9.5		5.5	6	11	6.80
Le	Air		36	39	41.5	45.5	53	52.25					
	Rad.		31	32	36	40	47	47.5					
	Diff		5	7	5.5	5.5	6	4.75					5.80
Gwalior	Air			78.5			86.25			87.75			
	Rad.			77.0			87.00			87.00			
	Diff			1.5			0			.75			

In the lofty table-land of Ladak, the greatest depression, which usually took place at 9 A. M., was 11° lower than the temperature of the external air. This was in Rukchu; but even in Ladak Proper the depression was no less than 9^0. The mean hourly depression throughout the day was 8^0 92' in Rukchu, but only 6^0 30' in Ladak.

VII.—SUPPOSED MILDNESS OF FORMER CLIMATE

Various circumstances induce me to believe that the climate of Ladak was formerly much milder and much less dry it is at present. The occurrence of vast quantities of fossil *fresh-water* shells in the sandy alluvium above the level of the present *salt-water* lakes of Ladak, proves that these lakes must once have been very extensive sheets of fresh water. In the case of the *Tsho-kar* or "White Lake," this is proved beyond all doubt, by the occurrence of fossil shells on the plain of Kyang, and in the deep gorge through which the waters of the lake once had exit into this place. As the plain itself had a gradual slope from the foot of the Thung-Lung Pass to the Sumgal River, the whole extent of this double lake can be seen by a glance at the accompanying sketch-map, which illustrates the ancient lake system of Ladak in those parts of the country which I have visited.

1. *The Kyang-Tsho* formerly extended from the foot of the Thung-Lung Pass to near the source of the Sumgal River, a length of thirty-five miles. It is difficult to ascertain the mean breadth, but it must have been about five miles. This would give an area of 175 square miles.

2. *The Tsho-kar* formerly flowed into the Kyang-Tsho, and was about twenty-five miles in length by five miles in breadth. The old beach-marks are distinctly visible on the mountain-sides, both to the north and south of the lake. I traversed along, the southern end of the Tsho-Kar in two different directions in 1846, and in 1847 along the northern end, and through the

gorge which formed its old exit into the Kyang-Tsho. Its principle feeder is a small fresh-water lake to the south, which once formed part of the old lake. The greatest extent of the Tsho-kar must have been about twenty-five miles by five miles, or 125 square miles. The two lakes together covered about 300 square miles.

3. *The Tshomo-Riri* formerly included a small salt-water lake, now lying about eight miles to the northward of it. The greatest extend was about twenty-five miles by five miles, or 125 square miles. It seems highly probable that it once had an exit from its southern end into the Para River, or perhaps into the Sumgal River.
4. *The Hanle* Lake is still of considerable size; but the clay deposits, which are found adhering in horizontal strata to the small isolated hills in the middle of the valley, and in sheltered positions at the sides, show that this lake must once have been one of the largest sheets of water in Ladak. In greatest extent must have been about twenty-five miles by twelve miles, or 300 square miles, with a mean depth of at least 100 feet.
5. *Lam-Tsho* is now only a small piece of fresh water, but it was most probably once a fine sheet of water about fifteen miles long by three miles broad, or forty-five square miles in extent.
6. The bed of the Indus, like that of all the other rivers, has once been crowded with a series of lakes. Two of these which came under my observation are shown in Plate V. The smaller one must have filled the valley, opposite Nyimo and Mud, for a length of twenty-five miles by three miles, or for about seventy-five square miles.
7. About Le, the vast plain of Chachot must once have been covered with water for some miles above

> Marchalang down to Le and Pitak. At Pitak, the lacustrine deposits of fine clay are still adhering to the rocks in horizontal strata, to a height of 750 feet above the level of the river. The whole extend must have been about thirty-five miles by six miles, or 210 square miles. Below Pịtak, the former channel of the Indus can be traced for many miles, by Phyang and Tharu, to Nyimo.

It is impossible to say what may have been the whole extent of the former lakes of Ladak, but as the ancient lakes of Rukchu, which I have described, must have covered a space of 840 square miles, or nearly one-sixth of the whole extent of the district, a vague idea may be formed of the general extent of the lake system, which must once have prevailed over Ladak. The vast lake of Pang-kong was probably not less than twenty miles in breadth by 100 miles in length, and must have covered an area of 2,000 square miles. This lake, with the others which I have described, would have occupied about one tenth of the whole extent of the country.

The former existence of these vast sheets of fresh water rests neither upon general appearances nor upon the vague assertions of tradition but upon the distinct evidences of vast beds of fine clay, which are found adhering to the rocks in horizontal strata, and which could only have been deposited in comparatively still water. Their existence is further proved by the abundance of fossil *fresh-water* shells that are found in the sandy clay deposits around the present *salt-water* lakes, and on the dry plain of Kyang. These shells are of two kinds- *Lymnaa auricularia* of all sizes, and *Cyclas rivicola*, which is only found of very small size preserved in the interior of the larger shells. As these mollusca do not now exist in Ladak at a greater elevation than between eleven and twelve thousand feet, it seems a probable conclusion that the country must at some former period have enjoyed a very much milder climate than that of the present day. This conclusion might indeed have been deduced from the former existence of the vast lakes which have been described. For the water vapourized by the sun must have been condensed by the cold of night, and the plains would then have been fertilized by rain, and the mountains covered by snow. Numerous streams would have flowed down the hill-sides in all directions, and the overflowing lakes would have formed mighty rivers.

Throughout Ladak there are numbers of vast ravines, many of them 500 feet deep, and as many yards broad, which could not possible have been formed by the scanty brooks that are not nearly lost in their meanderings from side to side of these enormous channels. In one of these vast river-beds the scanty rill of the Sum-gal now purls along at the southern end of the plain of Kyang. The sides of this channel are masses of alluvial boulders are gravel, which once formed the bed of the Kyang-Tsho. The rocky. barrier,. below the junction of the Sum-gal rivers, was probably worn away, gradually at first, Until the plain of Kyang became almost dry: after which, on the occurrence of any sudden disruption, the water of the Sum-gal would have rushed violently onward, cutting for themselves a deep channel in the soft beds on the lake. The Kyang-Tsho must have been gradually drained; but I have a suspicion that the Tshomo-Riri Lake once had an exit into the Sun-gal, and that its accumulated waters were suddenly drained off by the disruption of the Sum-gal barrier. That the subsidence of the waters of the Kyang-Tsho must have been very gradual is proved by the abundance of shells now lying on the upper part of the plain, all of which would have been swept away by even a moderate current. Is it possible that the whole mass of the country can have been gradually elevated?

(From *Ladak—Physical, Statistical and Historical, 1853*)

6

Into Ladhak

By
A. Reeve Heber and *Kathleen M. Heber*

At daybreak next morning we were off again. On the whole there was less snow on this side of the pass, and by about six a.m. we reached the Roosevelt's camping ground on the hillside, the front of their caravan just debouching down the valley, those in the rear still standing about in groups, as their loads were fastened on. Ahead of all could be seen the sun-helmeted figures of the four sahibs. The stretch of road now to be covered brought vividly to the Doctor Memsahib's mind the last time she travelled upwards over it. That year the winter snow had been excessive and though the Zogi was not crossed till the middle of June there were still long stretches completely covered with it. To grown-ups this would have been no obstacle but we had with us then our two children, Helen the elder being five, and Josephine the younger not seven months. The former rode a pony, and, having no khud sense at all, was perfectly happy save when fatigue overtook her. The wee mite was carried in a wicker cot with a pole which the coolies swung on their shoulders passing under wicker loops attached below the roof. In this nest she slept serenely, and, even when her blue eyes opened on the white world around, she was blissfully unconscious of all danger. It was the mother who was all too susceptible to every difficulty, potential as well as real. When one of the coolies slipped in the track on the steep hillside sloping acutely down to the rushing river below, and the little cot swayed dizzily for a moment, it was she who caught her breath in dread suspense; but there was always another figure in attendance who was quick to give an extra hand. This was Choskyit, the children's Ladaki nurse, a faithful, delightful woman, and a picturesque lady as she rode along in her dark plum-coloured, full-skirted Ladaki home-spun, with a fur-lined waistcoat fastened on the shoulder in Tibetan style, and her red velvet Ladaki hat turned up at the back and sides, showing the black lamb-skin lining. Large round hoops of seed pearls with a few small turquoises and red stones adorned her ears and framed her kind cheerful face, which gave the lie to the rather barbarous leather horsewhip she carried. Riding behind her baby's dandy, scolding the men roundly when they carried it crookedly or loitered, she was off her pony in a minute to lend her aid in any time of need, to adjust the curtain to a change in the direction of the sun at a turn in the road, or to see that the little one was comfortable and happy. So trustworthy was she that she and the baby were always sent off first in the early morning, the parents catching up before the stop for the roadside meal. And now again the Memsahib had reached the piece of road where the track led over the frozen ice and snow, undermined by the rushing river, so that every now and then it ended abruptly where another large piece had cracked off the bank and remained tilted up at an acute angel into the river. At such places a new path was beginning to be trodden out further up the hillside, but, when it joined the old one again, one wondered how long before any new piece would in turn yield to the pressure; whether perhaps one's own pony would prove to be "the last straw," and pony and rider suddenly find themselves taking a sideways somersault into the river. However, the baby was now safely in Srinagar, so there were no fears for her, and such dangers as the road presented merely acted as thrills to the grown-up mentality. Again Dromar went ahead and his rider found herself in the company of the head cook of the expedition. Going along together with his help every now and then to hold the stirrup for remounting after a nasty bit, and conferring with him as to the track advisable to pursue when the path suddenly broke off into the now increasing river, they conducted such conversation as the Memsahib's limited Hindustani would allow. So over snow and stream we journeyed, then, coming at last to an open plain free from snow, where Dromar could indulge in his favourtie amble, we parted like "ships that pass in the night."

It was on this part of the pass that we distinguished the call of some of its inhabitants. Not only the shrill cry of the marmot was heard in the stillness of this wilderness of bare stone and rock peeping out of the patches of snow a silence only broken by the rushing stream, but even the spring call of the cuckoo came frequently across the clear air, while nearer Ma'tayan the song of the soaring lark trilling in exquisite joyousness, floated on the air. The song of the cuckoo recalled a previous crossing in mid June of another year, with late snow, but far less than at this time, for just about the same place its call was heard, and could be traced to one pathetically lonely tree up on the hillside. Here also at a bend in the river, which was a fierce, wide, rushing torrent by June, a zo, the hybrid between the yak and the cow, was seen struggling in the water. We thought it had arrived there by a mishap, but were surprised to be forced to the conclusion that it was purposive, for, steering a calculated course very slantingly across the tremendous current, it ultimately was deposited on the other side, got out, shook itself, and walked calmly on to seek pasture, as though such an immersion were a daily occurrence.

Dromar soon overtook the walking expeditionary sahibs, and, as on the previous day, drew up at the head of the whole procession at Matayan Rest-house, the pass with all its dangers and difficulties now well behind. One pleasing ceremony was missing at this snowy crossing. It is usual when a white man crosses the pass for the first time, for the ponymen to present him as he nears the rest-house with a little posy of flowers, which he is supposed to acknowledge with the usual rupee, an exchange of mutual compliment and congratulation on the safe accomplishment of the crossing of man and beast, but with the pass covered in its white mantle, there was too much concern for real safety to attend to this little ritual, even had nature been able to prepare her spring favours. It was amusing to recollect how on coming down from Leh one August with their five-and-a-half months' baby who had been born up there, the Doctor and his wife had paid toll for the infant's first crossing though they themselves were exempt. On this second day several of the travellers suffered with sore eyes, and a bottle of eye lotion which the Doctor Memsahib happened to have with her was in great request. Two or three natives were passed, heads directed downwards, one with a precious umbrella, another even holding and end of his puggaree across his painful eyes. One of our party had a severely inflamed eye in spite even of glasses and veil, and this snow blindness is extremely painful. Among the patients was the elder son of the Rajah of Khaplu, who was found with his family at Matayan, and, although we arrived there at just after nine a.m., they had not started off on the next march, Matayan being the full stage from Baltal which they had actually achieved the previous day. The Doctor Memsahib went in to see the purdah lady and found her perfectly composed and cheerful and ready for her next bumping. Meanwhile the Roosevelt party had passed on to Dras, twelve miles further, having only come four or five miles from their camping place. The Doctor's party stopped to lunch or rather "brunch" (for this roadside meal is usually a combination of breakfast and lunch) on the bungalow verandah, and, when, the ponymen came up, they said they would prefer to go on to Dras rather than stay the night at Matayan, as there is no pony fodder there. So we took to the road again, the snow having now receded to the distant hills and left our path clear, and by about three p.m. reached Dras.

But we must not, in all fairness to the Zogi, leave it as though its presiding demons always held sway. In the three months of July, August and September, this dreaded road loses all its difficulties and is transformed into one of nature's most beautiful flower gardens. A visitor to Leh re-crossing it at the end of August describes it as follows: "The Zogi on our return journey was one vast flower garden and rockery, impossible in its wealth of beauty to describe. From my pony's back, I counted seventy different wild flowers crossing the Zogi La alone. There were carpets of edelweiss and blue gentian, mauve daisies, yellow ragwort, pink 'coralflower' and rich purple pelargonium. The whole hillside in one part would be sky blue with a sheet of forget-me-nots, further beyond the rich verdure of the grass there would be a mass of pink or mauve where the flower grew in rich profusion." After the bare hills of Ladak, the green slopes are extraordinarily verdant, and large flocks of sheep and goats are brought up here from the Plains in summer to pasture. We were particularly interested, one August, when stoppping for the night at Machoi on our way down, to notice one of these enormous flocks pass near the rest-house in single file. One after another they came in unceasing procession, over one thousand of them, tall Kashmiri goats with their look of foolish fearfulness ludicrously mixed with the patriarchal solemnity lent by their tufted beards, all of them so expressive, and many with irrisistibly humorous resemblances to one's human acquaintances, sheep of all sorts, mothers bleating and young ones following: it seemed as if they would never end. Fortunately for us their shepherds had set up a little camp quite near us at the foot of the great glacier behind Machoi, and we were able to procure a little fresh goat's milk from them instead of resorting to tins. With the words and tune of the song "The Lord God planted a garden" running in the writer's ears, the following adaptation evolved in response to the surrounding scenery :

SONG OF THE ZOGI LA

The Lord God planted a garden,
　　Up here on the roof of the world,
Where in winter the snow was warden,
　　And the wild winds swept and whirled.

So near to the gates of heaven,
    Its Gardener lived in the sky,
And colour and fragrance blended
    To gladden the passer-by.

And there on the verdant hillside
Were pastures clean and sweet,
    Tucked in with fleecy cloudlets
Where sky and hilltop meet.
    And many a glistening glacier
Gave birth to a shining stream
    That bore the life-giving water
To where the great rivers gleam.

(From *Himalayan Tibet and Ladakh, 1903*)

7

Ladhak : The Plateaus

By
Drew F.

Though Rupshu, taken as a whole, may be called a table-land, its valleys being,15,000 and its mountains 20,000 feet above the sea, yet the valleys themselves I have preferred to call "high-level valleys" rather than plateaus, thinking the former phrase more likely to convey to the mind a true notion of their form. Now, however, we come to certain tracts to which the words "plateau" and "table-land" may fairly be applied. They are not, indeed, of that complete table form which consists in a mass of high land descending at once on all sides; here, as in every case I have met with in the Himalayas, the lofty flat is surrounded by yet loftier mountains, the plateau is edged by ranges, or by a ring, of mountains. Still, in the cases we are coming to, as contrasted with Rupshu, the width of the flat is very great, the height of the bounding mountains bears to it a much smaller ratio.

Between the country which drains into the Shayok and that whose streams flow into the Karakash or into other rivers of Eastern Turkistan, is an elevated mass of ground- plains surrounded and crossed by rocky ridges-whence water finds no outlet, but dries up on the plains themselves. The level of these elevated plains or plateaus is 16,000 and 17,000 feet; the area of the isolated drainage-basin (as near as can be estimated from the explorations hitherto made) is no less than 7,000 square miles, the space being 100 miles long from north to south, with an average width from east to west of 70 miles.

Our knowledge of this tract is but scant, and of a portion of it only conjectural. It is truly a part, "where mortal foot hath ne'er or rarely been." The first European to cross it was one who did not return to describe it. In the year 1857 Adolphe Schlagintweit, in company with Muhammad Amin, an Arghaun, of Yarkand, went from the Changchenmo Valley across these plateaus to Yarkand. Thence Schlagintweit went on to Kashgar, where he was killed (in August 1857) by Walli Muhammad, the then ruler, who himself later met his death from Yaqub Beg, the present Amir. The first written account of the tract is that taken from the mouth of Muhammad Amin, the guide, and given in the 'Punjab Trade Report, 1862,' in the form of an itinerary. The next European who crossed it was Mr. W.H.Johnson, who at the time was on the staff of the G.T.Survey. In the 1865 this bold and enduring traveller took advantage of an invitation from the agent of the ruler of Khutan to visit that city, and on his way to it he followed the route, as far as the foot of the Kuenlun, which Schlagintweit and Muhammad Amin had taken. Mr. Johnson, the first (and as yet the last) European who in later times has reached the city of Khutan, has given us, besides details of the way, an account of the country he visited as it was during the short period of its history between the break-up of the Chinese power in Eastern Turkistan and the establishment of that of Yaqub Beg. But we are here more concerned with the intermediate highlands, of which a map constructed by Mr. Johnson has been published by the G.T.Survey. This necessarily has not the same degree of detail as the maps published by them of tracts which have been regularly surveyed, for it was made on a hurried journey over ground where to halt was to starve; still, for the opportunities, it includes a large amount of information, and it has been the foundation of every map of that region constructed since. A few years afterwards, Mr. Hayward, Mr. Shaw, and Dr. Cayley went separately over the plateaus, the last to explore for a trade-route, the other two on their adventurous journey to Yarkand. In the next year, 1869, I myself went across the plateaus to the eastern branch of the Karakash River, following partly in Mr. Johnson's and partly in Dr. Cayley's footsteps, and in this journey made the observations which I shall now put down. In 1870 Mr. Forsyth's party, on the first mission to Yarkand, went over the plains; they returned by a new route on the west. Then, in 1873, one party attached to the second Yarkand mission took the old route, but as yet no detailed news of their doings have been made public.

In the regions through which the reader has hitherto followed me-in the high-level valleys, among the bare mountains, of Rupshu-no great difficulty in providing supplies and means of carriage presents itself to the traveller. The inhabitants of Rupshu, though few, are enough in number to attend to the wants of those who pass through their ground, and their cattle do all that is wanted for the carrying of baggage. Bare as that country is when looked at as a whole, yet, with very few exceptions, there are to be found, at distances which are practicable for a day's march, water, some amount of pasture for the baggage animals, and fuel, either furze or *burtse*, or sometimes (as at one or two of the halting-places in the Indus Valley) the dung of the kyang, or wild ass. But now, in going beyond the basin of the Indus, especially in traversing the high plains with their enclosed drainage-area, one is put to straits to provide carriage for the necessaries of one's camp, and to procure food for the beasts of burden themselves. For at some stages fuel is wanting, at other grass, at others water even. Hence special arrangements are necessary to accomplish the journey; and even with these some loss of baggage animals may be expected.

Tanktse is the place whence a start should be made; it is the last large village, and contains a Government store-house, and is the head-quarters of a *kardar*, or manager, under the Governor of Ladakh. The smaller one's camp, the lighter the baggage, the more likely is one to get comfortably through the journey. With half-a-dozen men of my own, and an equal number of people from the Tanktse and Pangkong region, we took for our luggage and supplies eleven yaks and five ponies, and brought back, after a month's marching, six yaks and four ponies. This and other experience shows that ponies are far better for the work than yaks; for ponies can carry, besides a light load of baggage for their master, barley for themselves, which yaks, not being used to eating it, will not be able to live on; ponies also do the day's march quicker than the yak, and therefore have so much the more time to graze on the scanty, thin, pasture that here and there is found. My own journey was the more trying for the animals in that, after passing through the most desert part to where the valleys begin to decline to Turkistan and to become less bare of vegetation, they had to return over the same desert, without recruiting themselves in the lower pastures.

From Tanktse, or Pangkong, the road leads one over ground that was described in the last chapter to the Changchenmo Valley. This it leaves by the valley in which is situated Gogra, which is the last place where water, grass, and fuel are all to be found in plenty. I shall not trouble the reader to follow me through each day's march as I made it, but shall rather try to give him an idea of the character of the country such as I myself derived from observing it in the outward and homeward journeys, with the help, I must add of Mr. Johnson's map. A list of the marches will be found in Appendix IV., Route 27.

THE SOUTHERN WATERSHED

The Southern Watershed of the plateaus lies to the north of the eastern portion of the Changchenmo Valley, and is continued eastwards beyond the head of it. The ravines that lead up from that valley to the watershed are in their lower parts bounded by steep, more or less rocky, hills; as we get to the sources of them, they rise with a more gentle inclination, and their sides become more smooth. The ridge which here makes the watershed is a line of rounded hill, of a height of from 19,500 to 20,000 feet. The Passes over it are not cut deep; the one that we crossed, as I found by means of the Boiling

Point thermometer, which gave 178·9° as the temperature of boiling water, was 19,500 feet, this being but a hundred or two feet below the general level of the ridge; one or two other Passes are somewhat lower. Even at that high level the Pass was free from snow; there were some snowbeds near, but these were not permanent ones. The difference in the character of the form of the ground on the two sides of the pass was very striking. On the north side there were low hills of rounded form, down-like; to the south the summits were no higher than these, and the rocks were the same, but, the ground being cut into deeply by steep ravines, it had the ruggedness, and the degree of elevation above the immediate valleys, which give the more usual mountainous character. The rock here is not a hard one; it is shale, with interstratifications of sandstone, the strata of which are continually undulating. This rock was disintegrated so as to make a comparatively smooth dark-brown surface, either altogether of loose stones or of stones and mud intermingled, or sometimes with the two arranged, by the melting and sliding snow, in alternate lines on the slopes. All is completely bare of vegetation.

Over the watershed, for some miles to the north, extend these hills, rounded at top, and gently sloping to the valleys, not deep, which lead away northwards. These valleys, may be 500 feet, may be 1,000 feet, below the summits, are sometimes dry; but those which reach far back have small streams flowing in them, which unite into one that flows away to the eastward, and, it is believed, empties its waters into a saline lake, where they evaporate.

From the watershed ridge northwards for 15 or 20 miles extend these hills, varied by some ridges more rocky. Then, near the place marked Burchathang (or Burtse-thang), begins ground of another kind. On rising to the summit of the last low ridge, we suddenly acquire a wide view over an immense plain, which begins a few hundred feet below us, and extends without a break, in front, from south to north, for 16 or more miles, and from right to left for a distance that must be 50 or

60 miles. This plain has of late years been called by the Ladakhis *Lingzhithang,* and the name has been adopted by other travellers, and may well be continued. It is the southern division of the plateaus which lie between the ridge north of Changchenmo (the watershed we have just been looking at) and the Kuenlun Mountains. For the northern division, which we shall come to later, separated from this by ridges of hill (which I call the "Lokzhung Mountains"), I propose the name *"Kuenlun Plains."* These reach to the very foot of the Kuenlun Range; they consist not of one wide open plain, but of a plain a good deal divided, though not absolutely separated, into tracts by long branch ridges. These three, Lingzhithang, the Lokzhung Mountains, and the Kuenlun Plains, we will now successively examine.

LINGZHITHANG

The lateral dimensions of this plain were given above. Its elevation,as near as I could calculate from two sets of Boiling Point observations which were taken from Pangkong as a datum, is 17,300 feet on the southern side, and 17,100 feet on the northern. There is a very gradual slope from south to north, or from south-west to north-east, one imperceptible to the eye, but marked by the course of the streams. Besides this general slope there are minor variations of level; these, however, do not (as far as I saw) exceed 20 feet; the plain, therefore, is wonderfully even. In character it is bare and earthy; in colour it is brown and white in alternate spaces, according as the whitish clay which is the foundation soil of the whole is exposed on the surface or is strewn over or covered with stones. It is indeed "a weary waste, expanding to the skies."

If, from upon this plain, we survey the mountains around, we see that on the south, the side we have come from, it is bounded by low-sloping hills. On the west come bolder hills and even snowy peaks; in these there is a gap, to follow which would lead one down to the river Shayok. All along the north of the plain is the range of the Lokzhung Mountains, whose direction is west-north-west and east-south-east; this begins on the west with two peaks between 20,000 and 21,000 feet, and continues at from 18,000 to 19,000 feet, a range of irregular hills, steep, rocky, and peaked. To the east-south-east the plain at first seems boundless, but again, from some points, summits of mountains become visible, which probably belong to an enclosing ridge.

The climate of this high plain is one of almost daily extremes. The sun may rise in a clear sky, and, as it climbs, warm the ground with a speed proportioned to the thinness of the air that the rays have to pass through, increasing its warmth till two or three hours past noon; the air being still, the lowermost layer of it becomes somewhat raised in temperature, but the traveller feels chiefly the double effect of the direct rays and the radiation from below, and he labours over the desert plain oppressed by the heat. When the sun has declined but half-way to the horizon, there springs up a wind from the south-west or west-south-west, a keen and searching wind, that quickly makes one suffer from cold more than before one did from the heat. So it continues till nightfall, then gradually the wind dies away; in the still night the ground loses its heat, and a severe frost occurs by morning. On the 26th August 12°, and on the 11th September 10° Fahr. were the temperatures recorded by my minimum thermometer. This, I think, is the usual course in summer time, but, exceptionally, cloud, or a storm of wind, comes on that tends to lower the day and perhaps to raise the night temperature. One cannot tell to what depth snow falls on this plain in winter; I have never heard of anyone having traversed it at that season, but I saw it white with snow on the 12th September; the whole plain was covered with snow, while of the bounding mountains the lower slopes were of the brown colour of their own rocks, their summits only being whitened by the fresh fall; but at that time of year such a fall would be sure to melt. The winter's snow certainly stays on the hills till summer is well on. The streams which the melting snow supplies are apt to dry up by the middle of August; in crossing the plain at that time, and again in September, I found but a few pools of water in one of the chief stream-courses; of these one was brackish and one fresh. One day I was on the look out, as the goal of the day's march, for the salt lake marked in Mr. Johnson's map. Several times a mirage deceived us by imitating a lake; at last we reached the very spot where it was marked to be, and there found but the bed of the lately-dried-up lake. The lake seemed to have been three miles across, but very shallow; doubtless it fills in the early summer, receiving the drainage of some of the southern and of the western portion of the plain. By evaporation it becomes saline, and as the season advances dries up altogether. This wide plain, dry and bare, and exposed at noonday to rays of the sun untempered by thick air, is well calculated to produce mirage, which depends on the differing temperatures (and therefore differing densities) of different horizontal layers of air. The first time I crossed it, a striking and somewhat puzzling mirage prevailed. Eastwards the plain seemed to end in a boundless ocean, in which were strange-shaped islands, some bearing masses of snow; the inverted image of them was reflected from below, and a repetition of the double image beneath that. As one stoops low to the ground the ocean seems to ripple to but a hundred yards from one; sometimes the appearance of water was very distinct to us as we were seated, but disappeared on our rising. From other points the mirage made the plain look like a beautiful lake with steep banks, backed by high snowy mountains.

The area of the plain itself and of the inner slope of the surrounding mountains makes an isolated basin of drainage. In the western part the waters flow towards the temporary lake above mentioned, some very probably drying up on the way to it; in the eastern part they go to the larger lake marked on the map, which has, I believe, been viewed from a distance by some member of the G.T.Survey. The isolation of the basin was the last considerable change that occurred; that a lake, whether of enclosed drainage or communicating with the sea, existed for a great length of time, is proved by the composition of the ground; the whole soil that covers the flat *has been deposited in a lake.* Mr. Johnson on his journey recognized the fact that the plain had been a large lake, and a close examination of the substance of the ground clearly proves it, as will now be seen. The small differences of level that have been spoken of resolve themselves, speaking generally, into a higher tract and a lower, with 20 feet, or less than that, of difference between them; there is also an unevenness of the higher plateau, made by watercourses having been cut through it as the surface-water drained down to the lower tract. This is extremely like what we saw in the Salt Lake plain of Rupshu; but there is a yet more important resemblance in the substance of the plateau. Small cliffs at the edge of it, or the minor ravines cut into it, show that below, as at the surface, there is a whitish or a drab clay; some of this is a massive clay, some of it is laminated; some of it is calcareous. Interstratified with the clay is sand, some so fine as to be impalpable. Again, there are laminae of flat water-plants, and in places a mass of these plants some inches in thickness, with earth intermixed. These phenomena, repeated whenever one gets an opportunity of seeing into the substance of the plateau, leave no doubt in my mind that the strata were deposited in a still lake. The sections only enable us to say this of 20 feet in thickness of the material; how much deeper the lake deposits exist-to what extent the levelling of this wide flat surface is due to a filling up by such deposits-we have at present no means of ascertaining. The lower tract has stones on its surface from a quarter of an inch to three inches across, most of them angular or nearly so, some rounded, of limestone or of sandstone. That, in part at all events, this lower tract has been denuded out of the higher plateau, is proved by an outlier of the clay and plant-beds left in the lower space at a considerable distance from the rest. It is probable that the lower plain was cut out both by the water of the lake, acting at its margin, when it had already much diminished and had become localized in the lowest parts, and later by streams, which widened their way by denuding laterally. At one part, over a considerable space, was a curious result of the denudation of the substance of the plateau-a strange form of the portions of the clay which were left; this I saw four or five miles south and south-west of Tsothang, over a tract of some square miles. The rough sketch shows the form in question. There are mounds of a peculiar shape, with a steep and a sloping side, the steep face always looking in one direction, which is 15° south of west. The mounds are from two to twelve feet above the hollows between them. I have been much puzzled to account for these forms; their direction is most probably to be connected with the direction of the prevailing strong winds with it about coincides; one feels inclined to speculate on the possibility of the wind itself, by drifting fine sand, to act on a surface already made irregular by stream-denudation, having carved them thus. The lacustrine deposits hitherto described are clearly those of the deeper water of the former lake; we will now go to the edge of the plain to see if any marginal traces of the water of it can be found. Approaching the irregular Lokzhung Range, we see that the light-coloured flat of hard clay ends off with a marked boundary against ground sloping slightly upwards; the slope is at an angle of about 2°. At first the soil of this incline is clay, with stones strewn over it; farther up is sand, more or less in lines; and farther up still the substance was all sandy or shingly, with slight ridges in it; these are clearly the littoral deposits of our lake. Then as we go up still higher, and especially as we examine the ground on the north-west of Tsothang, we meet with complete beaches, parallel curved shingle-banks; some of the shingle was cemented by carbonate of lime dissolved from the stones themselves, which are of limestone. Beaches of this ordinary kind are seen up to 150 feet above the flat plain; at a higher level still there are deposits the mode of whose occurrence will be understood from the next diagram. There is a line of rocky cliff between 50 and 100 feet high; at the foot of it are distinct beaches; above it is a mass of rounded stones, forming the top of the hill, which may be as much as 300 feet above the plain at Tsothang. We have, therefore, in the intermediate or lower beaches, evidence of the lake having at one time had its shore along the edge of these Lokzhung Mountains; in the upper masses of shingle, evidence of a still higher water-level. Of this we will try to understand the full bearing as we go farther on and become acquainted with the form of the ground in the Lokzhung Range and beyond. Hitherto we have looked only on the north side of Lingzhithang for shore-marks, but we must not forget to trace them, if possible, on the south. Both times that I came to the southern edge-going and returning- I was under disadvantages; the first time night was falling, and it was impossible to make any examination; the second, a storm of wind and snow came on which much hindered it. This, however, I saw; that the ridge, of a height about 300 feet, which the path crosses as one approaches Lingzhithang from the south, has at its upper part a conglomerate of stones of the two kinds of limestone that occur near; the conglomerate is in beds which slope northwards 35° or 40°. It reaches also on to the northern side of the ridge.

Leaving for the present further discussion as to the history of the lake, we will go to the next division of the region, and afterwards return to the subject.

THE LOKZHUNG MOUNTAINS

These are a complex range of mountains running in a west-north-west and east-south-east direction from the western to the eastern bounding-ridge of the Plateaus. Its length is 60 miles, its width from 15 to 20 miles. It is a region of rocky hills with flat dry stony valleys between them. The map but partly expresses the character of this range; it would require a more detailed survey than has been made for their complications to be represented. It is not one range with branching spurs, but it may be spoken of as a tract occupied by parallel hill-ranges (running from west-north-west to east-south-east) of various outline, according to the kind of rock each is composed of; these ranges are broken or cut through by valleys which lead from the southernmost edge of the hill-tract towards the north-east; the breaks in the different ranges are not opposite to each other but are in echelon, so that each valley zigzags, now flowing south-east between two ranges, now breaking through one to the north-east, again turning south-east, and ultimately leading out to the Kuenlun Plains.

I have put in a sketch of one of the widest of the stony valleys among the Lokzhung Mountains; it leads up to the western range, in which is a conspicuous peak of 21,000 feet, a peak too steep is bear snow, except a little in the saddle-like hollow.

None of the valleys drain out to Lingzhithang; the rounded ridge which is about 300 feet above that place, that bears coarse shingle on the top, makes the watershed between Lingzithang and the Kuenlun Plains; for this is continuous, while the higher, the rocky, ridges behind it are broken through.

I said that the different ridges vary in character according to the rock they are composed of. There is an older encrinitic limestone, dark grey in colour, which usually is dipping high; this makes hills not the most rugged. Ferruginous sandstone, and above that a limestone that contains hippurites, lie unconformably on the older limestone; these sometimes make isolated hills of various forms, sometimes, with a high dip of the strata, make a rugged serrated ridge. Some portion of this newer formation gives, in the weathering, a reddish-brown surface; other portions, of a light-coloured limestone or crystalline marble, make conspicuous white rocks.

The path traverses this range from Tsothang to Thaldat; it takes two days' march in and out among the mountains to go through them. The road does not follow one valley, but passes from one to another by crossing low necks. More than one of these necks which I crossed were accumulations of rounded material-coarse shingle-like what composes the summit of the rounded ridge behind Tsothang. From one of these was a fall of 100 feet on one side and 200 feet on the other, but it is not certain that the whole mass was made of shingle; it may be that there was rock within.

THE KUENLUN PLAINS

This, as was said above, is the name I give to that part of these uplands which lies between the Lokzhung and the Kuenlun Mountains.

The place called Thaldat is on the north-eastern edge of the Lokzhung Hills; the ground slopes gently down from it, for 200 feet of fall, to the flat of the Kuenlun Plains. To the south-east the boundary of the Plains is not seen, except that from a commanding position we may get sight of the summits of some distant snowy mountains. The mountains which bound the Plains on the north are both massive and lofty snow-topped hills, part of the great Kuenlun Range. From the different mountain ranges long extending but not lofty spurs project, separating the various parts of the irregularly-shaped area of the Plains.

The level of the Plains is 16,000 feet above the sea, that is 1000 feet below Lingzhithang. The surface is sometimes of hard clay, sometimes of a softer mixture, half sand, half clay. The variations of level are greater than any we met with in Lingzhithang; from one upper plateau there is a fall of 60 feet to a lower watercourse plain, and numerous small ravines, cutting through nearly to that depth, make very irregular ground. Partly from these ups and downs and partly from the yielding character of the dry loamy earth (which certainly increased the labour of walking by one-half), we found the way very laborious; for here also, one must recollect, any increased exertion immediately makes the rarity of the air to be felt. The upper plateau is in parts covered with fragments of a brown calcareous cake, an inch or less in thickness-biscuit would be the more descriptive word. At the lower levels there are shallow saline lakes here and there. The flats of greatest extent are those to the north-east and east from Thaldat; from these many ramifications extend; a branch runs up between spurs (by the place called Yangpa) to the Kuenlun, with a width of some five miles; this again branches to the west and opens out into that most saline portion of all (which we shall examine later) between Patsalung and Londing. At the head of some of these branches, the plain, narrowing, changes into a slightly sloping alluvium of streams that come down from the Kuenlun Mountains; higher up this changes into steeper-sloped alluvial deposits in among the spurs of these mountains. These are part of the foremost ridge of the Kuenlun; it is a bold dark line some 4,000 feet above the plain; behind it is the lofty snowy range that reaches to close on 22,000 feet. On the southern face of the highest ridge the easternmost branch of the Karakash River has its source. The drainage of the Plains does not communicate with that river; there is a barrier which we shall presently look at. The Eastern Karakash, at its nearest point, flows in a valley between the north-west corner of the Plains and the foot of the great mountains; here it is 15,000 feet above the sea, 1,000 feet below the plain-level; there is a steep descent to it in a narrow side ravine. The Eastern Karakash Valley is here a few hundred yards in width; it slopes down to the west-north-west at an angle of about 3°. On the north it is bounded immediately by the main Kuenlun chain; on the south by spurs from a more southerly, nearly parallel, line of mountains. These southern mountains are of slate and shale, and the same rock extends some way up the slope of the Kuenlun opposite; but at this part the ridge itself of the Kuenlun, and farther east the whole height of the slope, are of granite; the road on its descent from the Plains to the Eastern Karakash Valley is about on the junction-line of the two rocks. The Kuenlun Mountains make a continuous ridge, with some higher peaks covered with permanent consolidated snow-beds; these tower 6,000 or 7,000 feet above the valley; just north of the high peak at the corner, a glacier, pure white, comes down in a hollow to a level some 3,000 feet lower than that of the ridge. All is, as usual, bare; above are surfaces steep but not precipitous, below are taluses and other stony accumulations; down the valley rocky spur after spur from both sides comes forward until the curving of the northern ridge with its high mountains shuts in the view.

Having thus considered the general form of the ground as far as I myself have seen it in this direction-for, after going a few miles down this Eastern Karakash Valley, I turned back towards Ladakh-we will return to the Kuenlun Plains and examine them with the same attention that we gave to Lingzhithang.

I have explained that the various parts of the flat communicate with each other, for they are separated only by ramifying, not by interlacing, hills. The substance of this flat consists of interstratifications of white or drab clay with sand and some calcareo-argillaceous flakes-such as we saw on the surface broken up in a biscuit form. This is quite parallel to what we found in Lingzhithang; it is clearly the deeper deposit of a lake; the biscuit-stone frequently, or generally, has impressions of plant-stems, and we sometimes find the same in layers in the clay. We conclude then that the small lakes scattered over are but the remnants of one that covered all the flat. To continue the same kind of investigation, we will now look along the foot of the lines of hill, at the edge of the flat, for those marginal evidences of a lake that our eyes or minds have now become accustomed to. At various places we see these as clearly as could possibly be desired. About Thaldat, though there is no beach proper, there is found a sloping littoral deposit of clay with small angular stones. Some fifteen miles north-north-east from Thaldat (at the farther side of that stretch of flat), when about a mile short of the hills, we reached again to the littoral deposit of the old lake-clay, with small stones, unrounded and half-rounded, within it. Then, right at the foot of those hills, we came on lines of shingle-beach, of unrounded and slightly-rounded stones, at successive levels up to 80 to 100 feet above the plain; these beaches stretched from spur to spur of the hill, sometimes connecting two headlands as by an isthmus of shingle, with a hollow left between it and the line of the hill. At the extreme point of this branch of mountains a high bank of beach connects it with an isolated hill beyond; again, at the north side of the branch, was a great accumulation of shingle, extending both in length and width towards the flat, first in ridges and afterwards in a flatter form, constituting a subaqueous littoral deposit, some of which has been cemented hard by carbonate of lime.

Now again come the questions—what made the lake? where would have been the outlet? is there any sign of a dam?

In trying to obtain facts in answer to these questions I wished for means of getting more accurate levels than I was able to obtain; I wanted both appliances for this and time for using them. But as far as I could judge by eye and by Boiling Point observations, the outlet of all this branching flat was once to the Eastern Karakash Valley. Further, I saw that the cause of the stoppage of this outlet, the dam which made the lake—the lake, I take it, which covered all the flat—also existed here. It is possible that at different times the dam may have been at different spots, and even may have been of different kinds. If, as is possible, the lake existed during part of the glacial period, then a glacier itself, with its moraines—perhaps a glacier occupying the head of the Eastern Karakash Valley—may have formed the dam. However that may have been, there is now, at the spot we are speaking of (four or five miles in a direction 30° east of south from Brangsa encampment on the Eastern Karakash), a neck between the Eastern Karakash drainage and that of the basin of the Kuenlun Plains; this neck is made by two alluvial fans, from opposite sides of the outlet valley, coming down and meeting. I do not say that this particular fan-made neck is high enough to account for the highest of our beaches, but I both believe that it acted as a dam at some stage of the lake's existence, and also that here or within a snort distance existed each and all of the barriers of the lake on this side.

We have now come to a corner of the Plains which I have not specially described, but it shows some points of peculiar interest. From the fans that make the neck, southward for more than 20 miles, is a comparatively narrow flat (from one to three miles in width) which communicates on the south-east with the wider plain. We descend into this from the neck, and at once come on lake-deposits. We see flaky clay, the deposit of still water, and upon this we see parallel curves of beach reaching across the valley, which in succession shut off the end of the lake (at its different stages of level) in that northerly direction; the lake at one time extended beyond them, and deposited some clay-beds, and later, on a recession, caused by a lowering by drying, of the waters, the beaches were formed in ribs upon it. Side valleys that join in on the west were once arms of the lake; the marginal indications extend for some distance up them; but of one that I saw the mouth had been closed by a bank of shingle that had formed right across it. Where one of these valleys comes in the old high margin of the lake is beautifully shown out by the beaches; these consist of flat stones, with their edges rounded; angular pieces have lately fallen from the cliff, but to distinguish them from the shingle matter is not difficult; the beaches are at various levels, up to 200 feet above the lowest part of the valley near. Here the downward succession of deposit is shown with great completeness; in the uppermost 120 feet, there are steep slopes of beach; below are flatter, shelving, beaches; lower still the ground is nearly flat, composed of dry mud and stones; again lower is a flat all of dry clay. The level of this hardened clay-bed of the lake is of course below that of the neck made by the two fans, but I think that the level of the highest beach is above it. This neck then, considered as a dam, would not account for the highest rise of the waters; as before said, other dams—of ice or moraine—probably came into action near the same spot. At this part of the Plains we are, I believe, in the lowest portion of the whole basin. Being nearest the original outlet of the valley that preceded the lake, it would naturally have the lowest level, unless disproportionately raised by the lake deposits. I believe that on the waters lessening by evaporation they receded into this corner, and for long occupied this space in a narrow lake, during which time a concentration, and ultimately a precipitation, of the saline materials they contained and were being supplied with, were going on. For this tract is the one of all where there is the greatest deposit of salts. At other parts, indeed, there had been seen a thin cake, or else an efflorescence, of salts, sometimes of carbonate of soda and sometimes of sulphate of magnesia. But here, over many square miles is a thick bed of salt which I believe to be chiefly sulphate of magnesia. There are three or four forms in which this occurs; first mixed with sand to a depth of many inches, but with a thin cake of unmixed saline matter at the surface; as one passes over this, the foot, crackling through the cake at top, sinks deep in the soft saline sand; secondly, a powdery form of the white salts, this being probably a changed state of the material to be mentioned next; lastly, a hard crystalline colourless cake of the salt; to what depth this may reach I do not know, but as much as 10 feet of thickness have I seen. The surface of this cake is often irregular, in hard rough narrow ridges, two or three feet high, of the consolidated salt, with the soft powdery salt, or the mixture of earth and salt, between them; these may have been forced up by the frost at the margin of the lake, in the same way as the frost-margins are made which we saw by Pangkong Lake; for I observed such a line of ridge along the edge of one of the present pools of water.

The water of the small lake now remaining, though very saline, yet was frozen when I saw it on the morning of the 6th September; for the cold had even then begun to be intense. Where the flat widens out, and connects eastward with the rest of the Plains, its surface bears much less of the salts.

GENERAL OBSERVATIONS

We have now considered these uplands in their separate divisions of the two plains and the dividing mountains. There are yet some observations to be made which will refer more generally to the whole tract.

First we will recapitulate the facts which have been more or less detailed as to the form of the ground. A nearly but not quite complete barrier of mountains encloses the two table-lands, one 16,000 feet the other 17,000 feet high, which are themselves separated from one another by the Lokzhung Range. Of what is *outside* this mountain barrier we do not know equally well for all the sides. On the north Mr. Johnson has shown how the ridges and the valleys lessen in height till the plains of Khutan are reached. On the west Mr. Hayward found that the mountain-ridge is succeeded by the main Karakash Valley, and that again by the high ground, partly mountains, partly table-land, that extends towards the Karakoram and Suket Passes. On the south is the mass of rounded hills which we dwelt on in the beginning of this chapter. There remains the eastern side. Here the ground has never been at all explored, nor even reached, by any European, nor, till some distance beyond, by anyone from whom information could be got. I believe there to be a bounding ridge of mountains on the east as there is on the west. Beyond that, I heard from the mouth of a Ladakhi who took the route from the Rudokh to Khutan, there is a long valley somewhat corresponding to the Karakash Valley on the west.

So much for the form of the ground. Next, a last word on the formation of the lake or lakes, for now that we have acquired a general idea of the ground we shall be able better to judge of the weight of the various facts, bearing on this subject, that were recorded. At the north-west corner we found an opening for former drainage, between the Kuenlun Mountains and spurs from the western ridge; this opening is now, to a certain extent, closed by alluvial accumulations, and was formerly in all probability obstructed to a still greater—perhaps to a much greater—height, either by similar deposits or by glaciers and moraines, glaciers at that time being more numerous and larger than now. At the extreme south-west corner I have been informed by Mr. Shaw (from his own observations and on the authority of Mr. Reynolds of the Survey) that streams which flow down to the Shayok interramify with those that flow into Lingzhithang, that the watershed between is quite unmarked. That here, too, or else somewhat lower down, existed a dam, in nature similar to the one observed or to those inferred, for the other end, I have but little doubt. Now, on the theory that the lake or lakes were dammed at these two points, we must allow the dams to have had a height at least equal to the highest beach or margin-mark. Some of the highest of the shingle observed is by the Lokzhung Mountains, *between* the Lingzhithang and Kuenlun Plains; indeed we saw that the watershed between these two drainage-basins (as they are at present) is made by a ridge of a height of about 17,300 feet (300 feet above Lingzhithang), *which bears or is made of shingle at its summit.* I can then but infer that at one time, when the two dams locked the waters to a great depth, there was *one lake* stretching from near the Changchenmo Watershed to the Kuenlun Mountains, which made, over what is now Lingzhithang, a wide sea, 60 miles by 20, which reached through straits among the various ridges of which the Lokzhung Mountains are composed, and which spread northward over what are now the Kuenlun Plains, penetrating far between the mountain spurs to the very base of the Kuenlun Mountains. At this stage there was *no watershed* between the indian and the Turkistan drainage; or if there were one it could only have been the higher of the two dams that confined the lake; it is possible that each dam alternately became the watershed, the waters of the lake sometimes going one way, sometimes another; and it is just possible that at some period the waters simultaneously flowed out both ways. The sinking of the surface of the water may have first begun by a lowering of one of the dams, but must at the last have been due to a change of climate, the present ratio of supply to evaporation of water not now availing, while formerly it must have availed, to spread the waters over the enclosed drainage-basins. At a stage in the sinking of the water the one lake must have become two. The waters themselves, by their currents and their shore-action, had accumulated deposits along the line of the Lokzhung Mountains, which, on their retreating, became bars separating the two watery tracts, and have since become the watershed between the two enclosed drainage-areas.

There is another subject—the extent to which this region can support animal or vegetable life—about which the little I have to say may be worth telling, since the place is so seldom visited. In the description hitherto little has been spoken of but earth and stones and rocks; but in this I have been guilty of hardly any omission, so few are the traces of either animal or vegetable life. Vegetation exists but here and there; generally every 10 or 15 miles is to be found some *burtse*, or Eurotia, the plant that serves for fuel, though at one halting-place moss is obtained in its stead, and at another neither *burtse* nor moss can be got. Pasture is still rarer; on leaving the last halting-place in the Chonglung branch of the Changchenmo Valley wę had to pass over 60 or 70 miles before reaching any grass; the first find was at Lokzhung, a halting-place in the middle of the mountains of the same name. On the Kuenlun Plains grass is equally scarce, and it is only when one gets well into the Eastern Karakash Valley that this cause of difficulty in keeping one's baggage animals alive disappears. Of wild animals one would think from the foot-prints that great numbers must live in the plains and the surrounding mountains; but one sees few., and on reflection it appears that the many foot-prints are the work of a comparatively small number of individuals, for in this country a mark made may stay unobliterated for years. I saw Kyang, the Wild Ass, but only singly, at Thaldat, which is a watering-place of his; a track had been made straight to it for two miles, beaten and cleared of stones by continual passage. Hare also are now and then to be seen, and foot-prints of Antelope were observed at various places on the plains. Beyond, on the Eastern Karakash, Kyang and Antelope, are Hare were more plentiful. A beast I had not before seen, was the wild yak; him I met among the Lokzhung Mountains—a solitary bull—an animal in form exactly like the domesticated yak, but of larger bulk; form his sides hung long hair, but his back was comparatively bare. At first, on seeing us, he went away with a short quick trot, but he afterwards broke into a heavy lumbering gallop. It has been doubted whether the domestic yak comes from this wild one, or whether the wild yak may not have sprung from some that have escaped from the camps of travellers, for every now and then these beasts of burden are overcome, and, unable to carry their loads, are relinquished; these may, perhaps, recover, and, finding subsistence on some scant pasture, live and reproduce their kind in a wild state.

There is one other phenomenon that deserves a moment's attention before we leave this interesting ground. There are at least two instances of *ice-beds,* or, as some have called them, *snow-beds,* occuring in the plains. I prefer the former name as being more truly descriptive, although at first sight they look just like beds of snow. Colonel H. Strachey described two or three of these in Rupshu and Pangkong, but gave no explanation of their origin. Mr. Johnson mentioned the one at Thaldat, which was the first I ever saw. On the plain, a mile or two from the nearest hill, a space about a mile long and a quarter of a mile wide is occupied by the ice-bed; it lies in the bed of a stream, with the water flowing beneath part of it; the greatest thickness that I saw was four feet; some of it was like *neve,* and some was more icy. A similar bed which I saw in Rupshu (one of those noticed by Colonel Strachey), I find described in my notes as being made in great part of layers from a quarter inch to one and a half inch thick of prismatic ice, the prismatic crystals being of course at right angles to the surface of the layers; there, too, was some that is described as like *neve.* At other parts, again, the length of the prisms (and therefore the thickness of one layer of ice) was as much as eight inches.

I think that these ice-beds are the unmelted ice of the streams, formed especially in spring, when the successive rising levels of the water that flowed from the melting snows would make layer after layer of ice, as the still severe cold at that time froze the surface at night, until a thickness had accumulated too great to be made to disappear by one summer's sun, and so the bed had become permanent. The limit to its vertical increase would be the impossibility of the water reaching to a higher and higher level beyond some certain height; only as it wasted away, as in summer it must waste, from the sun melting its upper and the stream its lower surface, would, when the mass of ice settled down, additions again be made to it from above in the same way as before. It may not unlikely happen that snow fallen on the surface sometimes becomes enclosed and consolidated by the overflowing water.

(From *Landmarks in Indian Anthropology—Jammu and Kashmir Territories, 1875*)

8

Rivers of Ladhak

By
Alexander Cunningham

I.—GENERAL REMARKS

From the lofty mountains around the holy lake of Manasarovara, spring four celebrated rivers, the Indus, the Sutluj, the Gogra, and the Brahmaputra. These four sources are represented in the ancient Chinese maps; and the well-known story regarding them is common both to the Hindus and the Tibetans. The classical Ganges is fabled to flow from a cow's mouth; and to each of these four rivers is assigned an equally wonderful origin. The Indus is said to flow from a lion's mouth, *Singge-kha-bab*; the Sutluj, from an elephant's mouth, *Langchen-kha-bab*; the Gogra, from a peacock's mouth, *Macha-kha-bab*; and the Brahmaputra, from the holy horse's mouth, *Ta-chhog-kha-bab*. The fable is evidently of Indian origin, as elephants and pea-fowl are only known to the Tibetans by pictures, and because the source of the Brahmaputra, or river of Lhasa, is ascribed to *Ta-chhog*, the holy steed of Shakya Thubba, or Buddha.

The most remarkable feature about the Indus and its tributaries, is the general parallelism of their courses, which has been determined by the directions of the principal mountain-chains. In the "Novum Organum", Bacon has noticed the "similitudines physicae in configuratione mundi", and the same similarity may be observed in the peculiar knee-bends which are common to all the Panjab rivers. For the curious southward sweep which occurs in the Sutluj below Bilaspur, is also found in all the other rivers: in the Byas, below Hajipur; in the Ravi, near Bisoli; in the Chenab, below Kashtwar; in the Jehlam, below Mozafarabad; and in the Indus, at the gorge of Makpon-i-Shang-Rong. The same returning bend also occurs in the Kishen Ganga, above Mozafarabad.

The most common name for a river is *chhu;* as, *Singge-chhu,* the Lion river, or Indus; and *Zanskar-chhu,* the river of Zanskar. When a river is spoken of generally, it is either called *Chhu-chhen,* or *Tsangpo,* or *Tsangchhen.* The first means simply the "great river", but the latter is a genuine name for a river, and is applied to the Indus as well as to the Brahmaputra, although it belongs strictly only to the great river of the Lhasan, territory, which flows through the province of Tsang. It is now used to signify any large river, in the same way as Ganga is applied in India. Smaller streams are called *Dok-po,* the narrow water", or brook; and *Drag-po,* the "rapid water", or torrent; or *Tsang-chung,* the "small stream;", but *Dok-po* is the common term.

The river system of Ladak consists entirely of the three great mountain-feeders of the Indus, the *Singge-chhu,* or Indus Proper, the *Shayok,* and the *Zanskar* rivers. But as my account of Ladak Embraces the districts of Lahul and Spiti, which once belonged to it, my description of the rivers must necessarily extend to the Chenab and Sutluj: and to complete the subject I will add some short notices of the other three rivers of the Panjab,—the Jehlam, the Ravi, and the Byas.

II.—THE INDUS

By some the real source of the Indus is at present considered an unsettled point, notwithstanding the distinct and explicit statement of Moorcroft, that "the Smh-kha-bab rises from the Gangri or Kailas range, a short way to the south-east of Gartop" (Garo). The information collected by Moorcroft agrees exactly with that which I obtained from different people, that the Garo river is the Singge-chhu or Indus, and that there is no *great* eastern branch. My principal information was derived from, Anant Ram, the vazir of Shasso, in the Sungnam valley, who was despatched to Garo by the late Wans Agnow and myself in September 1846, with the Governor-General's letter to the Governor, of Lhasa. He went from Hanle *up the valley of the Singge-chhu* to Garo, or rather to Higong, which is the winter residence of the Governor. For the Garo of our maps, which was visited by Moorcroft, is chiefly a summer encampment, as its name implies, on the right bank of the Higong-chu, while the other Garo is situated two marches lower down the river, and on the left bank. The former is called Gar-Yaru, or upper encampment, and the latter *Gar-gang,* or the snowy encampment, because the people retire to it during the winter, or snow season. Anant Ram passed by Tashigong, but he saw nothing of the great eastern, branch which I believe owes its existence entirely to Gerard, who could only account for the two names of Higong-chu and Singge-chu by supposing them to belong to different streams.

Thornton, who never misses an opportunity of sneering at Arrowsmith, states in a note that "the existence of this river and confluence is alleged on he credit of the map accompanying Moorcroft's Travels, and stated to have been compiled from his notes and field-books". Now the man referred to, which was published. 341 represents the eastern Sinh-kha-bab by a dotted line, whereas in Arrowsmith's map of Northern Asia, published in 1834, the eastern branch is defined as distinctly as the Garo river. This branch is just as boldly delineated by the "accurate" Walker in Sheet XI. of the map of India, published in 1836, by the Society for the Diffusion of Useful Knowledge. These dates prove that previous to the publication of the map of Moorcroft's and Trebeck's Travels, an eastern branch of the Indus had been inserted in our *best* maps, and that Arrowsmith, after he had seen Moorcroft's and Trebeck's notes and field-books, was so doubtful of its existence, that he only represented it by a dotted line in the map illustrating Moorcroft's travels.

According to may information, the true source of the Indus lies to the north-west of the holy lakes of Manasarovara and Rawan Hrad, in the south-western slopes of the Gangri or Kailas mountain, in north latitude 31^0 20', and east longitude 80^0 30' and at an estimated height of 17,000 feet. From its source to Garo, the Indus was followed by Moorcroft in 1812. Within eight or ten miles of its source it was 240 feet broad and 2½ feet deep in July, and at Garo, about forty miles from its source, it was "a clear, board, and rapid, but not deep river". On the 19th September, 1847, I measured the Indus at an uninhabited spot named Ranak, a few miles above the junction of the Puga rivulet, and about 260 miles from the source. The stream was there 240 feet broad, with a mean depth of 1.7916 feet, an an extreme depth of only three feet. Its greatest surface velocity was 3.658 feet per second, or 2½ miles per hour, and its mean surface velocity was 2.727 feet per second, or nearly one mile and seven furlongs per hour. From these data I found the discharge of the Indus to be only 774 cubic feet per second. The stream was quite clear, but sluggish, running between grassy banks, half sand, half mud, the sand being quick, and the grass coarse, long, and yellow. The banks were flat and low, and the bottom generally muddy. Below this the character of the stream was quite changed, and the waters rushed impetuously down a narrow channel full of huge boulders and enormous rocks.

It will be observed that the Indus at Ranak had the same breadth, and but little more depth than where Moorcroft saw it above Garo; but as the current was "rapid," its velocity cannot be estimated at less than five or six miles an hour. This would give a discharge of about 1,500 cubi feet for July, and of 560 feet for September. If this estimate be correct, it is certain that no large stream can join the Garo river above Ranak.

The course of the Indus from its source to Ranak is to the north-west, and distance is about 260 miles, and the fall 2,600 feet, or about ten feet per mile.

From Ranak to Pitak, opposite to Le, the distance is 130 miles, and the direction the same as before, almost due north-west. The fall of the river is 3,200 feet, or 24.6 feet per mile. Above Ranak the Indus is generally fordable, but from thence to Le it can only be crossed by bridges. From Le to the junction of the Dras river, a distance of 125 miles, the river changes its course to west-south-west. From this point to the junction of the Shayok river, a distance of seventy-five miles, its course is generally north-north-west, and from thence to Skardo, a distance of thirty miles, it makes a sweep up to the northward, and returning to the south resumes its former course to the north-north-west.

At Nyimo, just twenty-five miles below Le, the Indus is joined by the Zanskar river, a dark and turbulent torrent of equal, or perhaps of greater size. The junction of the united Waka, Suru, and Dras rivers with the Indus takes place at Moral, and confluence of the Shayok and Indus just above Keris (7,500 feet).

On the 26th of November, Dr. Thomson found the Indus at Skardo 520 feet broad, with a mean depth of 7.11 feet, and an extreme depth of 9½ feet. The mean surface velocity was 2.128 feet per second, or about 1½ mile per hour. The greatest surface velocity was 2.586 feet per second, or rather more than 1¾ mile per hour.

From these data I calculate the discharge at 4,525 cubic feet per second in the winter. Of this amount about, 2,000 cubic feet are probably supplied by the Shayok river, and the remaining 2,500 cubic feet by the Indus Proper. The small rivers of Wanla, Waka, Suru, and Dras probably supply 500 cubic feet, and the Zanskar river about 1,000 cubic feet; thus leaving 1,000 cubic feet for the discharge of the Indus at Le during the winter season.

From Skardo to Rongdo and from Rongdo to Makpon-i-Shang-Rong, for upwards of 100 miles, the Indus sweeps sullen and dark through a mighty gorge in the mountains which for wild sublimity is perhaps unequalled. Rongdo means the "country of defiles", and Makpon-i-Shang Rong means the "craggy defile of Astor". Between these points the Indus raves from side to side of the gloomy chasm, foaming and chafing with ungovernable fury. Yet even in these inaccessible places has daring and ingenious man triumphed over opposing nature. The yawning abyss is spanned by frail rope bridges, and the narrow ledges of rock are connected by ladders to form a giddy pathway overhanging the seething caldron below. At Makpon-i-Shang-Rong, 4,500 feet, the Indus cuts the Trans-Himalayan Chain of mountains by a bold and sudden sweep round to the southward, where it receives the waters of the Gilgit river, a mighty stream, perhaps not inferior to any one of the mountain tributaries. From Skardo to Rongdo the distance is 40 miles, and the fall of the river 800 feet, or 20 feet per mile. From Rongdo to the Shang-Rong the distance is 75 miles, and the fall 1,700 feet, or 22.6 feet per mile.

From the junction of the Gilgit river to attock, 1,000 feet above the sea-level, the course of the Indus is to the south-west. The distance is 300 miles, and the fall of the river 3,500 feet, or 11.6 feet per mile. This part of its course is but little known; but even at Ohind, 15 miles above Attock, I found the current of the Indus much more rapid than that of any other river of Panjab.

From its source to Ranak, the Indus is a broad and fordable stream, rolling its sluggish waters through open grassy plains. Its general width is about 250 feet. From Ranak to the junction of the Zanskar river, the stream is a brawling rapid from 100 to 150 feet broad; and thence to the confluence of the Shayok it is a furious torrent, raving from side to side of a narrow ravine. At the Khallach bridge, the channel is only 50 feet wide below and 60 feet above. In the winter the lower part of the Indus is frequently frozen over, and in 1841 Zorawar Sing's troops crossed the Indus on the ice.

The whole length of the mountain course of the Indus from its source to Attock is 1,035 miles, and the whole fall is, 16,000 feet, or 15.4 feet per mile. From Attock to the sea the length is 942 miles, and its whole length from he Kailas mountain to the Indian Ocean is 1,977 miles. The minimum discharge of the Indus between Attock and Mithankot is about 16,000 cubic feet, which I have estimated in the following manner:—

Discharge at Skardo	4,500	cubic feet.
Shigar, Gilgit, and Astor rivers	4,000	
Small unknown streams	2,500	
	11,000	
Kabul river	5,500	
	16,500	
Loss by evaporation between Attock and Mithankot	1,500	
Total discharge	15,000	

In May, when it has been increased by the melting of the snows, its discharge is six times as great, or 91,791 cubic feet; and in July and August, when swollen by the seasonal rains, it reaches its maximum discharge of 135,000 cubic feet, or nine times that of the winter discharge. These estimates are for the Indus itself above the confluence of the Panjnad. Below the confluence, the minimum discharge of the Indus is about 27,000 cubic feet. The discharge in May is 160,674 cubic feet, and the maximum discharge is 230,000 cubic feet.

The discharge of the Indus at Ranak has already been stated at 774 cubic feet in September; and I estimate its winter discharge below Le at 1,000 cubic feet. As the Zaṇskar river is about the same size, the minimum discharge of the Indus Proper may be taken at 2,000 cubic feet; and the maximum discharge, at nine times the minimum, will be 18,000 cubic feet. The this estimate is not too great, can be proved by the known rise of the river (35 feet) at the Khallach bridge, where the stream is confined between almost perpendicular rocks, only 55 feet apart. A discharge of 18,000 cubic feet at this point would require a surface velocity of not more than 8½ miles per hour, or of 12.46 feet per second.

The waters of the Indus are supplied by the rivers of the Panjab in the following proportion.

		Cubic Feet	Authority
1	Sutluj	5,700	Major Baker, Engineers.
2	Byas	3,100	Major Cunningham.
3	Ravi	2,700	Col. Napier, Engineers.
4	Chenab	4,700	Major Cunningham.
5	Jehlam	4,000	Estimated.
		20,200	
	Loss	8,200	by evaporation, permeation, & c.
	Panjnad	12,000	cubic feet, discharge.
	Indus Proper	15,000	
	Minimum discharge	27,000	cubic feet.

The following table exhibits the discharge of the Indus below Mithankot in several months of the year.

	Dr. Lord corrected	Wood	Burnes corrected
In March	26,357	—	—
In April	66,660	—	67,837
In May	160,162	160,674	—
In June	163,483	—	—
In July	223,678	—	—
In August	230,177	—	—
In September	217,110	—	—

In his Memoir on the Indus, Sir A. Burnes has assigned to the Indus a discharge of 80,000 cubic feet in April, and then contrasted this amount with the minimum discharge of the Ganges, as published by George Prinsep. But the comparison is doubly incorrect, for the lowest state of the Indus occurs in March, when, as we have seen, the discharge is not more than 27,000 cubic feet: and the discharge of the Ganges, at Sikrigali, as stated by George Prinsep, is so manifestly wrong that it is quite astonishing how any one could have repeated such an absurd mistake. On turning to George Prinsep's statement, I find that he assigns 21,500 cubic feet as the discharge of the Ganges at Sikrigali, and 20,000 at Benares. The latter, as Burnes remarks, "differs in but a trifling degree from that at Sikrigali;" and the near agreement of these two, he conceives to be a proof in favour of the correctness of the estimated discharge. Had any one told *him,* that the discharge of the Indus at Mithankot was the same as at Dera Ghazi Khan, *above the junction of the Panjnad,* he would at once have exposed the absurdity; and yet he takes the Ganges at Sikrigali to be the same stream as the Ganges at Benares, although between these points it receives the tribute waters of the Gumti, the Gogra, the Son, the Gandak, the Baghmati, the Gogari, the Kosi, and the Mahanadi; of which the Gogra alone is fully equal to the Ganges at Benares.

As the comparison of the two rivers is a subject of much interest, I will here state all that I have gathered regarding the discharge of the Ganges. The estimated discharge at Benares was, without doubt, derived from the measurements of James Prinsep, who was for several years Assay Master of the Benares Mint, and whose high attainments in all branches of science are sufficient to guarantee the correctness of his calculations. Indeed the accuracy of James Prinsep's discharge of the Ganges at Benares is most satisfactorily proved by the measured discharge at Ghazipur, which from data published by the Rev. R. Everest, I have calculated at 21,757 cubic feet. The only other minimum calculation which I possess, is luckily that which is most wanted, the minimum discharge of the

Ganges at the head of the Delta. For this I am indebted to the late Colonel Wilcox, who was formerly employed on the Great Trigonometrical Survey, and afterwards in the Observatory of the King of Oude. The measurements were taken above Comercolly and Pubna, and included the streams of the Jalinghi and Bhagirathi, as well as the main river. The discharge of the Ganges at this point was found to be 96,000 cubic feet, or more than three and a half times that of the Indus. The maximum discharge of the Ganges at Ghazipur, calculated from the data furnished by the Rev. R. Everest, I find to be 476,761 cubic feet, or more than double that of the Indus at its greatest height. The maximum discharge of the Ganges, at the head of the Delta, cannot therefore be estimated at less than, 1,500,000 cubic feet, or just six times that of the Indus. George Prinsep states the maximum discharge at Sikrigali, at 1,850,000 cubic feet; but my calculation, from his data, gives only 1,430,800 cubic feet. This result might have been anticipated from the much greater extent of the Himalayan chain, drained by the Ganges, and from the known greater fall or rain in the Gangetic basin. The latter cause is probably the chief one, as it is known that the annual fall of rain increases rapidly from the Jamna, eastward.

III.—THE SHAYOK RIVER

The principal mountain tributary of the Indus is the Shayok, or Khundan river, which rises in the Karakoram mountains, to the northward of Le, in N. latitude 35^0, and E. longitude 78^0, and to the south-eastward of the Karakoram Pass. From its source to the neighbourhood of Sassar, it makes a bold sweep of sixty miles to the west and south. Thence, for fifty miles, to Mandalik, it takes a south-easterly course; and onward, to the town of Shayok, which gives its name to the stream, it flows due south for fifty miles more. From the source to this point, the whole length of the river is 170 miles, and the fall 6,000 feet, or 35.3 feet per mile. A short distance above the great north-western bend, the Shayok receives the waters of the *Chang-chhen-mo*, or Great Chang river, whose course has been explored by Captain H. Strachey; and below the bend it receives the waters of the *Long-Konma*, from the south-east. From Shayok to Hundar, the course is west-north-west, and the distance is about eighty miles. Near this place it receives the Nubra river, considerable stream, about 100 miles in length, from the north-west. Beyond this point it pursues the same direction to its confluence with the Indus, at Keris, a distance of 150 miles. From Shayok to the junction, the distance is 230 miles, and the fall is 4,500 feet, or 19.6 feet per mile. From its source in the Karakoram to Keris, where it joins the Indus, the whole length of the Shayok is just 400 miles, and the total fall is 10,500 feet, or 26.4 feet per mile.

The general character of the Shayok is exactly the reverse of that of the Indus. Its upper course is rushing and turbulent, down a narrow glen, but its middle course is either broad and rapid, or divided into numerous channels, in an open valley; and in these places where the waters are much scattered, the river is generally fordable, although not without difficulty. Between Tertse and Unmaru, there are seven distinct branches, of which three are between 300 and 400 feet in width, and the others much smaller, with an average depth of two feet. The Surmu, the Shayok is also forded by two separate channels, each 300 feet broad, with a depth varying from two to three feet. At the Turtuk bridge, the river narrows to seventy feet, and in the lower part of its course, the Shayok is generally a furious rapid, confined between precipitous cliffs. In the height of summer, when the stream is much swollen by the melted snows, the fords are always difficult. In the winter, the passage is easy; and even in the lower part of its course the Shayok is frequently frozen over, and the stream is crossed upon the ice. I estimate the winter discharge of the Shayok at 2,000 cubic feet, the increased discharge in May at 12,000 and the maximum discharge in August at 18,000 cubic feet.

IV.—THE ZANSKAR RIVER

The *Chiling-chhu*, or Zanskar river, is formed of two principal branches, *Zanskar* proper, and the *Sum-Gal*, or river of the "Three Fords". The head-waters of the Zanskar river are the Yunam, the Serchu (or Yellow River), and the Cherpa, all of which rise to the north of the Himalaya range, near the Bara Lacha Pass. The head of the Cherpa river, which is the most remote source of the Zanskar river, is situated in N.latitude 32^0 40', and E.longitude 78^0. The united stream, below the junction of the Cherpa, is not fordable until the end of September; and the Cherpa itself is not fordable after mid-day, even in the beginning of September, as both the rapidity and depth of the stream are much increased by the daily melting of the snow. The united stream, called Lingti, follows a north-westerly course, as far as Phadam, the chief place in the Zanskar district. From its source to Phadam, the distance is 130 miles, and the fall 4,000 feet, or 34.6 feet per mile. At Phadam the Lingti receives a small stream from the west, and then takes a due northerly course for upwards of eighty miles, to its junction with the Indus, opposite Nyimo. In this part of its course the fall is only 1,500 feet, or 18.7 feet per mile. The whole length of the Zanskar river is 210 miles, and the total fall is 6,000 feet, or 28.5 feet per mile.

About twenty-five miles above its junction with the Indus, the Zanskar river receives the waters of the Sum-Gal, or river of the "Three Fords." The head-waters of this tributary rise in the mountains to the westward of the Tshomo-Riri lake, in N. latitude 33^0, and E. longitude 78^0. Three branches, of about equal size, joint their waters to form this river; and as each of these streams is forded separately within the short distance of one mile, the united stream has received the descriptive name of *Sum-Gal*, or the river of the "Three Fords." From its source to its junction with the Zanskar river, the course of the Sum-Gal is north-north-west; its length is 110 miles, and its fall is about 5,000 feet, or 45.4 feet per mile.

I estimate the discharge of the Zanskar river at 1,000 cubic feet in the winter, at 6,000 cubic feet in May, and at 9,000 cubic feet at its maximum, in August.

V.—OTHER TRIBUTARIES

Of the other mountain tributaries of the Indus, there are only four that are deserving of particular notice: the rivers of Dras, Shigar, Gilgit, and Astor.

The Dras river is formed of the united streams of the Waka, the Suru, the Dras, and the Kuksar rivers. The Waka-chu is formed of two main branches, the Waka and the Phugal, both of which take their rise to the north of the Himalaya, near the Vingge-la, in N. latitude 33°40', and E longitude 76° 30'. Each stream is fordable above the junction, but the united stream is crossed by bridges. The whole length of the Waka-chu is about 100 miles, the general direction being north-north-west. The Suru river rises to the north of the Himalaya range, in N. latitude 34°, and E. longitude 76°. Its length is about sixty miles, and its direction about north-north-east. The Dras river rises to the north of the Himalayan range near the Scoji La Pass, in N. latitude 34°12', and E. longitude 75°45'. Its whole length is about eighty-five miles, and its general direction is north-east. The Kuksar river rises to the westward, in about 34°40' N. latitude, and 75° E.longitude. The length of its course is unknown; but it is probably not less than 100 miles. Its general direction is easterly. The whole of these streams unite near Kargyil, below which they cut the Trans-Himalayan range, at the narrow gorge called the Wolf's Leap, and join the Indus opposite Mural. I estimate the discharge of the Dras river at not less than 500 cubic feet.

The Shigar river rises in the Karakoram mountains, in N. latitude 36°20', and E. longitude 75°. It takes a south-easterly direction for 100 miles, and then turns to the south-south-west for nearly forty miles, to its junction with the Indus, opposite Skardo. The discharge of this stream is probably about 500 cubic feet.

The Gilgit river is one of the principal mountain-feeders of the Indus. Its upper course is formed of two principal branches, the Yasan and Parasot rivers. The former rises in

N.latitude 37°, and E.longitude 73°, at the point where the Karakoram merges into the Hindu Kush. The source of the Parasot is in 36°10 N.latitude, and 72°40' E.longitude, on the eastern face of the range which gives rise to the Chitral, or Kunar river. After a separate course of seventy-five miles each, the two streams join above Roshan, in latitude 36°20', and longitude 73°30' and take an easterly course for twenty-five miles , to Gakuch, where they are joined by the Chator-Kun river, from the north. Thence to the town of Gilgit its course is east-south-east, for fifty miles, below which it receives the joint tribute of the Hunza-Nagar rivers. It continues the same course for about thirty miles further, to its junction with the Indus below the defile of Makpon-i-Shang-Rong. The general direction of the stream is to the east-south-east, and its whole length not less than 180 miles. The minimum discharge is probably 2,000 cubic feet, or even more.

The Astor, or Hasora river, falls into the Indus in latitude 35°30', and longitude 74°35'. Its rises to the east of the great mountain of Dayamur, and takes a northerly course of about 100 miles.

VI.—CATACLYSM OF THE INDUS

Since Moorcroft visited Ladak, there have been no less than three inundations of the Indus, of which the last and greatest occurred in 1841. Vigne was the first to make known the second of these cataclysms, which, from the information of the people, he attributed to its right cause, the bursting of a glacier in the upper course of the Shayok river. In 1812, when Izzet Ullah went from Le to Yarkand, he travelled up the Shayok river, from its great western bend to its source in the Karakoram mountains; and in 1822, when Moorcroft was at Le, the road by the Shayok was still clear. The information which I obtained regarding the shayok or Khundan glacier, dates the first stoppage of the river in the fourth year after Moorcroft left Ladak, and in the same year that Jehangir Khoja came from Yarkand, or in A.D. 1826. The river was dammed only for a short time, but the road was permanently obstructed.

The second cataclysm happened in 1833, when, to use Vigne's account, "the protecting glacier gave way, and the mighty flood, no longer confined, rushed down the valley of the Shayok, destroying every village that came within its reach." The third cataclysm occurred in 1841, when the gallant Syam Sing Atariwala (who fell at Sobraon) was encamped in the bed of the river. Suddenly down rushed the wave of the inundation, thirty feet in height, and the whole camp took to flight: most of the men were saved, but the baggage, camp equipage, and guns, were swept away.

The cataclysm of the Val de Bagnes, a small feeder of the Rhone, is the only great flood of this kind of which I can find any account; but the Val de Bagnes is scarcely five miles in length, while the glacier of the Khundan river is not less than 800 miles from the fort of Attock, past whose walls the flood rushed in one tremendous wave about 30 feet high, and continued its overwhelming course to the Indian Ocean, a distance of 1,750 miles.

> Who that from Alpine heights his laboring eye
> Shoots round the wide horizon, to survey
> Indus or Ganges rolling their bright floods
> Through mountains, plains, through empires black with shade,
> And continents of sand, will turn his gaze
> To make the windings of a scanty rill? *Akenside*

The Val de Bagnes is a petty brook, while the Khundan is a mighty river, scarcely inferior to the Indus itself at their junction above the fort of Skardo.

As a magnificent natural catastrophe on so grand a scale as that of the cataclysm of the Indus is worthy of the most particular examination, I trust that the following detail will prove both interesting and valuable.

When Vigne and Dr. Falconer were at Skardo in 1837, they heard that the Shayok or Khundan river had been often "blocked up by avalanches and masses of ice," and that a flood had occurred not many years before. Both of these travellers heard of a lake in the upper course of the Shayok river, but as Mir Izzet Ullah does not mention it, I conclude that my information regarding the origin of the lake is correct. In two different parts of the Shayok or Khundan river, above and below Sassar, the bed of the stream is completely spanned by enormous glaciers. The upper glaciers above Sassar were seen by Dr. Thomson in 1848. They had descended from two lateral ravines on the western bank, and had been thrust right across the bed of the river by their own weight. But the lower glaciers on the Khundan are those to which my informants attributed the obstruction of the river, and they were unanimous in ascribing the flood to the long stoppage and sudden escape of the accumulated waters of the Khundan. The exact position of the great glacier is known within a few miles. It is situated somewhere between Sassar and the junction of the Changchhenmo, and as the distance between these points is only 50 miles, we may place the glacier with tolerable certainty at about 30 miles below Sassar, and 20 miles above the junction of the Chang-Chhen-mo. This part of the course is now quite inaccessible, owing to the accumulated mass of fice and snow. The high road from Le to Yarkand formerly ascended the bed of the Khundan or Shayok river the whole way to its source in the Karakoram mountains; but since the obstruction of the channel, the road now takes a more westerly direction up the Nubra river, and then crosses a lofty pass to Sassar on the Khundan. At this point it again leaves the Khundan, on account of the upper glaciers seen by Dr. Thomson, and proceeds over a rugged and elevated tract to the head-waters of the river.

In these cold and lofty regions, almost every ravine is filled with a glacier, which, except during a very warm summer, never moves, but is bound to the rocks every night by the icy chains of frost. A glacier is melted on its under surface by the higher temperature of the soil, and on its upper surface by the thawing of the snow under the direct rays of the sun. The heated stones that lie on the top form hollows and clefts that admit the external air, and little rills of water trickle over the sides in all directions. The glacier is thus furrowed by holes, penetrated by cracks, and undermined below, until it becomes narrower than the ravine which contains it. It then descends by its own weight, and is either rent to pieces by unequal pressure, or checked by some opposing obstacle. In a very warm and dry summer the glaciers in the lateral ravines of the Khundan would be so much diminished by melting and evaporation, that they would be impelled onwards by their own gravity right across the channel of the river. This I suppose to have been the case towards the end of September 1826, from which time the channel of the Khundan river has never been clear, and the accumulated waters have formed a lake of considerable size, to which the people have given the name of *Nubra Tsho*, or the Nubra Lake. The accounts which Vigne received were "various and most conflicting, but all agreed that it was very large;" and he concluded that it might be "three or four miles in length and less than a mile in width." My informant, who had seen the lake, said it was four or five kos (eight or ten miles) in length, and less than a quarter of a kos (half a mile) in breadth; and such is the shape, that I should suppose it must take in the confined channel of the Khundan river.

In 1833 this barrier was burst, and the accumulated waters rushed down the valley of the Shayok, destroying every village within their reach; from Nubra to Skardo, a distance of 120 miles, the flood-wave descended in a single day, at the rate of ten miles an hour; and the marks of its fury were still to be seen at Skardo in 1837. So well was the cause of this inundation known to the people, that it was believed "that the same terrific visitation might be expected to occur again at no very distant period."

The expected cataclysm occurred in June 1841, but it was immensely greater in volume and more devastating in its effects than the previous inundation of 1833.

During December 1840 and January 1841, the Indus was observed to be unusually low between Torbela and Attock. In

February and March it became lower, and was even fordable not far above Attock; but in April and May, though still very low, it was no longer fordable, as the depth of the stream had been much increased by the melted snows. Early in June the barrier was burst, and the collected waters of nearly six months rushed with overwhelming violence down the narrow valley of the Shayok, sweeping everything before them. Houses and trees, men and women, horses and oxen, sheep and goats, were carried away at once, and all the alluvial flats in the bed of the river, which had been irrigated with laborious care, were destroyed in a moment. This happened in the middle of the month of Jyeth in the Sambat year 1898, or about the 1st June, A.D. 1841.

According to the testimony of the people of Chulung and Tartuk, on the western boundary of Chhorbad, the wave of inundation passed their villages at two o'clock in the afternoon. As these villages stand on opposite sides of the river, and are ten miles apart, the concurrence of testimony may be taken as a proof of its correctness. Two days afterwards, and exactly at the same hour, the flood passed by Torbela, a distance of 550 miles. The rate is 11.4583 miles per hour, or 16.81 feet per second, being only just half that of the flood-wave of the Val de Bagnes in 1818 at its first burst into the valley of the Rhone. The fall from the Khundan glacier to Torbela is 16,000 feet, or just 20 feet per mile.

The devastating effects of this terrible flood were still quite fresh in 1847. At Tertse, one of the widest parts of the valley, they could be traced to a height of more than 20 feet above the stream, where straws and twigs were massed together in lines two or three feet broad, and upwards of half a mile from the channel of the river in October 1847. But the most striking effect of the flood was the entire absence of trees in the valley of the Shayok, while the lateral valley of Nubra was full of trees upwards of a hundred years old. There were of course many young trees in the bed of the Shayok, but they were the growth of only a few years. At Surmu and at other places in the Khapolor district, numbers of fruit-trees were observed standing amidst large tracts of sand and gravel.

The following table shows the loss of life and property in most of the villages along the Shayok from the junction of the Nubra river to the fort of Skardo.

Districts	Houses	People	Horses	Oxen	Sheep, Goats.	Khals of Land	Trees
Nubra	19	83	18	114	1,040	178	—
Chhorbad	140	8	—	—	—	364	140
Khapolor	163	1	1	4	—	859	—
Keris	20	—	—	—	—	127	4,900
Skardo	9	—	—	—	—	107	1,190
Parguta	—	—	—	—	—	10	1,200
Total	351	92	19	118	1,040	1,645	7,430

From this list we learn that the principal loss of life occurred in the Nubra district, where the valley of the Shayok expands to about half a mile in breadth. There the shepherds and herdsmen, with their flocks and herds, were overwhelmed in the midst of the open plain, without a chance of escape. In the lower part of the valley, where the channel is confined, and where the villages are generally built high above the stream, there was no loss of life. Even amongst the low-lying hamlets in the bed of the river, the loss of life was trifling, for the distant roar of the rushing waters was a sufficient warning to the people who had beheld the inundation of 1833, and with a few exceptions they all made their escape up the mountains.

The effect of the inundation at Torbela has been so graphically described by Major James Abbott from the lips of an eye-witness, Ashraf Khan, of Torbela, that I will quote it entire. "At about 2 P.M. a murmuring sound was heard from the north-east among the mountains, which increased until it attracted universal attention, and we began to exclaim. `What is this murmur? Is it the sound of cannon in the distance? Is

Gandgarh bellowing? Is it thunder?' Suddenly some one cried out, `The river's come.' And I looked and perceived that all the dry channels were already filled, and that the river was racing down furiously in an absolute wall of mud, for it had not at all the colour or appearance of water. They who saw it in time easily escaped. They who did not, were inevitably lost. It was a horrible mess of foul water, carcases of soldiers, peasants, war-steeds, camels, prostitutes, tents mules, asses, trees, and household furniture, in short, every item of existence jumbled together in one flood of ruin; for Raja Gulab Sing's army was encamped in the bed of the Indus at Kulai, three kos above Torbela, in check of Painda Khan. Part of the force was at that moment in hot pursuit, or the ruin would have been wider. The rest ran, some to large trees which were all soon uprooted and borne away; others to rocks, which were speedily buried beneath the waters. Only they escaped who took at once to the mountain-side. About five hundred of these troops were at once swept to destruction. The mischief was immense. Hundreds of acres of arable land were licked up and carried away by the waters. The whole of the Sisu-trees which adorned the river's banks, the famous bargat-tree of many stems, time out of mind the chosen bivouac of travellers, were all lost in an instant."

Throughout the mountain-course of the Indus the devastation casued by this terrible flood in the low lands along the bank of the river was complete. All the cultivated lands were swept away, and not even a single tree was left standing to mark the spot where careful tillage and laborious irrigation had for hundreds of years wrung luxuriant crops from the thirsty soil. The fields, the houses, and the trees, were all overwhelmed in one common ruin; while man and the animals which he has domesticated, horses and oxen, sheep and goats, generally managed to escape.

The ruin caused by this awful inundation in the bed of the Indus, between Torbela and Attock, was so over-whelming and so vast, that "it will take hundreds, if not thousands of years, to enable time to repair, with its healing hand, the mischief of that terrible hour. The revenue of Torbela has in consequence dwindled from 20,000 to 5,000 rupees. Chach has been sown with barren sand. The timber, for which the Indus has been celebrated from the days of Alexander until this disaster, is now so utterly gone, that I vainly strove throughout Huzara to procure a Sisu-tree for the repair of the field-artillery carriages. To make some poor amends, the river sprinkled gold dust over the barren soil, so that the washings, for several successive years, were farmed at four times their ordinary rent."

Opposite Attock, the waters of the Kabul river were checked and forced backward for upwards of twenty miles, by the mighty wave of inundation. The fort of Akora, and the village of Messabanda, were overthrown; and when I saw them in January 1848, were mere scattered heaps of ruin.

As everything connected with this tremendous inundation must be interesting, I have attempted to ascertain, approximately, the mass of the accumulated waters in the Nubra Tsho, or Lake, formed by the glacier barrier, as well as the mass and height of the cataclysmal wave. In calculating the accumulation of water, I have estimated the usual winter discharge of the Khundan river at 800 cubic feet, or less than one-half of the discharge at its confluence with the Indus. The increased discharges in April and May are based upon the known rates of increase in the discharge of the Indus, which have already been given. The accumulation began in December.

Date		Velocity			Accumulation	
December	1840	800	cubic ft. per sec.		1,249,920,000	cubic ft.
January	1841	800	"	"	1,249,920,000	"
February	"	800	"	"	1,128,960,000	"
March	"	800	"	"	1,249,920,000	"
April	"	2,000	"	"	5,064,000,000	"
May	"	4,800	"	"	12,918,320,000	"
					22,861,040,000	"

From this amount a considerable deduction must be made for loss by evaporation and percolation. I do not, therefore, estimate the whole mass of accumulated waters at more than 20,000,000,000 cubic feet. But even this would be sufficient to form a lake twelve miles in length, with an average breadth of 526 yards, or 1,578 feet, and an average depth of 200 feet. The surface of the lake would have been half a mile or more in breadth, and the depth at the lower end, against the glacier, would have been 400 feet. As the fall in this part of the bed of the river is somewhat less than thirty-five feet, a lake of this depth would be exactly twelve miles in length.

The bursting of the barrier was, I have little doubt, caused by the cutting powers of the overflowing waters, which must quickly have worked enormous clefts in the outer face of the glacier. In a few days these clefts would have been worn deeper and deeper, until the icy mass at length gave way under the mighty pressure of the vast liquid body. Then the imprisoned waters burst forth with a roar of exultation, lashing themselves into foam against the rocks, careering madly from side to side, and sweeping all things before them in the wild might of their untamed strength.

According to the information given by the people of Chulung, on the Shayok, and flood was three whole days in passing off; two days in full height, and the third day considerably decreased; on the fourth day the flood had mostly gone by, but the stream was still much swollen. The following calculation shows the daily discharge of water for each of the three days of flood, with a small allowance for the fourth day.

				Daily discharge	
1st day at	100,000	cubic feet per second		8,640,000,000	cubic feet
2nd "	80,000	"	"	6,998,400,000	"
3rd "	40,000	"	"	3,499,900,000	"
4th "	20,000	"	"	1,728,000,000	"
Total discharge in four days				20,866,300,000	"
Total mass of accumulated water				20,000,000,000	"

By dividing the maximum discharge of 100,000 cubic feet per second by the ascertained velocity of 11.4583 miles per hour, or 16.81 feet per second, we obtain 5,948 square feet as the sectional area of the cataclysmal wave. From this I have deduced the rise of the river in different parts of the channel according to its width. These heights, however, do not give the actual rise of the water, which must always have been greater immediately above every narrow part of the channel.

	Width of River	Rise
Above Tertse	250 feet broad	23.79 feet
Near Turtuk	100 feet broad	59.48 feet

The height of the flood below Tertse was ascertained to have been between twenty and thirty feet, by the broad lines of straw and twigs which marked the extreme limit of the inundation. In the open plain of Unmaru, the waters must have been kept at the same level as at Tertse, by the obstruction offered to their passage in the narrow channel between Chulung and Turtuk. This would account for the lines of straw and twigs begin observed about half a mile from the present bed of the river.

The valley of the Indus, below the junction of the Shayok, narrow in some places to 100 feet, and even less. At these points, therefore, the flood must have risen to a height of sixty feet at least, and must have caused a considerable back wave up the confined channel of the Indus proper, or Le river. And this was actually the case, for the effect, of the inundation is said to have been felt for nearly thirty miles up the Indus, while at Sarmik, ten miles above the confluence, the lower cultivated lands were destroyed, and no less than 1,200 fruit-trees were swept away by the back-water flood.

At Skardo, where the river expands to 520 feet in width, and where the sandy flats rise at least thirty feet above the general level of the stream, it is probable that the flood did not spread much beyond the usual limits. The rise would, therefore, not have been more than ten feet. But below Skardo, in the confined and rocky channel, which is the prevailing character of the bed of the Indus throughout the Rongdo district, the flood-wave would have risen to its full height of sixty feet; and at the "Craggy Defiles" of Makpon-i-Shang-Rong, the curbed waters must have been massed up at least 100 feet in height.

At Ghori Trap, below Attock, where the width of the river is not more than 250 feet, the wave of inundation must have attained a height of at least 23.79 feet; and this will at once account for the height of the waters at Attock, which are said to have submerged the fort of Khairabad by their sudden rise of nearly thirty feet.

From Attock to the sea the inundation pursued its ruinous course, but I have no information as to the extent of the country flooded, or the numbers of people swept away. According to the papers of the day, the devastation of the three Deras, — Ismail Khan, Ghaze Khan, and Fateh Khan, was very great; and I trust that full particulars of this extraordinary flood may yet be collected by some of the many British officers now stationed along the Indus.

VII. —THE JEHLAM RIVER

The *Jehlam* river takes its name from the town of Jehlam, beneath which it flows. In Kashmir, it is called *Behat*, a contraction of the Sanskrit *Vitasta*, which the Greeks slightly altered to Hydaspes. The Jehlam drains the whole valley of Kashmir: and the reputed sources of its principal feeders are all esteemed holy. The Behat takes its rise in the small pool of Vira Nag, which Jehangir walled round; but its true source is some miles further to the south-west, in N.latitude 33°30', and E. longitude 75°25'. Its most distant source is in the lake of Sesha Nag, at the head of the Lambodari, or Lidar river, which joins the Behat below the town of Islamabad. Between Shahabad and Islamabad, it receives the river of Brang; and a few miles below Bij Bihara, it receives the united waters of the Veshau and Shupyen rivers. The Veshau, or Veshavi, rises in the holy fount of Kosa Nag; and the Shupyen river in the Lake of Nandan Sar. Below the city of Srinagar, the Behat is joined on the east by the Sindh, which is the largest of all its tributaries. From this junction the river continues its north-westerly course to the Wular lake, which it leaves above the town of Sopur, and then flows on in a south-west direction to Barahmula, receiving midway the waters of the Lolab river. The whole length of the Behat, from its source to Baramula, is 150 miles. From Shahabad to Baramula, the river is navigable. The fall is only 400 feet in 120 miles, or 3.33 feet per mile; and the usual rate of the current is about a mile and a half per hour. Vigne says that a piece of wood thrown into the stream at Kanibal, will reach the city in 24 hours. As the distance is about 64 miles, the rate will be 2¾ miles per hour: but I was 2¼ hours in descending the stream from the Islamabad bridge to the Bij Bihara bridge, a distance of little more than six miles, with two men gently paddling the boat. Again, in descending the stream from Bij Bihara to Wantipur, I went on shore to warm myself by walking, and I distanced the boat, although it was paddled by two men. I do not therefore estimate the velocity of the current at more than 1½ mile per hour, and I believe that it is considerably less.

At Islamabad, the breadth of the stream is 120 feet, with a maximum depth of 12 feet 3 inches. It is spanned by a log bridge, 118 feet in length, with two openings. At Bij Bihara, below the junction of the Lidar river, it is spanned by a bridge 250 feet in length, with four openings. Between these points the water is beautifully clear, and the bed of the river is generally sandy, and ripple-marked, and covered with shells and broken pottery. In a few places the bottom is stony, but the stones are all small and rounded. At Pampur the Behat is spanned by another log bridge, 325 feet in length, with five openings; but the water is slightly muddy, and the bed of the river can no longer be seen. Below Pampur, and opposite Panthasok, the abutments and two piers of a stone bridge are just visible above the water. In its course through the city of Srinagar, the channel of the river is narrowed to 250,and even to 200 feet, with a varying depth of from six to twelve feet. The stream is very sluggish, and the surface of the water in many places is covered with the green slime common to stagnant pools. In December, Moorcroft found the river 210 feet broad, with a mean depth of nine feet, and a velocity of 2,400 feet per hour, or of 0.6666 feet per second; which gives a discharge of 1,150 cubic feet per second.

At Sambhal, or Sambhalpur, below the junction of the Sindh river, the Behat is spanned by another bridge, 340 feet long, with five openings. The average depth of the water is about fourteen feet at the same place. On the 16th December, Trebeck found the depth of water from one to three fathoms. Assuming twelve feet as the average depth in December, and the rate of the current at 2,400 feet per hour (the same as at Srinagar), the winter discharge of the united streams of the Behat and Sindh rivers will be 2,480 cubic feet. At Barahmula the discharge is most probably not more, as the waters of the Lolab river may be supposed to supply the great loss by evaporation on the Wular lake.

From Barahmula to Mozafarabad, the Behat pursues an easterly course for 100 miles. The total fall between these places is 3,800 feet, or thirty feet per mile; and the character of the river entirely changes from a placid and sluggish stream to a raving torrent. Below Tattamula, and about sixteen miles from Barahmula, the rocky cliffs rise almost perpendicularly from the river to a height of 300 and 400 feet; and in some places that I noticed, the bare steep cliffs were not less than 800 feet above the stream.

As the height of the Behat, near Tattamula, is about 5,000 feet above the sea, the whole of Kashmir must have been submerged by the waters of the river, before the wearing down of these cliffs. The level of the Kashmirian lake would have been about 5,800 feet above the sea, and from 50 to 100 feet above the Karewahs, or isolated alluvial flats now remaining in Kashmir. The great Karewah of Nonagar, opposite Avantipur, which rises from 200 to 250 feet above the plain, is a mass of lacustrine deposit. I searched in vain for shells as I crossed over the Karewah to Payachh: but I was more fortunate at Wantipur, where I obtained numerous specimens of *Cyclas rivicola* in the horizontal strata of clay and sand at different heights up to nearly 200 feet above the present level of the river, and about eighty feet below the presumed level of the lake. The high level land of Marttand was probably not submerged, but the horizontal beach-marks are still quite distinct on the limestone cliffs above the cave of Bhaumajo and the holy spring of Bhawan. Above Ramuki Serai, on the Shupyen river, the Karewah forms a bank about 100 feet in height, in horizontal strata of different kinds. The uppermost twenty feet are composed of stiff alluvial soil; the next twenty feet of rolled stones and loose earth; and the lowermost sixty of indurated blue clay. The last must have been deposited by the lake in its state of quiescence; but the middle stratum could only have been formed by the first grand rush of waters on some sudden burst of the rocky barrier below Tattamula; and the uppermost would have been deposited by the subsiding waters as they reached the newly-formed level. Then, as the rocky bed was gradually worn down, the different streams worked new channels for themselves in the former bed of the lake, until the present Karewahs of Nonagar, Pampur, and Kanikpur were left first as islands in the decreasing lake, and eventually as long flat-topped hills in the midst of the open plain, just as we now see them. The Karewah of Nonagar is about five miles in length by two and a half miles in extreme breadth.

Above Uri the Behat has once been spanned by a stone bridge thrown across a very narrow part from cliff to cliff; but to judge from the lowness of the remaining portions of the abutments, the bridge must have been swept away by the very first extraordinary rise of the river. High up on the right bank stands a ruined serai of the Mogal emperors. Opposite Uri the river is now crossed by a suspension-bridge of leather ropes. Above Hatiya there is a second suspension-bridge of twisted leather ropes 258½ feet in length.

At Mozafarabad the Behat is joined by the Kishen Ganga, a considerable stream which rises in the mountains to the north of Kashmir, in N. latitude 34°34', and E.longitude 75°20'. It flows first to the westward through the districts of Gures, Suti, and Drawa, then turning to the south-west it pursues its course through Kerigam and Karna to Mozafarabad. The late Mr. Vans Agnew ascended this river on his way to Gilgit; but as he was not a surveyor, his travels were confined to a mere descriptive account. The whole length of the Kishen Ganga is not less than 180 miles, and its probable discharge about 1,000 cubic feet. The total discharge of the Behat below Mozafarabad will therefore be 3,500 cubic feet.

Below Mozafarabad the Behat sweeps suddenly round to the southward, and after receiving the Kunihar river continues the same course to the town of Jehlam, a distance of 150 miles. The fall in this part of the river is 1,200 feet, or only eight feet per mile. The Kunihar river rises in the Nila mountain, eight days' journey to the north or Mozafarabad. Its whole length is about 100 miles. From the junction of the Kunihar to Dhangali the Behat has been surveyed by Mr. Ingram, an assistant to Lieut. D. Robinson, of the engineers; and in this part of its course it receives no tributary worth mentioning. Near Mangali, at the foot of the hills, it is joined by the Punach river, a considerable stream, which is said to rise in the lake of Nandan Sar, in N. latitude 33°35', and E. longitude 74°40'. It takes an easterly course between the Pir-Panjal and Ratan-Panjal, ranges past Bahramgala to Punach, where it turns to the southward, and follows a south-westerly course to its junction with the Behat or Jehlam. Its whole length is 140 miles, and its discharge about 500 cubic feet.

The whole discharge of the Behat or Jehlam as it enters the plains is therefore just 4,000 cubic feet; this estimate is borne out by the statements of Moorcroft, who says that the river at Jehlam in October was 450 feet broad and from twelve to sixteen feet deep, with a current of about a mile an hour. These data give a discharge of 4,800 cubic feet per second for October, which would certainly be reduced to 4,000 cubic feet by February and March. The whole mountain course of the Behat, from beyond Virnag to Mangali, is 380 miles, and its fall is about 8,000 feet, or twenty-one feet per mile. From the hills to its junction with the Chenab between Jhang and Uch, its general direction is south-south-westerly, and its length about 240 miles. Its whole length from its source to its confluence with the Chenab is therefore about 620 miles.

VIII.—THE CHENAB RIVER

The Chenab is formed of two principal feeders, the Chandra and the Bhaga, from which it derives its Sanskrit name of Chandra Bhaga. Ptolemy calls it Sandabal; but the Greek historians of Alexander named it the Akesines, because its proper name was one of ill omen. The Chandra and the Bhaga rise on opposite sides of the Bara Lacha pass, in N.latitude 32°45', and E.longitude 77°22', at an elevation of 16,500 feet above the sea. The Chandra flows at first to the south for fifty-five miles, and then sweeps suddenly up to the north-west for sixty miles farther, to the junction of the Bhaga river at Tandi. The fall to this point is 7,500 feet, or sixty-five feet per mile, for the Chandra river, and 125 feet per mile for the Bhaga river, which has a course of only sixty miles to the southwest. At Koksar, twenty-five miles above Tandi and 10,000 feet above the sea, the Chandra river averages 200 in feet width, with a mean depth of two and a half feet, and a current of not less than four miles per hour in October, when it is fordable with every great difficulty. The discharge at that time is therefore not less than 2,000 cubic feet per second; and the minimum discharge is probably about 1,500 cubic feet, or of the united stream below Tandi about 2,000 cubic feet. From Tandi the Chandra Bhaga pursues a north-westerly course to Kashtwar, a further distance of 115 miles. The whole length to this point is 330 miles, and the fall is 11,500 feet, or 34.8 feet per mile.

Between Tandi and Kashtwar the Chandra Bhaga receives many snow-fed torrents of considerable size, of which the largest are the Chukam and Chatrgarh rivers. The discharge at Kashtwar cannot therefore be less than 4,000 cubic feet, or just double that at Tandi, which is half-way between the source and the town of Kashtwar. Below the town it receives from the north the large river of Wardwan, about sixty miles in length, by which the discharge is probably increased to 4,500 cubic feet.

At Koksar, 10,000 feet above the sea, which is the highest inhabited village on the Chandra river, a suspension-bridge of twisted birchen ropes is annually constructed. A second suspension-bridge of the same kind formerly spanned the mouth of the Bhaga river at Tandi, but this was carried away some time after Dr. Gerard's visit in 1830. In 1839 I saw the ropes lying high and dry on the northern bank; but when I visited Tandi again in 1846, there was no trace of them. A small wooden bridge of thirty-eight feet span, and forty feet above the stream, is thrown across the Bhaga river about four miles from Tandi. Fifteen miles below Tandi, and five miles above Treloknath, the Chandra Bhaga is crossed by a couple of spars covered with loose planks. The bridge is eighty-five feet long and forty-three feet above the water. Two miles above this bridge the river was not less than 300 feet broad. Above Chatrgarh and opposite Kashtwar, the Chandra Bhaga is crossed by suspension-bridges.

From Kashtwar the river sweeps suddenly round to the south-west as far as Doda. It then turns due west towards the fort of Riyasi, where it resumes its south-westerly course to Aknur, at the foot of the hills, a total distance of 150 miles. In this part of the course the fall is 4,000 feet, or 26.6 feet per mile. It receives the Banahal and the Budhil, above Aknur, and the two Tohis of Rajaori and Chaneni above Vazirabad. By these and some other small streams, its winter discharge is increased to 4,750 cubic feet per second. This discharge has been calculated from my own data obtained at Ramnagar in January 1849. Our military bridge of boats afforded me every facility for obtaining the most accurate measurements, and I have therefore full confidence in the correctness of the result. The river was divided into two streams; that on the left bank having a maximum depth of fifteen feet four inches, and that on the right bank a maximum depth of ten feet six inches. The total breadth, including the sand-bank in the centre, which was barely covered with water, was 646 feet, or, excluding the sandbank, 533 feet. The greatest surface velocity was 3.6666 feet per second, or just two miles and three-quarters per hour. The mean depth was exactly five feet, and the mean surface velocity 2.3 feet per second, or nearly one mile and five furlongs per hour. I have calculated each portion of the stream separately, and the result gives a discharge of 4551.038 cubic feet per second. A similar result may be obtained from the rough measurements of Sir Alexander Burnes, made at the same place in the middle of February. His data make the breadth 900 feet, greatest depth nine feet, and current one and a half mile per hour. Taking four and a half as the average depth, the discharge will be 4,860 cubic feet. I only give this to show the correctnes of my own measurements.

From the Bara Lacha pass to Aknur, the length of the Chenab is 380 miles, and the whole fall is 15,500 feet, or 40.8 feet per mile. From Aknur to Mithankot the length is 570 miles in a south-south-west direction, and the whole length from its source to its junction with the Indus is 950 miles.

During the dry season the Chenab is fordable in many places between Sodra and Ramnagar. Opposite Sodra in 1848 there was a good ford, crossing no less than seven branches of the stream. The Ramnagar ford was open during the whole of our operations in December 1848, and January and February 1849. The other fords were constantly liable to shift, but three days before the battle of Gujrat I discovered a good ford between Vazirabad and Ramnagar, by which Brigadier Markham's brigade crossed the Chenab on the 19th February.

I have no means of ascertaining the maximum discharge of the Chenab during July and August. Macartney measured it in July at Vazirabad, when the stream was 7,590 feet (nearly one mile and a half) broad, with a depth of fourteen feet, and a current of five miles an hour; but these data are too vague for even an approximate result. The depth for one half of this breadth was probably not more than one or two feet.

In July 1839, I found the main channel of the Chenab above Vazirabad to be 2,760 feet broad, but the depth could not be ascertained with any certainty; in many places it was more than eighteen feet. The mean depth was probably about nine feet, and if we allow two and a half miles as the average rate of the current, the maximum discharge would be 56,000 cubic feet, or with the six small branches to the westward, not less than 60,000 cubic feet. The increase of the Indus is nine-fold, while that of the Ganges is fifteen-fold. The mean between these is twelve-fold, which, if applied to the Chenab, would give a discharge of 54,600 cubic feet for the maximum. The actual maximum discharge is probably between 50,000 and 60,000 cubic feet.

IX.—THE RAVI RIVER

The Ravi is the smallest of the Panjab rivers. In the hills it is generally called Rawa or Rawati, which is only a spoken form of the Sanskrit Travati, from which the Greeks made Hydraotes. The Ravi is formed of three principal branches,—the Ravi proper, the holy Budhil, and the Nai, which make a triple junction below Wulas, in the district of Chamba. I have seen all these rivers myself, and am indeed the only European who has yet visited the head-waters of this stream.

The Ravi rises in the petty dismembered state of Bangal, in N.latitude 32°20', and E.longitude 77°0'. It takes at first a south-westerly course, and then bending to the north-west receives its principal tributaries at Wulas, a distance of sixty miles from its source. Its highest springs rise at the junction of the Dhaola Dhar and Lahul mountains, at an elevation of not less than 16,000 feet. As the height of the river at Wulas is only 5,000 feet, the fall is 183.3 feet per mile. From Wulas to Bisoli it continues its easterly course for fifty miles, and then turns to the south-west for twenty miles, to the neighbourhood of Tirikot, where it enters the plains. Its whole length is only 130 miles, while its fall is 15,000 feet, or 115.4 feet per mile.

The sacred Budhil rises in the Lahul mountains, to the north of the Ravi. Its whole course is not more than thirty-five miles from east to west, while the fall is 11,000 feet, or 314.3 feet per mile. Below Barmawar, the former capital of Chamba, the Budhil is crossed by a wooden bridge formed of spars covered with loose planks. The width is four and a half feet, the span sixty-eight feet, and the height above the river ninety-eight feet. This bridge has a hand-rail knee high on each side. A petty feeder of the Budhil rises in the small and holy lake of Mani Mahes.

The Nai river rises on the western face of the Kali Debi mountain, in the Lahul range. Its general course is to the south-west, and its whole length is only thirty miles. Its fall is therefore 366.6 feet per mile.

The Rawa or Rawati, just above the junction of the Budhil and Nai at Wulas, is spanned by a birchen-rope suspension-bridge 116 feet in length. It is therefore about double the size of the Budhil river. Below Wulas the road leaves the river and crosses over the mountains, to avoid the precipitous cliffs which overhang the stream. At Mahila, ten miles above Chamba, the Ravi is crossed by another suspension-bridge of 169 feet span. Between the bridge and Chamba the river takes a sudden sweep to the left, between overhanging rocks not more than fifteen feet apart. A curling wave returns to meet the rushing stream, and a shower of mist is perpetually rising from the shock. Then all is smooth, and the stream pours headlong into a gulf below, and is instantly dashed back by the opposing rocks in a huge curling wave.

Just below Chamba the Ravi receives a considerable feeder from the north. This is the Sawa, or Sar Nala which rises in the Saj Joth, in the Lahul range. On entering he plains the Ravi takes a south-westerly course past Lahore for 430 miles to Chichawatni, where it turns to the west, and after seventy miles more falls into the Chenab below Sirdarpur. The whole length of the Ravi from its source to its confluence with the Chenab is 630 miles, and its minimum discharge is 2,700 cubic feet. The Ravi is fordable throughout the winter season, but the bed is full of quicksands.

X.—THE BYAS RIVER

The Byas is perhaps the best known of all the Panjab rivers, from its source to the foot of the hills below Mirthal. Its Sanskrit name is *Vipasa*, from which the Greeks made Hyphasis and Bibasis. The common name of Byas is derived from the small pool at the source of the river, which is called Vyas Rikhi or Vyasa Rishi. This sacred spot is situated in the Rotang pass, at the head of the Kullu valley, in N.latitude 32^0 25', and E.longitude 77^{0}10', at an elevation of 13,000 feet above the sea. For seventy-five miles the river flows nearly due south past Sultanpur, the capital of Kullu, to the village of Larji, where it is joined by two large tributaries—the Sainj and the Tirthan. Above this it receives the Parbati and the Gomati rivers from the east, besides many smaller streams. The Gomati is fordable with difficulty, but the others can only be crossed by bridges. The Sainj has course of about fifty miles, the Parbati and the Gomati of forty miles, and the Tirthan of thirty miles. From the source to Larji the fall is 9,400 feet, or 125.3 feet per mile. From Larji the Byas sweeps suddenly to the westward through a narrow chasm in the rocks several hundred feet in depth. The stream is deep and rapid, but before the wearing down of this cleft the whole of the lower part of the valley must have been submerged. From Larji to Mandi the distance is not more than twenty-five miles, while the fall is 1,000 feet, or forty feet per mile.

The Byas continues its westerly course through this narrow channel to Mandi, above which it receives the Ul river from the north, and the Sukhet river from the south. The former is upwards of fifty miles in length, and the latter about thirty miles. At Mandi the river is crossed by a boat for the greater part of the year, but during the height of the seasonal floods the current is too strong for a boat, and the passage is then made on inflated skins. Between Sultanpur and Larji the river can only be crossed on skins, but from Sultanpur upwards it is spanned in many places by spar bridges.

From Mandi to Mirthal the general direction of the river is to the west; but the course is very winding, and the length cannot be less than 150 miles. Between these points it receives several large streams from the north, of which the chief are the Binwa, the Nigwal, the Ban-Ganga, the Gaj, and the Chakki.

The *Binwa* rises in the Dhaola Dhar range, and after a southerly course of forty miles past Baijnath falls into the Byas opposite Kamalagarh. The road from Kangra and Mandi ascends this stream to its source, and crosses over the Surai pass into Chamba on the upper course of the Ravi.

The *Nigwal* rises in the same range, and after a southerly course of forty miles through the beautiful districts of Palam, falls into the Byas opposite the large town of Shujanpur-Tira.

The *Ban-Ganga* is formed of two principal feeders,— the Ban-Ganga and the Patal-Ganga, which rise in the Dhaola-Dhar, and join immediately below the fort of Kangra. The general direction as far as Kangra is south-west, but below the fort the stream winds very much, and changes its direction first to the south and then to the west as far as Haripur and Guler, from whence it resumes its south-west direction, and falls into the Byas at the village of Nireyana, after a course of about sixty miles through the district of Katoch.

The *Gaj* or *Ghar-Gaj* is one of the largest feeders of the Byas, and was thought worthy of mention by Abu Rihan, who accompanied Mahmud of Ghazni to Kangra. It is formed of the united streams of the Gaj, the Kohli, the Bral, the Dehar, and the Bhet, all of which rise in the Dhaola Dhar range, and flow to the south through the district of Guler. The whole length of the Gaj to its junction with the Byas below Siba is not less than sixty miles.

The *Chakki* rises in the western end of the Dhaola Dhar, and is the smallest and longest of all these northern tributaries of the Byas. Its whole length from its source near the Chuari pass to its junction with the Byas at Biyanpura below Mirthal is not less than seventy miles.

On the south the Byas receives only one feeder of any consequence,—the Kunihar, which joins it a few miles above Nadon; but except in the rains, it contains very little water.

From Mandi to Mirthal, a distance of 150 miles, the fall of the river is only 1,600 feet, or 10-6 feet per mile. The whole fall from the source to Mirthal is 12,000 feet, or forty-eight feet per mile. In this part of its course the Byas maintains its supremacy as the most beautiful river in the Panjab. From Biyanpura, below Mirthal, the Byas flows in a south an south-westerly direction past the towns of Rahila, Bhairowal, and Govindwal, to its junction with the Sutluj at Hariki-patan, a distance of 100 miles. The whole length of the Byas, from its source to its confluence with the Sutluj, is 350 miles, and its minimum discharge is not less than 3,000 cubic feet.

On the 10th November, 1838, I measured the Byas a few mils above its junction with the Sutluj. Its breadth was 450 feet, and its greatest depth seven feet four inches. Its greatest surface velocity was 4.04 feet per second, or a little more than two miles and three-quarters per hour. The discharge was then 3,425 cubic feet, from which we may calculate the minimum discharge at not less than 3,000 cubic feet.

During the melting of the snows the Byas rises every night in the plains from one foot to one foot and a half. It attains its maximum in the morning and subsides during the day. When I was making the bridges at Govindwal for the passage of the army in March, 1846, I pitched my tent on the sand close to the water's edge, and in the morning I was surprised to find one line of tent-pegs completely under water. This rise is caused by the melted snows of the Dhaola Dhar, which are brought down during the day by the Binwa, the Nigwal, the Ban-Ganga, and the Gaj, and which do not reach

Bhairowal and Govindwal until past midnight of the second day, after a lapse of 36 hours. The Byas is fordable in many places in the plains.

XI.—THE SUTLUJ RIVER

The *Sutluj* is the largest and longest of all the Panjab rivers. Its Sanskrit name is *Satadru,* or the "hundred channelled," from which the Greeks made Hesudros and Zadadros; but the common names throughout the hills Satludr, or Satrudr, and Sutluj. The Tibetans call it *Lang-chhen-kka-bab,* or "elephant-mouth-fed" river, according to the commonly received notion of the descent of rivers from animals' mouths.

The rise of the Sutluj in the holy lakes of Manasarovara and Rawan-Hrad has been satisfactorily ascertained by the adventurous journeys of Captain II. Strachey and Lieut. R. Strachey. The most remote sources of the Sutluj are the eastern feeders of the holy lakes, in N. latitude 30°35; and E. longitude 81°35'. Numerous small streams flow from all sides into the great lake of Manasarovara, which overflows at its north-eastern corner into the lake of Rawan-Hrad. From this point to its junction with the Spiti river, at the base of Porgyal, the Sutluj takes a west-north-westerly direction through a country but little known, but which I believe to be similar to that of the upper valley of the Indus. From its source to the confluence of the Spiti river the length of the Sutluj is 280 miles, and the whole fall is 9,400 feet, or 33.8 feet per mile.

From the base of Porgyal to Bilaspur the Sutluj takes a west-south-westerly direction for 180 miles. In this part the fall increases to thirty-nine feet per mile, and the river becomes a furious torrent. Many old channels still exist to show that the Sutluj once flowed at a higher level, and that all the alluvial flats must have been the deposits of a series of lakes. Eddy-worn holes also may be seen high up in the rock, even up to 1,000 feet above the present level of the river. Two of these ancient channels are on the left bank, one just above Rampur, and the other opposite the Wongto bridge. The Rampur channel is 150 feet above the stream, and 100 feet broad, between large dykes of quartz, the intervening micaslate having been scooped out for some depth. A little higher up, the river has made a perpendicular cut through one of these quartzose dykes about sixty feet deep.

From Bilaspur the Sutluj makes a sudden sweep to the north-west, and then back again to the south-east, round the end of the lowermost range of hills, and finally enters the plains at Ropar. The distance is 100 miles, and the fall about 500 feet, or five feet per mile. The whole length of the Sutluj, from its source beyond Manasarovara to the foot of the hills at Ropar, is 560 miles, and the whole fall about 17,000 feet, or thirty feet per mile. From Ropar, the Sutluj takes an easterly direction for 120 miles past Lodiana, to the confluence of the Byasat Hari-ki-patan, beyond which it flows to the south-west for 400 miles to its junction with the Chenab opposite Uch. The whole length of its course is, therefore, 1,080 miles, or 130 miles more than the length of the Chenab.

The minimum discharge of the Sutluj at Ropar is 5,400 feet. As a small addition must be made for the Sirsa Nadi, the Kali Vehi, and the Dḥaoli Vehi, we may reckon the discharge of the Sutluj, above its confluence with the Byas, at 5,500 cubic feet, or just 1,000 cubic feet more than that of the Chenab. The Sutluj is fordable in many places above the junction of the Byas, below which it becomes deeper, and is usually called the Ghara river.

Like the other Punjab rivers, the Sutluj has a daily rise and fall, owing to the increase and decrease of the melted snows: On 29th May, at Kepu, below Kotgarh, I measured a rise of ten inches, the higher level being obtained at 3 A.M. In July the Spiti river at Kyi attained its maximum of four inches and a half at 3 P.M. This is in fact the hour at which I have found that all these snow-fed streams reach their highest level. If, therefore, we assume that the Sutluj, at the mouth of its last great feeder, the Baspa, reaches its maximum at 3 P.M., we shall obtain a mean velocity of six miles and a quarter per hour as far as Kepu, a distance of seventy-five miles.

XII.—THE SPITI RIVER

The Spiti river, which is perhaps as large as the Sutluj itself, is formed of two principal branches,—the Spiti and the Para-ti or Zang-sum river. It takes its rise near the Bara Lacha Pass, in N. latitude 32°4', and E. longitude 77°40', at an elevation of 16,500 feet (the height of the Bara Lacha Pass). From its source to the village of Mane, it flows in a south-easterly direction for eighty-five miles, and then turns to the eastward for thirty-five miles to its junction with the Para river. The fall is 6,000 feet, or fifty feet per mile. From Chang-Razing the river turns to the south for twenty-five miles, through a narrow rocky channel to its confluence with the Sutluj. The fall to this point is 2,000 feet, or eighty feet per mile; and the whole fall, throughout its entire course of 145 miles, is 8,000 feet, or fifty five feet per mile.

In the upper part of its course, the Spiti river partakes of the general character of the Tibetan streams, and spreads its waters over a breadth of nearly half a mile. It thus becomes fordable, during the winter season, as far as Dangkhar, where it receives the Pin river from the south. Below this, it is crossed by several suspension-bridges. Opposite Rangrig, it is spanned by a spar bridge with a hurdle footway. At Shalkar, below the junction of the Para, it is crossed by another spar bridge ninety-two feet long; and there is a third wooden bridge between Liya and Nako.

The Para-ti, or Para river, was considered by Alexander Gerard to be larger than the Spiti; but there is no comparison between the two. The Para is only a very large rushing torrent, while the Spiti is a very deep rapid river. The Para rises in the Parang Pass, to the north of the Bara Lacha range, in N. latitude 32°25', and E. longitude 77°50', at an elevation of 18,000 feet. It first flows for about twenty-five miles to the north-east, and for about twenty-five miles to the north-east, and for about twenty-five miles to the east as far as Chumur. From this point it turns to the south-east, and afterwards to the south-west, to its junction with the Spiti at Chang-Razing. Its whole length is 130 miles, and its fall about 7,500 feet, or 57.7 feet per mile.

Just above the confluence of the two rivers, there is a hot spring named Zang-sum, and the lower part of the Para is sometimes called by this name. Alexander Gerard took the Zang-sum for another river, and has accordingly entered it in his map. But it is quite evident that he mistook the Gyu, a small tributary which joins the Spiti just above the confluence of the Para, for the Para itself. I surveyed this locality with some care, and can therefore state positively that Alexander Gerard was mistaken.

Four miles above its confluence with the Spiti, the Para river is spanned by a single block of granite, which forms a vast natural bridge eighty-five feet in length, and from twenty-five to thirty feet in breadth and depth. The stream below is contracted to a raging torrent, not more than fifteen feet in width.

XIII.—CATACLYSM OF THE SUTLUJ

About midnight on the 26th day of the month of Kartik, and in the Sambat year 1819 (10th November, A.D. 1762), the shoulder of a vast mountain gave way, and fell from a great height headlong into the Sutluj. The slip took place in the neighbourhood of the hot springs at Seoni, about twenty miles north by west fom Simla, where the river is confined between precipitous cliffs that rise several thousand feet above the stream. The narrow channel was instantly choked with a vast mass of rock, earth, and rubbish, to a height of more than four hundred feet, and the stream for the space of forty days was so completely dammed that the water ceased to flow below the barrier. The bed of the Sutluj was reduced to a succession of deep pools, scattered amongst the huge boulders and angular masses of rock, and the people passed over with dry feet. The waters of the river accumulated till they rose nearly four hundred feet in height opposite the Rana's residence at Bhaji, and the effect of the obstruction is said to have been felt as high up the river as Rampur, a distance of forty kos, or about sixty miles. At Bhaji, a lofty semal, or cotton-tree, which was half-submerged, is still pointed out; and as the height of this cotton-tree above the Sutluj is estimated by the Rana at 120 yards, the rise of the river cannot have been less than 400 feet.

A similar account was obtained by Alexander Gerard in 1817, when numbers of people who had witnessed the flood were still alive. "About fifty-five years since, forty or fifty miles above this town (Bilaspur), an immense mountain gave way, filled the bed of the Sutluj, and arrested the stream for six weeks. During this time the inhabitants were anxiously looking out for the bursting of the embankment. When it did give way, the rush of such an overwhelming body of water may be more easily conceived than described. People were stationed on the heights all along from the place where the stream was stopped as far as Bilaspur, and they gave notice of the approach of the flood by firing matchlocks. The news arrived in time to save the inhabitants, but the whole of the town was swept away."

This account is not quite correct, for it was only the lower town that was swept away, as the houses of the upper town, including the Raja's palace, and several old temples, are situated on an elevated flat far above the reach of any inundation. The distance from Seoni to Bilaspur is not more than forty-five miles by the river, and about thirty miles by land. The wave of inundation would therefore have reached Bilaspur in three hours, at the rate of fifteen miles per hour, while the news of the bursting of the barrier could have been signalled by matchlocks in half an hour.

As my information is derived from the Rana of Bhaji, in whose principality Seoni is situated, I have full confidence in the general accuracy of my account, even including the statement that the bed of the Sutluj became quite dry for the space of forty days. At first I was disinclined to believe this startling fact, but a little reflection showed me that it must have been the case; for as the fall of the Sutluj in this part of its course is not more than twenty feet per mile, the accumulated waters must have filled the bed of the river for twenty miles before they attained a height of 400 feet, level with the top of the barrier. To fill this gulf would have required the accumulated discharge of the river for about forty days. The minimum discharge being 5,400 cubic feet at Ropar, the discharge at Seoni in November cannot be less than 5,500 cubic feet. This discharge accumulated for forty days would have amounted to 19,008,000,000 cubic feet, a mass of water which would only just have been sufficient to fill the gulf in the bed of the Sutluj for twenty miles above the barrier to a mean depth of 200 feet, with an average breadth of 900 feet. The flow of the river must therefore have been quite stopped below the barrier for the whole period of forty days.

When the accumulated waters once began to pour over the obstructing barrier, the mass of loose earth and rocks must have been speedily cut up in all directions, until it soon yielded to the pressure of the mighty body of water; and the long-imprisoned river burst its fetters and rushed headlong down its rocky channel in one mighty wave, from fifty to more than one hundred feet in height. This occurred on the fifth day of the month of *Paush*, or the 19th of December. Of its progress in the hills I know nothing more than what I have already quoted from Gerard of the destruction of the lower town of Bilaspur. But after reaching the plains, the mighty wave was swept more and more to the northward by its own speed off the Sewalik hills at Ropar, and thus took a new course under Phalor to the north of the old channel until it joined the Byasat Hari-ki-patan, where its further course to the northward was stopped by the stiff high cliffs on the right bank of the Byas. From this time the Sutluj, when swollen by the annual rains, continued to pour its waters down the new channel until about A.D. 1790, when the whole body of water finally deserted the old bed by Lodiana and Dharmkot, and joined the Byas at Hari-ki-patan, some thirty miles above the former point of junction at Firozpur. For six months the Sutluj remained above its usual level until the rise of the river in June, when the last remains of the once mighty barrier were swept away by the swollen river.

The following table embodies all the principal points of information contained in the preceding pages.

	Rivers	Length			Fall per mile		Discharge	
		In Hills	In Plains	Total	In Hills	In Plains	Min.	Max.
1.	Indus Proper	1,035	942	1,977	15.4	1.06	16,500	
2.	Shayok	400	—	400	26.4	—	2,000	
3.	Zanskar	210	—	210	28.5	—	1,000	
4.	Jehlam	350	240	620	21.0	—	4,000	
5.	Chenab	350	570	950	40.8	—	4,550	54,000
6.	Ravi	130	500	630	115.4	—	2,700	
7.	Byas	150	100	350	48.0	—	3,000	
8.	Sutluj	560	520	1,080	30.0	—	5,500	
9.	Panjnad	—	—	—	—	—	12,000	100,100
10.	Indus alone	—	—	—	—	—	15,000	100,177
11.	Indus and Panjnad	—	—	—	—	—	27,000	230,117
12.	Ganges at Ghazipur	250	1,500	1,750	52.0	0.66	21,757	476,761
	Ganges at Pubna	—	—	—	—	—	96,000	1,500,000

(From *Ladhak — Physical, Statistical and Historical, 1853*)

9

The Indus Valley

By
A.H. Francke

A
LADHAK

We crossed the Thag-lang Pass (17,500 feet high) on the 19th August, and marched to the village of rGya (13,500 feet high), the first village of Ladakh, on the road from Rubshu. Before entering rGya, we passed by the ancient remains of the village of Rum-rtse (map Ramcha) which is asserted to have been a Mon settlement. When Moorcroft halted here in 1820, the whole population of this little village, who had never seen a European before, fled in terror, leaving their houses empty.

What may be called the necropolis of the ancient Mons of Rum-rtse, is situated on a plain above the trade road, about two miles above rGya. It consists of a number of large single *mchod-rten*, and many well-preserved rows of 108 little *stupas*. The present inhabitants of Run-rtse, said that all those *mchod-rten,* having been the work of Mons, were not reverenced by them. The Mons and the Tibetans had nothing in common, the said. Although we examined some of the ruined *mchod-rten* at the site, we did not find any inscribed tablets in them. We took a photo of a rather well-preserved specimen of these *mchod-rten* which was of the so-called ladder type, as we find it represented among the ancient rock carvings near the Alchi bridge. The lower part showed remains of stucco frames which, I suppose, originally enclosed stucco figures of Buddha. This kind of ornamentation is not found on Tibetan *mchod-rten*. If a Tibetan *mchod-rten* has stucco relievos, they represent lions, Garudas and other animals. These are not found round the base, but round the middle portion of the *mchod-rten*. Another of our photos shows some of the well-preserved rows of little *stupas*.

Opposite, and a little below the necropolis, on the other bank of the rGya brook are the ruins of the ancient castle and town of the Mons, called Run-rtse-mkhar, with cave dwellings close by. The most conspicuous building in the old town was a round tower of great dimensions. Unfortunately, our limited time did not allow us to visit the site. The rGya district altogether is so full of ancient remains that an archaeologist could profitably spend a couple of weeks here.

There is another ruined castle (called *mKhar-gog*), on a spur in a side valley to the left, between Rum-rtse and rGya. Although I could not trace any traditions regarding it, it is apparently of Mon, *i.e.*, pre-Tibetan, origin. Besides, there are many ancient Mon *stupas* in various places between Run-rtse and rGya. The two large *mchod-rten* seen by Moorcroft on the road before entering rGya, are apparently still in existence. They are of Tibetan origin, and probably not more than two centuries old.

The site of the old settlement of the Tibetans at rGya is called *rGya-mkhar*. It is situated on a spur of the right bank of the rGya brook. From Moorcroft's account it appears that in 1820 A.D., the site was no longer inhabited and that Moorcroft's town of rGya was identical with the present, which is situated on the left bank of the brook. He says : "Opposite to the town, on a lofty ridge of rocks, was a large pile of houses, formerly inhabited by the raja; and lower down, one belonging to the lama." The ruins of this ancient Tibetan town are still very picturesque. Higher up on the same hill are several ancient watch-towers. When Moorcroft was in rGya. He found one of the ancient chiefs of the district still in authority. He had friendly intercourse with this man whom he calls a raja. He says : "The raja whose name was Tsimma Panchik, was a short stout man about fifty." Of course, there were no kings of rGya, not even a vassal king. The title of raja (*rgyal-po*) may have been given to the chiefs, because they were related to the Ladakhi kings. Now the line is extinct, and all records being lost, I found it impossible to establish the identity of Moorcroft's Tsimma Panchik. It is even difficult to make out what Tibetan name may underlie Moorcroft's spelling of it. I suppose that the man was called Thse-dbang Phun-thsogs, pronounced Tsewang Puntsog. I asked several people at rGya if they could remember the names of the last members of their line of chiefs, and they gave me the following three names ; (1) bKa-blon-Thse-bstan; (2) Nono bSod-nams jo-rgyas; (3) bKra-shis (or Thse-ring) bZang-grub. More they could not remember. It is, however, possible that on a votive tablet on one of the *mani* walls at rGya the name of Moorcroft's friend may yet be discovered. Thus an inscription on a *mani* wall below rGya, of the time of bDe-ldan rnam-rgyal (c. 1630 A.D.) contains the name of one (or two ?) probable ancestors of Moorcroft's Tsimma Panchik, *viz.*, Nono bSod-nams-lhun-grub, `father and son.' In this inscription the castle of rGya is called rGya-mkhar-rmug-po, `the dark red castle of rGya.' On another *mani* wall in the vicinity of the preceding I found a tablet which is of interest on account of its reference to the state of Ladakh during the times following the battle of Basgo, 1647 A.D.

It gives the name of the Lhasa commissioner who for a time was regent of Ladakh and who, as the chronicles prove, intended to make himself the independent ruler of the country. His name is given here as rGyal-bai rgyal-thsab rJe-btsun Mi-pham-mgon. But unfortunately, there was no time for copying these inscriptions in full, nor for making impressions of them.

Behind the present village of rGya, on the left bank of the brook, there is a plateau studded with a number of ancient, mostly ruined *mchod-rten*. They are still held in veneration by the present inhabitants of rGya. This is remarkable, because many of these *mchod-rten* which are called *Lha-bab-mchod-rten,* undoubtedly go back to Mon times. And had not the people of the neighbouring village told us plainly that they were indifferent to everything connected with the Mons? The difference may be this, that whilst the Mons of Run-rtse did not succumb to Tibetan influences, the Mons of rGya did. We found several types of cremation tablets with Indian inscriptions, containing the *Ye dharma* formula. The characters employed are of c.700—900 A.D. according to Dr. Vogel's estimate. But there were also several tablets which showed the same formula in Tibetan characters. The difference between the Tibetan and Indian characters rests mainly in this, that in the Tibetan version the aspirated mediae are indicated by an ordinary media furnished with a subjoined *h,* whilst in the Indian version *gh, dh,* and *bh* are expressed in simple characters. Besides, the Tibetan version has the tripartite *y,* whilst the Indian version has a later from of the *y.* In two cases, there were two tablets showing almost exactly the same design, but the characters used for the inscription were Tibetan on one of them, and Indian on the other. Among the *Lha-bab-mchod-rten,* there were also the ruins of an ancient monastery of unknown origin, built of sun-dried bricks. I am almost convinced that the town of rGya is mentioned in the time of King Sadna legs, c. 850, in the chronicles of Ladakh. There it is stated that King Sadna legs built the temple of sKar-chung-rdo-dbyings in the province of rGya (*rGya-sde*). This could, of course, also be translated by "Indian Province" or "Chinese Province." But it is very unlikely that a Tibetan king should have built a monastery in a district, the hold on which was always uncertain. It is a pity that the name of the ruined temple in the middle of the *Lha-bab-mchod-rten* has become entirely lost.

On the 20th August, we left rGya for Mar-rtse-lang (map Marsahing), the Marsilla of Moorcroft. Below rGya, we passed by a high *lhatho,* an altar of the pre-Buddhist religion, with a few houses and fields in the vicinity. It is the *Latu* of Moorcroft, and soon we reached the houses and fields of small settlement, called Rong.

We made a short halt at this place, because I wished to examine the site of some ancient graves, called *Mon-gyi-rom-khang*, "graves of the Mons." The first who told me of the existence of these graves, was our evangelist dGa-Phun-thsogs of Kyelang, who is a native of rGya. He had told me that he had been inside them when a shepherd boy. He said that then the graves were quite accessible; that he went down a staircase and came to rooms furnished with boards of pinewood, on which were placed numbers of skulls. A native of Rong whom we met, also asserted that the graves were very deep and furnished with masonry walls. As regards pinewood, I must say that it is a very rare article at rGya, which place is nowadays 150 miles away from the nearest pine tree. When we looked at the graves, we saw only pits in the ground for the superstitious people of Rong had closed them up with earth. As my observations later on in Leh showed me, it is very probable that these ancient graves of Rong belong to the same period as those of Leh, which I have much reason to attribute to the period of the "Empire of the Eastern Women.' This State bordered on Ladakh, if it did not include parts of Eastern Ladakh. The Leh graves as well as those of Rong are furnished with masonry walls. Both contained numbers of skulls, a circumstance which points to the custom prevalent in that empire of burying all the higher officials along with the chief. The fact that the skulls were placed on boards in Rong, seems to show that the corpses were cut to pieces. Also at Leh the skulls as well as the vases containing the bones were originally placed on boards which became rotten when irrigation water entered the graves. Most of the larger pots at Leh had holes in the bottom, which shows that they probably had fallen down from a higher position. As excavations in Rong would have been possible only at a considerable sacrifice of time and money, I abandoned the idea for the present.

The next village on the road along the narrow valley from rGya to the Indus is Meru, pronounced Miru. It has a monastery in ruins which was famous in olden days. It is situated on a hill above the trade road. Its temple occupies the uppermost position on the top of a little conical hill, and the now ruined cells of the monks surround it below. It used to be one of the important monasteries of Ladakh, but its founder is not known. It lost much of its glory, when King Seng-ge-rnam-rgyal made it the "mother" of the Hemis monastery which he built in the Shang valley. On that occasion, not only the "spirit" of the Meru monastery was carried off in a bundle of twigs, but also most of the images were transferred to Hemis. But Meru had to suffer a still greater injury during the Dogra wars, when it was plundered, and the monks expelled. At present, there is not much remaining in the temple hall; one of the frescoes is, however, of unusual interest as it represents Gob-bzang-lha-mo, the mother of Kesar and one of the great pre- Buddhist deities of the Ladakhis. This picture is probably of ancient origin, although it had apparently been renovated from time to time. It was painted at a time when Bon-po art was largely influenced by Buddhist art. The complexion of the goddess is a beautiful white, whilst her hair is black. The hair is raised over the forehead and furnished with a ribbon and a diadem of pearls. Her ear ornaments (probably shells) are white and spiral-shaped, and her dress is white with blue and red seams. In her hand she carries a white cup.

Opposite the monastery, there is a hill with cave dwellings, probably the most ancient inhabited locality at Meru. It is called *Baho* ('Caves').

The place where the inhabitants of Meru had to live before they built their present houses in the bottom of the valley, is a hill spur on the right bank of the rGya river where there are extensive ruins of houses. As has been stated above, during the ascendancy of the Ladakhi kings people were not allowed to live among the fields, probably to prevent their trespassing too much on valuable ground. But, as we learnt from Moorcroft's account of rGya, the lofty sites on the top of rocks were already partly abandoned during the times of the last king. Thse-dpal-don-grub-rdo-rje-rnam-rgyal (1820 A.D.). From his account it appears that at Meru also people lived in their present houses in 1820.

Several miles below Meru, the rGya brook discharges into the Indus, and at this place is situated the village of Ubshi (Moorcroft's *Ukshi*). In this village we noticed several *mchod-rten* of great age which were known to the inhabitants as *mchod-rten* of the Mons. We examined the interior of one of them and found the walls inside covered with ancient frescoes which were apparently painted with two colours only, indigo blue and brownish red. There were any number of rows of figures of blue complexion seated corss-legged. Their garments were white with red seams. The larger pictures in the centre of the four walls were too far gone to allow of any identification. The headdress of these blue figures was somewhat unusual; it looked as if the ends of a long hair-pin projected on each side. Later on, when I had examined several more similar frescoes at other ancient sites, I came to the conclusion that the Ubshi pictures represent Nagas (*Klu*), and that these ancient *mchod-rten* may be Bon-po, and not Buddhist, structures.

We spent the night of the 20th and the 21st August at Martselang. Here I had a pleasant surprise in meeting one of the Leh mission ladies, Miss Schurter, who had travelled through the desert wilds of Rubshu from Kyelang to Leh, accompanied only by two Christian Tibetans from the former place. I might have caught her up much earlier, if she had not been alarmed by rumours of the approach of a very untrustworthy sportsman (myself !) which caused her to make double marches to escape him.

Martselang is situated at the lower end of the Shang valley the *Changa* of Moorcroft), which contains the Hemis monastery. This monastery which was built by king Seng-ge-rnam-rgyal only about 300 years ago, has acquired quite unusual fame among European visitors to Ladakh on account of its devil-dances. These are performed here in June (originally probably on the occasion of the summer solstice), a convenient time for Europeans to attend them, whilst most of the other monasteries have the same performance in winter. The monastery was also frequently referred to fifteen or eighteen years ago, when the Russian traveller Notovitch surprised the world by stating that he had found in it a copy of a new Christian gospel written in Pali. A great deal of learned correspondence then took place which proved that Notovitch's extraordinary find was a forgery. The interesting Tibetan account of the foundation of this monastery was brought to Europe by the Schlagintweits, and the Tibetan text with an attempt at a partial translation was published by Emil von Schlagintweit. I hope to find time to prepare a reliable version of this interesting document. Although the Hemis monastery is not very ancient, yet it contains images of a type which is found only in monasteries of the 10th or 11th century. When the monks are asked to state the place of origin of such statues, they say that they were brought here from Lhasa. I wonder if that can be true. It seems to me that a more likely explanation is that these images were brought here from Meru, which is, as already stated, the "mother" monastery of Hemis.

At Martselang we saw again many ancient *mchod-rteṅ* of the Mon type, and all along the road, from this place to Chushod, these *mchod-rten* were much in evidence. I may add that it is very much the same on the other bank of the Indus, *e.g.*, at Khrigtse, Ranbirpur, and Sheh, where they are numerous. At Ranbirpur, I remember having seen even several specimens of the ladder type in fair preservation. The conviction that we are travelling here on ancient Buddhist ground, grew very strong on me. It is not impossible that the present village and monastery of Khrigtse are identical with the castle of Khri-btsegs-abum-gdugs mentioned before Srong-btsan-sgam-po, who was the first Buddhist king of Tibet, and with the monastery of Khri-rtse mentioned under King Mes-ag thsoms (705—755 A.D.). Local names in Sanskrit which are found here and there in Ladakh, date from the times of this more Indian than Tibetan form of Buddhism. The names of Meru, and Sakti (Skr. *Sakti*) have already been mentioned. I may add the names of Muni and Kanika (=Kanishka ?) in Zangskar, and Tar (Skr. *Tara,* on account of the Svayambhu *Taras* at that place), Hari rtse (Summit of Hari). The greater part of the Ladakhi local names are certainly Tibetan; but not a few are of Dard origin. In connection with the latter statement let me point to the many names which have the Dard word *hem* (Skr. *hima*) or *hen* "Snow," as one of their component parts, *viz.*, Hembabs (Dras), Henasku, Hemala, Hemis. Of other plainly Dard names like Hanu, Hunupatta, Garkunu, Chanegund, Hibti, Esu, etc., I cannot yet explain the etymology. The name *Ranbirpur* is a modern Dogra name. A few ancient Indian personal names also have been preserved in folklore and inscriptions. Thus, the ruined castle opposite Stag-sna is called the castle of king Surgamati (Skr. *Sury-amati,* "Sun-mind") and among the old royal names on inscriptions at Khalatse we find Shirima (Skr. *Sriman*) and (probably) Satyamati ("Truth-mind"), besides several others.

When riding along the left bank of the Indus river, we could see the villages, castles and monasteries on the right bank, a visit to many of which would amply reward archaeological research. The conical hill of the Khrigtse monastery always looks picturesque, and so it is with the Stag-sna monastery which is built on a rock between two arms of the Indus. The buildings of this monastery look almost like a royal castle. It was built with the greater care, because it was the residence of several members of the royal family who had taken orders in the 'a Brug-pa sect. The erection of this monastery in its present shape is attributed to Ngag-dbang -rnam-rgyal, the step-brother of Seng-ge-rnam-rgyal. The village of Sheh (*Shel*) on the right bank has also many attractions. It was apparently the capital of Ladakh, before the old kings of Leh, the professed descendants of the mythological king Kesar, were expelled. Here are the most ancient royal rock inscriptions, but the best preserved of them will probably remain inaccessible for some time for the natives of Sheh, being afraid of a devil who has his abode exactly in front of the best of them, have erected a wall which conceals the entire inscription.

We crossed the Indus at Choglamsa. The water was so high, that if flowed over part of the bridge, and we had to ride through deep water for several hundreds of yards on the bridge as well as on the left bank. At Choglamsa we met two ladies of the Mission who had come to the bridge to welcome Miss Schurter, and on the road through the sandy desert below Leh we were welcomed by several more members of the Moravian Mission. We rode along the royal *mani* walls south of Leh which had astonished Moorcroft ninety years ago, and entered Leh with thankful hearts, for we were all much in need of a good rest. Here in Leh we again received letters, the first since leaving Poo four weeks before, and also a remittance. But a more powerful inducement to continue our work was the approval of our past doings, which found expression in Dr. Marshall's letters.

B
LEH

The name of *La-dvags* is not mentioned in the Tibetan chronicles before the reign of King Niy-ma-mgon, c-900 A.D. when it is stated that it was in the hands of Gesar's descendants. The kings Lha-chen-she-srab and Khri-btsug-lde (c.1350—1400 A.D.) seem to have resided chiefly at Sabu; and only the kings from a Bum-lde onward, (after 1400 A.D.) resided permanently at Leh. As has already been mentioned, the original name of the town is not *sLel,* as it is now-a-days spelt, but *sLes,* which signifies an encampment of nomads. These nomads were probably in the habit of visiting the Leh valley at a time when it had begun to be irrigated by Dard colonizers. Thus, the most ancient part of the ruins on the top of the rNam-rgyal-rtse-mo hill at Leh are called aBrog-pai-mkhar (Dard castle), and of the supposed Dard graves at Leh, we shall have occasion to speak again.

The first European to visit Leh was apparently the Jesuit Desideri who visited Ladakh in 1715 during the reign of King Nyi-ma-rnam-rgyal whom he calls Nima namgial. The Jesuit was kindly received by the king, but as the Muhammadan traders plotted against him and undermined the king's confidence, he soon left the town and travelled to Lhasa. I regret to say that I have not yet seen a satisfactory account of this interesting and important journey. A relic of Desideri's mission was discovered by the next European visitor to Ladakh, Moorcroft. He found at Pashkyum an old Bible on which he makes the following remarks : "A Sayid, who seemed to act as his (the Pushkyum Raja *i.e.* vassal chief's) ghostly adviser , produced a book which had descended from his grandfather to the Raja, and which proved to be an edition of the Old and New Testament from the Papal press, dated in the year 1598. It was bound in Morocco, with the initials I.H.S. surmounted by a cross, stamped on each side of the cover. How it had come there no person could inform me, but it might possibly have been given to the former Raja by Desideri, who visited Ladakh, although it is very doubtful if he reached Le. The Khalun and Khaga Tan zin made, at my request, very particular inquiry regarding any evidence of a European having been at Le before us, and no proof nor tradition of such an occurrence could be traced." I feel confident that a critical edition of Desideri's diary will establish beyond doubt the fact that Desideri actually visited Leh.

But although Moorcroft was the second instead of the first visitor to Leh, his description of his visit is of the greatest importance in historical as well as geographical respects. Moorcroft visited Ladakh fourteen years before the kingdom lost its independence. He spent two years at Leh, and as he was a very keen and intelligent observer, his description of the kingdom is of unique interest. Trebeck, Moorcroft's travelling companion, who was a clever draftsman, made a pencil sketch of Leh, which was reproduced in the account of their travels, and this picture of Leh, the oldest known to exist, no archaeologist would willingly lose. The reason why

Moorcroft spent such a long time at Leh was his attempt to arrange for the king of Ladakh's tendering his allegiance to the East India Company. It took him a long time to win the confidence of the Ladakhi king, Tuntuk namgial (*Dong-rub-rnam-rgyal*) and his Prime Minister, Tsiva Tandu (*Thse-dbang-dong-rub*). But when they were ready to tender their allegiance, their offer was declined by the East India Company. How different the fate of Ladakh would have been, had it been accepted. Moorcrofts had no doubts then, that Ladakh would soon be swallowed up by Russia, for the Prime Minister showed him a letter from the Emperor of Russia to the king of Ladakh which had been brought there by a Jew, six years before. Moorcroft and Trebeck became eye-witnesses of some little warfare between the Ladakhis and Baltis, and between the Ladakhis and the Kụlu State; they also saw the seditious placard at Leh, in which the unsatisfactory rule of the king was contrasted with the excellent rule of his predecessor, his brother, who had died young. There is simply no end of most interesting information in Moorcroft's account, and I hope to be spared to edit the Ladakhi portion of his journal with notes from the Tibetan point of view.

Let me now quote Moorcroft's description of Leh, in 1820, and contrast it with the Leh of the present day. He writes: Le, the capital of Ladakh, is situated in a narrow valley, formed by the course of the Sinh-kha-bab (*Sengge kha-bab*, i.e., the Indus), and bounded on the northern and southern sides by a double chain of mountains running east and west, the highest of which are from eighteen hundred to two thousand feet above the plain. It is built at the foot and on the slope of some low hills, forming the northern boundary of the valley, and separated by a sandy plain about two miles broad from the river it is enclosed by a wall, furnished at intervals with conical and square towers, and extending on either side to the summit of the hills. It is approached by a double line of the sacred structures of manis, frequently noticed in the journal, and houses are scattered over the plain without the walls, on either hand. The streets are disposed without any order, and form a most intricate labyrinth, and the houses are built contiguously, and run into each other so strangely, that from without it is difficult to determine the extent of each mansion. The number, it is said, is about a thousand; but I should think they scarcely exceeded five hundred. They vary from one to two or three stories in height, and some are loftier. The walls are in a few instances wholly, or in part of stone, but in general they are built with large unburnt bricks: they are whitened outside with lime, but remain of their original colour inside. They are usually furnished with light wooden balconies; the roofs are flat, and are formed of small trunks of poplar trees, above which a layer of willow shoots is laid, which is covered by a coating of straw, and that again by a bed of earth."

From this description we learn that in 1820, although the general character of the houses was the same as it is nowadays, yet the ground plan of the old town must have been very different from that of the present town. It is true that even then some houses existed outside the walls, but the town proper was enclosed by a fortified wall. The two large bazaars which form such a conspicuous feature of the present town of Leh were not yet in existence. As popular tradition asserts, the large bazaar of Leh was laid out by the Dogras after the war of 1834-1842, and the new bazaar was made in 1897 by Captain Trench, British Joint Commissioner. I have been told, the Schlagintweits give a very minute descritpion of Leh as it was in 1856, when the large bazaar was already in existence. Where this descritpion is to be found, I have not been able to trace. A few remains of the walls of Leh are found right in the middle of the present town, where there is also one of the ancient crooked gates. The gate, which is a little north-east of the great mosque at the end of the bazaar, marks the extent of the former town towards the south. All those houses which are found between the rNam-rgyal rtse-mo Hill and this gate, belong to the old town of Leh, of Moorcroft's time. He makes special mention only of three conspicuous buildings, *viz.* The royal palace, the Chamba

(Byams-pa, *i.e.,* Maitreya) and the Chenresi (sPyan-ras-gzigs, *i.e.* Avalokitesvara) Monasteries. These three buildings are still in existence, and will be referred to in due course. The following conspicuous buildings of the old town must also have been in existence in Moorcroft's time, although he does not make any reference to them. The house *Blon-po* ("Minister") is situated directly below the castle, on the south-west corner; the *dGon-pa-so-ma,* (New Monastery) is situated on the south-eastern corner of the same castle. It is the scene of the devil-dances which were witnessed by Moorcroft. Both these buildings can be distinguished on Trebeck's picture of Leh. Below the dGon-pa-so-ma and the Byams-pa monasteries, is situated the *mKhar-chung* ("the little Palace"), and exactly below the latter the ruined site of the house *bKa-blon* 'Prime Minister', possibly the very same house in which Moorcroft was received in audience by the then Prime Minister. West of the house *bKa-blon* we see the house *To-go-che.* The *To-go-che* used to be an official who ranked between a minister and a *Grong-dpon,* or mayor. The representative of the To-go-che is Munshi dPal-rgyas, the chronicler of Ladakh. To the west of his house we find the house *Grong-dpon* or "Mayor," and below it the old Byams-pa (Maitreya) monastery. But on Trebeck's sketch of Leh we see two high palace-like buildings behind the Maitreya and Avalokitesvara Monasteries, of which no trace remains. What were the names of these two buildings? From the chronicles of Ladakh we learn that a 'new palace" was built above the sPyan-ras-gzigs Monastery during the reign of King Thse-dpal-rnam-rgyal. That would account for one of those buildings. During the reign of the same king mention is also made of a *"Theg-chen-gong-ma* Hall." As, however, nothing definite is said with regard to its situation, we do not know whether it is a room in the old castle or the building shown on Trebeck's sketch between the large roayl palace and the "New Palace," behind the Avalokitesvara Monastery.

We could not possibly examine all the antiquities of Leh within four weeks, but we did some work, and I now wish to describe what we found.

We were just entering Leh, when I heard that somebody had again opened the ancient Dard graves near the *Teu-gser-po*, about two miles above the Commissioner's compound in the Leh valley. This is the same site on which Dr. Shawe and myself had done some excavation work, in 1903. As I did not wish anybody else to take away the more important objects of interest, I asked Mr. Schmitt of the Moravian Mission to go with met to the graves on the 23rd August. This we did, and the two Christian boys who accompanied us proved very useful in opening the graves, which involved very hard work. The roof of the grave is more than a yard below the present level of the ground. It consists of large unbewn stones of rectangular shape, each about 1½ yards long, and a foot or so broad. The walls of the grave consist of masonry of unhewn stones. It is about two yards long, 1½ yards broad, and at least six feet deep. We had not yet reached the bottom, when we stopped our excavations. Originally the roof of the grave was probably above the ground. Later on, the deposits accumulated and buried it. But destruction did not set in, as I believe, until a field was made above it. Then, the continual flood of the irrigation water destroyed all the woodwork and many of the bronze implements began to oxydize. I suppose that the Leh graves originally contained wooden boards just like those at rGya.

The grave contained clay pots of various sizes, a few entire, but most of them in fragments. The largest pot, of which only fragments came to light, may have had a height of three feet, and its diameter was probably not much less. The smaller pots, which were rarer than the large ones, had a height of 10 to 15 cm. There were also small, saucer-like vessels of clay, probably lamps. The natives who were with as at once asserted, that the pottery of the grave was distinctly different from present day tibetan pottery. The pottery of the grave is not wheel-made but hand-made and characterised by very small handles. When Dr. Shawe and myself visited this grave (or another in the neighbourhood) in 1903, we found two elegant pots of medium size which were ornamented with designs sin dark red colour. These pots were kept by Dr.

Shawe in his house, and photographed by Miss Duncan. This time we could not fine a single pot with painted designs in the grave. But there were linear ornaments impressed on several of them. The only places in Ladakh, besides the graves, where similar hand-made pottery with dark red ornaments has been found, are the ancient ruined castles of sBalu mkhar and Alchi Mkhor gog. A plate showing such pottery is reproduced in my article "Archaeological Notes on *sBalu mkhar*." Another collection of such ornamental sherds was made at *Alchi mkhar gog* on our expedition and brought to Simla. These ornaments are all of a very primitive type. They consist of spirals, ladders, and a zigzag band; and occassionally there are bunches of lines which may represent grass or reeds.

As most of the pots had holes in their bottoms, I was led to believe that they had fallen down from some higher position, probably from wooden boards (as are said to exist in the rGya graves). When the irrigation water entered, the boards decayed and gave way. As I had previously observed, when examining the graves with Dr. Shawe, most of the pots were filled with human bones. This circumstance seems to indicate that the ancient inhabitants of the Leh valley indulged in the gruesome practice of cutting the corpses to pieces and filling clay pots with the fragments. This custom, which is also found in other parts of the globe, is asserted by the Chinese to have been in vogue in the "Empire of the Eastern Women". Some of the pots had old cracks and carefully bored holes on both sides of them. Thus the art of mending broken pottery with strings must have been known to the race which built these graves.

There were, it appears, between fifteen and twenty skulls in one single grave. How many, exactly, it is difficult to state now, as we were not the first to examine the grave. When we opened a grave in 1903, DR. Shawe carried home three of the skulls. He took measurements of them and writes with regard to them in his letter of the 14th November 1905, as follows : "All the skulls I got are very decidedly egg-shaped. The measurements taken with an ordinary pair of compasses (we have no proper`calipers' here) along the antero-posterior and longest transverse diameter of the roof of the skull are (approximately) 6-3/1 × 5 inches, 6¾ × 5¼ inches, and 6¾ × 5¼ inches. Against these the similar measurements of a skull which I got in Baltistan from a Musulman grave, presumably that of the Balti, are 6-5/6 × 5-5/8 inches." If we convert these measurements into the ordinary centigrade formulas of cephalic indexes, we obtain the following numbers : three skulls from the Leh grave : 74, 70 ; 77,77 ; and 77,77. Balti skull 82,82. Unfortunately, on our visit to Leh last year, even a pair of compasses could not be obtained, and I therefore cannot give any numbers. But as I have acquired an experienced eye for forms of skulls, I venture to state that all the skulls we found in the grave last year, were most distinctly dolichocephalic, and the formulas 74 to 77 would probably suit them all. We had also an opportunity to compare them with two skulls taken by Mr. Schmitt from the graves below Leh which date from the last epidemic of small-pox in Leh, about a hundred years ago. These skulls from the small pox graves appeared to be decidedly brachycephalic, when compared with those from the ancient grave. As dolichocephalic heads are a characteristic mark of the Dards of Hanu, Da, and other Dard places of Ladakh, we are led to believe that the people who built the ancient graves were probably of Dard stock; at any rate they were not of Tibetan, but of North Indian origin.

Besides human skulls, a head of a sheep, and a horn of an ox were also found in the grave. These are apparently remains of a sacrifice, or gifts to the dead.

The grave contained also a number of bronze implements, some in fairly good preservation. Most of them were, however, much corroded, and covered with a thick layer of verdigris. First of all, I may mention small square leaflets of thin bronze furnished with an embossed ring, of which we found hundreds. Whether they were used for ornamental purposes, or as coins, I find it impossible to decide. Then there were numerous bronze beads, of round as well as oblong shape, small and large, the largest thicker than a finger. Later on we discovered little pendants of bronze, of bell-like form, with triangular holes and a ring at the top. They were probably inserted between the bronze beads of the necklace. When we took photos of the bronze implements and other articles, we found a glass bead among the bronze beads. It was of mother-o-pearl colour, and looked like Roman or Greek glass. Dr. Marshall informs me, however, that this kind of glass is found all over Asia.

Once, when I had made arrangements to go to the grave and continue my exploration, I was prevented from doing so by an attack of malarial fever. Then Mr. and Mrs. Reichel of the Moravian Mission offered to go in my place, and they brought home several more very interesting finds. In particular, there were a number of bronze buttons of various sizes witha loop on the reverse. Some of them were of ordinary size, about half an inch in diameter, but others were much larger, nearly two inches in diameter. The largest had a scalloped edge, like an Indian one-anna piece. None of them contained an inscription. The smallest were quite plain, the largest had an elaborate spiral ornament, and those of medium size, a star ornament. I suppose that these buttons were worn by ancient officials as distinguishing mark of rank, just as is the case in China nowadays.

Some other round pieces of bronze may have served as mirrors, such as are still found in Ladakh. Some fragments were probably the remains of bronze pots.

On the 28th August, three of our Christians went again to the graves of their own accord. They found many more bronze implemets, several of them in fairly good preservation; for instance, a can with a spout of excellent workmanship, though quite plain and without any ornament; a seal with a cross-pattern engraved on it; an entire bracelet with a pattern of little circles. Although we could trace decorative designs on several fragments, there was no vestige of any script.

In addition let me say that fragments of iron implements came to light also, and that Mr. and Mrs. Reichel discovered the only gold article that was in the grave. It is of a shape similar to the mouthpiece of a trumpet, but its purpose is not known. Its ornamentation is curved form of the Greek key.

After this description of the grave and our finds in it, let me enter into the question of its date and the nationality of the people who built it. As I have pointed out already, in connection with the rGya graves, the condition of these graves calls to mind at once the description of the form of burial practised in the "Empire of the Eastern Women," of the Chinese historians. There we read : "When a person of rank dies, they strip off the skin, and put the flesh and bones mixed with gold powder into a vase, and then bury it.... At the burial of the sovereign, several tens of the great ministers and relatives are buried at the same time!" The latter statement about this gruesome custom may account for the great number of skulls, sometimes as many as twenty, which are found in a single grave. As the grave contained large bronze buttons, obviously a mark of high rank, it is very probable that the Leh grave actually contained the remains of several "great ministers." This "Empire of the Eastern Women" has been described in the *Sui shu*, a book which was compiled in c.586 A.D. Here it is called Nu-Kuo. Hiuen Tsiang also heard of this empire, and a little after his time, we read that the last queen died and was replaced by a king. The frontiers of this curious empire are given by the *Sui shu* as well as by Hiuen Tsiang. They are : Khotan, Sampaha (Ladakh), Brahmapura (Chamba State), and Tibet. From these definitions we may conclude that the empire comprised the Tibetan provinces of Guge and Ruthog, and possibly Eastern Ladakh. The empire was a Tibetan one, according to our Chinese authorities, and it therefore appears strange that the skulls of the Leh grave are not those of Tibetans, but of Aryans. My explanation would be that it is very probable that portions of Ladakh were for a time at least included in this empire. The value of our grave finds lies in this that they afford us a glimpse of the general state of civilisation which prevailed in this empire. As regards its date, the presence of iron besides bronze precludes the fixing of any very early date, say before the Christian era. The absence of any form of writing in the grave would perhaps point to a time earlier than 586 A.D., at which time, according to the Chinese, the Indian characters were used in the empire. In my opinion the grave dates from between 1 and 500 A.D.

Fortunately for me, I had finished my investigations, when Mr. Chatterji, Director of Archaeology in the Kashmir State, arrived in Leh with the message that it was the wish of the Maharaja that no further excavations of any kind should be undertaken in Kashmir State territory.

The village of Skara (*sGa-ra* in native documents) is situated south of Leh and forms a kind of suburb of that town. On the 3rd September, I visited the ruins of the sGar-rtse Monastery at Skara. According to K. Marx this is the monastery "for four lamas only," founded by King a 'Bum-lde, about 500 years ago. It was built on a crag resembling an elephant. This little monastery was destroyed by the Dogras, at least so I was told. There was also another small temple erected below the ruin, occupied by one lama who belongs to the `aBrug-pa order. No tradition regarding King 'a Bum-lde has been preserved in the locality.

The village of Skara was formerly situated on a rocky spur to the right of the Leh valley, where there are still many ruined houses. The chief reason for evacuating the former site was said to be an epidemic. There are still many graves in a side-valley near it.

Probably the most ancient monastery at Skara is the one which is situated in a little ravine, between the rGar-rtse Monastery and the ruined village. Four walls are still standing, and there are traces of red colour (frescoes) on the walls. Close by is an underground room, in which we found a human skeleton of recent date.

Below this ruined monastery, there is a *mchod-rten* shaped like a "Mon *mchod-rten*." It consists of a lower square room, on the top of which is placed a round pyramid. Locally this *mchod-rten* is known as the grve of a king. It actually contained human bones, notably fragments of a skull.

Not far from it, on the plain, there is a group of three ancient-looking *mchod-rten* of the usual shape. A man from Skara had extracted from them several ancient house-hold utensils filled with grain. Out of these, he sold me a sieve cup made of very thin copper leaf.

At Skara my attention was drawn to a rather modern-looking round *mchod-rten* which was hollow and furnished with a door. Inside of it we found several cremation tablets of ancient style, some with Indian inscriptions. I was told that a few years ago an ancient *mchod-rten* was destroyed by a Muhammadan who built a house for himself at Skara. He carried all the tablets found in the old *mchod-rten* to the new one and hid them there. In the desert below Skara, there are the low mounds of several ancient *mchod-rten*. We found in them cremation tablets with Indian legends, very much like those at rGya.

In the desert between Skara and Spithug (*dPe-thub*) on the Indus, on a plateau below the western mountain range, there are the ruins of a large building called *Chad-pai-lha-khang*, "Temple of punishment." The outer wall towards the east has a length of more than 100 feet. There is no wall on the west side. Perhaps it was left incomplete. I made a plan of it. I was told that in the days of the Ladakhi kings (no personal name could be remembered) two men were ordered to erect this temple as a punishment for some crime. No woodwork remains, and there are no traces of images or frescoes on the site.

In the desert east of Leh, there is a large *mchod-rten* of yellow colour, which is called *Ma-ni-gser-mo*. Popular tradition asserts that it is one of the most ancient here. On the western side of the dome there is a niche with a complete figure of a seated Buddha. It must formerly have had such niches on all four sides. Attached to it are two or three *mchod-rten* of more recent date. One of them was open, and contained all sorts of old rubbish, *viz.*, fragments of idols, pages of books, charms, and cremation tablets. We took away some of the better preserved tablets. In 1906 we obtained from the same *mchod-rten* a few sheets of manuscript in a modern Indian dialect which were sent to Dr. Vogel, for examination. As King *Seng-ge-rnam-rgyal* (c 1600 A.D.) exhibited strong sympathies with the religions of India, the manuscripts may date from his time. Of more recent date are the pages of a Sanskrit book in Devanagari character. This book was used by the Dogras after the wars, 1834-1842 A.D., when they established a Sanskrit school at Leh; but the school soon came to an end, and the book was then placed in this *mchod-rten. mChod-rtens* of this kind, which serve chiefly as receptacles for old and useless manuscripts,remind me strongly of the Jewish Genizas.

The hill behind the town of Leh is called rNam-rgyal-rtse-mo. On the top there are the ruins of the royal palace which was built by bKra-shis-rnam-rgyal (c.1520 A.D). As I had often visited this site during my former stay at Leh, I had not intended to visit it again on this occasion. Owing, however, to the return of the Italian, Dr. Filipo de Filipi, of the Duke of Abruzzi's mountaineering expedition, with his wife and brother, it was decided to show them some of the sights of Leh. One forenoon was accordingly set apart for a trip to the top of rNam-rgyal-rtse-mo, Mr. Reichel of the Moravian Mission accompanying us. I had no reason to regret having been of the party, for on this occassion I noticed a few things which I had overlooked before.

The Maitreya temple on the rNam-rgyal-rtse-mo is apparently the oldest, and is in all probability identical with the "Red College" built by King' aBum-lde, 500 years ago. It contains an inscription in praise of the reformer bTsong-kha-pa; and, among many other frescoes, a picture of the bKra-shis-lhun-po Monastery in Tibet. This picture shows the group of buildings which make up the large monastery, and there is a long inscription attached to it which is distributed all over the picture. Although this inscription, as well as the other one, is in very bad preservation, several sentences can be made out. As masons or architects are therein mentioned, it probably refers to a restoration of the temple. The name of a great minister, Phyag-rdor, is given in one of the inscriptions. He is possibly the same minister Phyag-rdor who is mentioned in the Daru rock inscription. I am inclined to think, for reasons which I will state later on, that Phyag-rdor served under Lha-chen Bha-gan, c. 1470—1500 A.D. In that case the inscriptions in this temple may date from the latter half of the 15th century. I ordered both of them to be copied. On the right and left hand side of the huge Maitreya statue, there are fragmentary traces of two other statues which once stood there. This is in agreement with a statement in the *rGyal-rabs*.

There is another temple, of red colour, on the top of the same hill, namely, the temple of "the four Lords" (*mGon-khang*). This is the very one which was erected by king bKra-shis-rnam-rgyal c. 400 years ago, as stated in the chronicles. K. Marx was assured of its existence by bKra-shis-btsan-phel, his lama friend, but he was unable to visit it. It contains very artistically executed figures of "the four Lords" which are about from three to eight feet high. The principal figure represents rNam-thos-sras (Vaisravana). All four figures were covered with blankets; but these were removed with the exception of the one which covered Vaisravana. With regard to the latter image we were told that it is exhibited only once a year. The lama showed us, however, a fresco of Vaisravana on the wall, where he is represented in sexual union with his Sakti. As these images belong to the few in Ladakh which can be dated, they are of the greatest importance for the histroy of Tibetan art. Among the frescoes on the walls, I found one on the right hand side of the door which represented gorgeously dressed men with Yarkandi turbans on their heads. I could not understand the presence of these Muhammadan portraits in a Buddhist temple, until the lama in charge explained that they were Ladakhi kings. By the side of the picture, there is a long inscription in gold on indigo tinted paper, which mentions King bKra-shis-rnam-rgyal, the builder of the temple. From this inscription it appears that the picture represents this king who testified to his close attachment to the Turkomans by dressing exactly like them. As regards the Turkoman invasion under Sultan Haidar during his time, it is very difficult to reconcile the Tibetan with the Turkish account. The latter is found in the Tarikh-i-Rashidi. Not only according to the Tibetan chronicles, but also according to inscriptions from Ladakh, he gained a signal victory over the Turkomans. According to the Tarikh-i-Rashidi, on the other hand, he was a servant of the Turkomans who held him in little honour. I have come to the conviction that he was a very clever politician. bKra-shis-rnam-rgyal knew very well that he could not resist the first violent attack of the Turkomans with an armed force. He, therefore, concluded a treaty with them, and apparently took their side. He then very cleverly enlisted the energy of the Turkomans on his side, for co-ercing his disobedient vassal princes and unpleasant neighbours. Some of them were Muhammadans; for instance, the chiefs of Suru, Sod, Baltistan, and one in Nubra. It is rather remarkable, therefore, that the Turkomans actually went against and fought them. Whether the Lhasa expedition came to an end a few marches beyond the Manasarowar Lake, or eight marches from Lhasa, as stated in the Tarikh, does not matter much. In the eyes of the Ladakhi kings, the chiefs of Guge as well as the Central Tibetans required suppressing. After the Turks had spent all their strength on the enemies of the Ladakhis, the latter rose against them themselves, and turned them out of the country. As the Ladakhi chronicles tell us, the corpses of the slain Turks were placed before the idols of the temple of the four Lords (*mGon-khang*). This is the reason why the male members of the royal family of Ladakh are shown wearing the Turkestan dress in the frescoes, whilst the female members are dressed in true Ladakhi fashion, wearing on their heads the *berag*, a leather strap covered with turquoises.

Above the temple of the four Lords (*mGon-khang*) are the ruins of bKra-shis-rnam-rgyal's palace. They include a little Lamaist monastery which is of no particular interest. Ruins of other parts of the ancient palace, for instance watch-towers, are found all along the ridge of the rNam-rgyal-rtse-mo hill. Some of the ruins are of a decidedly earlier date than the reign of bKra-shis-rnam-rgyal. For instance, I am told that the foundations of a certain round tower are commonly known by the name of *'aBrog-pai-mkhar*, "Dard castle". It may, therefore, be attributed to a building which was erected before the Tibetan conquest of Ladakh, in c. 900 A.D. A man from Leh brought me a fragment of a copper pot, which he said he had found on the top of rNam-rgyal-rtse-mo. It contained an inscritpion in ancient characters, giving the name of a prince: *rGyal sras dBang-(nya.?) gsing dbang-po,* " Prince dBang (nya?) gsing dbang-po." As the word *rnam-rgyal* does not occuar in the name, it may be the name of a younger son of a king of the first dynasty of Ladakhi kings. In the Ladakh chronicles we read that one of their early kings had placed the bones of Buddha in his elephant incarnation on the top of the same hill. I made inquiries as to their whereabouts and was told that they had been deposited in a *mchod-rten* which was utterly destroyed by the Baltis about 1580 A.D. No trace of the relics remains.

On our way down from the top of the hill, we passed by the Great Palace of Leh which was erected by king Seng-ge-rnam-rgyal in c.1620 A.D. As I knew from fromer visits, it is practically empty. We did not enter it, but photographed the carved wooden gate, the famous "Lion Gate" of Ladakh. One of the rooms of the palace contains heaps of old manuscripts. All the paper is indigo-tinted, and the writing is in gold, silver and copper. As this collection probably represents the old royal library, or part of it, I asked Mr. Chatterji of the

Kashmir State, to make arrangements to put the manuscripts into order again.

I heard rumours of the existence of ancient Indian Buddhist manuscripts at Leh and in other parts of Ladakh, Munshi dPal-rgyas, the representative of the To-go-che family being reported to be in possession of one. Fortunately for me, Munshi dPal-rgyas himself arrived in Leh soon after I had heard this, and readily showed me his old book. It was, however, not of Indian, but of Tibetan origin, being the eighth volume of the Tibetan translation of the Prajna-paramita, and written throughout in 11th century orthography, gold on indigo-tinted paper. The wooden cover was ornamented with very beautiful ancient carvings, for which reason a photo was taken of the same. Munshi dPal-rgyas emphatically denied the existence of Indian manuscripts at the Hemis monastery, in spite of a rumour to that effect which had been brought to us. But he said that he had heard of the existence of a book, written in Lanthsa characters at the Sanid (or Muni) monastery in Zangskar. This book may be identical with the old 'palm leaf' shown to the Rev. Mr. Bateson on the occassion of his journey through Zangskar in 1908.

Mr. Meebold also makes the statement that he was shown 'palm leaf' books at the Rangdum monastery of Zangskar. These statements await verification. It is strange that Munshi dPal-rgyas should have bought his ancient book at Lhasa, as he says. The Prajna-paramita, as already stated was translated into Tibetan by Lama Rin-chen-bzang-po, who was a West Tibetan, and most of the copies of his book were distributed among the West Tibetan monasteries of his time. Sending them to Lhasa would have been of no use, as Buddhism had practically disappeard from Central Tibet in the 11th Century, being introduced into the conuntry again from West Tibet and Khams. But at a much later time, possibly only century or so ago, a number of important books were carried off to Lhasa. So I was told at the Alchi monastery where no ancient manuscripts now remain. The histroy of Munshi dPal-rgyas' book may therefore be as follows : It was originally written for one of the Western monasteries. Then it was carried off to Lhasa; and was there again sold to a pilgrim for a high price.

Here I may add that I made another find of manuscripts of a very different character at Leh. In the Mission library at Leh, I found a good number of my old hand-written books which I had collected in former years and quite forgotten. As they contain many hundreds of pages of hitherto unpublished folklore, I carried them off with me and sold them to Government for the benefit of the Mission, together with another collection of unpublished folklore which I had still in my possession. Among these latter manuscripts was a sheet which contained a kind of introduction to the cryptic alphabet used in Tibetan seals. The inscription on the Dalai Lama's seal, among many others, is written in this alphabet. How gratifying it was to find that my sheet from Leh proved to be the correct key to the reading of the Dalai Lama's seal. Among my treasures are several hymnals relating to the pre-Buddhist religion of Ladakh which, I hope it will be possible to translate in course of time.

At Changspa, a village half a mile from Leh, there is the large residence of a family of ministers (*bka-blon*) of the former Ladakhi kingdom. In a garden-house (*rab-gsal*) belonging to the minister's estate are the remains of frescoes illustrating the Kesar-Saga. Several years ago, I ordered one of them to be copied by a local painter. this time, I had photos taken of three of them, in addition to a copy in colours executed by a local artist. The frescoes in the garden house will soon be gone altogether, and as pictures relating to the Kesar-Saga are very rare, I was resolved to save for science what could be saved. All the frescoes in this hall refer to a chapter of the Kesar-Saga, entitled *Ljang-dmag*, "the war against the country of Ljang," as we find it in the literary version of the Kesar-Saga. Let me remark that the famous epic of Tibet, the Kesar or Gesar Saga, is preserved in two versions which are very different from one another. One of them, the oral version, exists only in the mouths of the people whilst the literary version is found in several manuscripts in Ladakh, and possibly even in woodprints. All lmy publications with regard to the Kesar-Saga deal only with its oral version. A manuscript of the literary version of the Saga is in the hands of the present ex-minister of Changspa. From an article by Schiefner it is evident that it was the Changspa minister's Gesar manuscript, which was copied for the Imperial collection of manuscripts in St. Petersburg. Upt to the present, nobody seems to have been able to read and translate it. This is very natural, considering the extreme difficulties of its language. K. Marx says that it is written in the *Khams* dialect. As there are people here at Changspa who can read and understand the Saga, their knowledge ought to be utilised for the benefit of science. I copied all the wall-inscriptions relative to the frescoes which it was still possible to decipher. The following notes on the dress of the pre-Buddhist divinities represented in the frescoes, may be of iconographical interest : dBang-po-rgyab-zhin has a red coat, and white cloak with blue seam; Gog-bzang-lha-mo is dressed in white , but her trousers are red, and she has a green shawl; one of her sons (Don-yod?) has a red jacket with green seams; another of her sons (Don-ldan?) has a white and green jacket and red trousers; Kesar has a red coat, and a white cloak with green seams; he sits on a red carpet, and the background behind him is blue.

There is a large pyramidal *mchod-rten* at Changspa which is called "the Kings' *mchod-rten*" by Europeans, and bKra-shis-sgo-mang by the natives. The present inhabitants of Changspa say that it was not erected by their ancestors, but by Turks of Mongols on one of their expeditions to Ladakh. The latter assumption is, however, difficult to believe. This old *mchod-rten* may go back to the times of the Mons or Dards. It is surrounded by rows of one hundred-and-eight *mchod-rten*. And this goes to prove that it cannot be of much later date than the 15th century, and may very well be of much earlier date. The *mchod-rten* has received its name *sgo-mang* "many doors" on account of the many little niches with which it is furnished. In all probability these niches once contained Buddhist images, but none now remain. On the whole, however, this old *mchod-rten* has been wonderfully well preserved and is still regularly whitewashed.

Not far from it are several stone sculptures in relievo which probably also go back to Mon or Dard times (c. 700-900 A.D.). The best of them shows a standing Buddha with Bodhisattvas on his right and left. The one on his right who carries a vase is Maitreya. The one on his left, and higher up, with a flower in his hand, is Avalokitesvara. Above him, in the air, we see two flying figures (Gandharvas?) On the reverse of the same stone is a four-armed figure, perhaps a Maitreya, and a *mchod-rten* is carved on one of the narrow sides. I will not now describe all the stone sculptures of Leh and surroudings, because it would take too long, for there are many of them. A number have been mentioned or described in my article, "Archaeology in West Tibet." But I will mention another sculpture at Changspa near a group of houses, lower down, not far from the brook. It is enclosed by a masonry wall. This figure is furnsihed with an unusual headdress and seems to represent a Buddhist priest of the Mon or Dard times.

On a rocky hill to the west of Changspa, there are several crematories and some ancient *mchod-rten*. Higher up, on the same hill, are the ruins of the Ribug (Ri-phug) monastery. As the monastery was reported to be of ancient date, I visited it but could not, however, discover any inscriptions or documents referring to it. One of the *mchod-rten* close by is of an ancient type, but the cremation tablets contained in it are unfortunately without inscriptions. The temple hall being roofless, nothing remains of former frescoes except a few traces of colour on the plaster.

The ruined *mchod-rten* called Teu-bkra-shis'-od-mtho is the largest in Ladakh. It is situated about 1½ mile from the Commissioner's compound, a little higher up in the Leh valley. We measured the circumference of its base at about 10 feet above the ground, a height at which the masonry rose clear above the surroudning rubbish, and found it to be 550 feet. It was erected by king' aBum-lde, in order to cover up a crag which was believed to be harmful to the country, and is now in a very dilapidated condition.

On the 9th September, I went to the Teu-gser-po orTiserru (as ordinary people call this ruined *mchod-rten*), accompanied by Mr. Schmitt of the Moravian Mission, Lobazang, a Christian and Meteorological Observer at Leh,, Pindi Lal, and the Khalasi. Our object was to study the inside of the structure. When we had climbed up to half its height, we found a hole in the surface, the opening of a narrow shaft. Lobzang went down first of all. He came to a narrow room of triangular shape, which was perfectly empty. We then tried to dig a new hole in a different place, when suddenly a number of men, who had been working in the fields, rushed towards us terrified. They implored us not to open the Tiserru, as such a procedure would bring incalculable misfortune to the country. From their remonstrances we learned something about the history of the old monument. The story reminds us of European fairy tales, such as that of the devil being caught in a bottle. In King'aBum-lde's times, there used to live a demon in a cavity of the rock Teu-gser-po. This devil, who had fire proceeding from his mouth, roamed about the country and destroyed the king's palace and portions of the town of Leh. To exercise him, the huge *stupa* was built above his abode. If we opened the *stupa*, the people feared that the evil spirit which had been kept under custody for 500 years, might once more attain liberty. We pointed to the old holes in the building, and observed that he might have escaped long ago. But that was of no avail. At the same time, we were told that the old *stupa* was not only a repository for devils, but for heavy gales also. When in the days of King'aBum-lde, the country suffered severely from storms, several large clay pots were held against the wind with their mouths open. As soon as the wind subsided, their mouths were closed, and they were stored up in the *stupa* with the storms contained in them. People were afraid we might find and open this ancient pottery, and that the country would be plagued with heavy gales again.

From the opposition which we met in this case from the peasants of Leh, it was plain to me that it is difficult to do archaeological work in an inhabited country. The chronicles of Ladakh have only a very short note on this *mchod-rten.* They simply state that it was built, because "some fatality" had occurred at Leh. I am still of opinion that the idea of a devil living in this place has something to do with the ancient graves described above. These graves are situated in proximity to, and some of them possibly below the *mchod-rten.*

On the same day, I went higher up the Leh Valley, following the desert road to the west of the cultivated area, accompanied by Pindi Lal and the Khalasi. Close to the village of dGonpa, we passed by the ruined site of an old town with *mchod-rten* of ancient type near it. There we found also a stone sculpture of some Bodhisattva, enshrined in a masonry wall, with a *lhatho* (altar of the pre-Buddhist religion), in front of it. As usual, the altar was furnished with many ibex horns. This ruined town may be the original site of the present village of dGonpa.

Marching upwards in the side-valley to the left of the village of dGonpa, we came to the ruins of an ancient temple, which is generally known by the name of Gya-mthsa. I had visited it occassionally, ten or twelve years ago, when I was stationed at Leh as a missionary. But the late Dr. Shawe of Leh was the first to draw attention to the fact that there are traces of circular medallions on two of its walls. In that respect rGya-mthsa reminds us of the ruined monasteries of Basgo and Chigtan. Inside and below the medallions, Drl Shawe noticed holes in the wall, as if sticks had once been stuck into it. He even found fragments of wood in two of the holes (according to his letter of the 27th October 1905). He supposed that these sticks had once served to support images. Our observations at the Tabo monastery of Spiti fully confirm Dr.

Shawe's supposition. As will be remembered, in the Tabo monastery we found thirty-two raised medallions on the walls of the temple hall, and an image placed in front of each of them. After digging only a little way into the mass of debris below one of the medallions at rGyamthsa, we came across several pieces of plaster composed of clay, straw, and linen. This is exactly the material these images are made of. From our observations it follows that rGya-mthsa is probably of the same time as the Chigtan, Basgo and Tabo monasteries, i.e. of the times of Rin-chen-bzang-po (c. 1000 A.D.). But let me add that my assumption is not supported by popular tradition. The present inhabitants of the valley do not even believe that the ruin is that of a temple, but assert that it once served as a summer house for a minister (*bka-blon-gyi-dbyur-sa*).

On the other side of some adjoining fields, there are several ancient ruined *mchod rten*. In one of them I found cremation tablets of the "miniature *stupa*," type. When I threw one of them to the ground, it broke to pieces, and out of it came a very neat little tablet with an inscription in an ancient form of Sarada. The inscription again contains the *Ye dharma* formula, and its characters belong to the 11th century. Owing to its extraordinary receptacle, the characters of the inscription were as distinct as any I had seen up to this. I made an accurate copy of the inscription on the same day, and I am glad I did so. For, when my collection of clay tablets arrived at Simla several months later, the distinctness of most of the inscriptions had suffered much, in spite of very careful packing. Although I opened several more "miniature *stupas*" in search of inscribed tablets, I did not find any other specimens.

On the 17th September, I visisted Munshi dPal-rgyas in his own house, called *To-go-che*, at Leh. Mention has already been made of his old Tibetan book. This time he showed us some of the contents of his private temple, several printed flags of no particular importance, a few idols of the ordinary type, and a mask of an *Agu* (hero) of the Kesar-Saga. This

Agu, dGra-lha, who is worshipped in the Munshi's house, is also represented among the frescoes of Changspa. As I am told, several more masks representing Agus of the Kesar-Saga can be found also at the Lamayuru monastery. According to popular tradition, Lamayuru used to be the centre of the Bon religion of Ladakh. Munshi dPal-rgyas told me plainly that he was fully. Convinced that the religion of the Kesar-Saga and the Bon religion were absolutely the same. As will be remembered, the study of the Songs of the *Shar-rgan* festival at Poo leads to the same conclusion. Then Munshi dPal-rgyas showed us the head of an ibex in his possession, with the right horn crooked like an ammonite. This head was found in Ladakh, and the famous lama bKra-shis -bstan-'aphel, who died in 1890, pronounced it to be the head of Buddha in his antelope incarnation. It is, of course, treated with proper respect by its owner, who will not part with it for anything. This is the second "bone of Buddha, " which we have come across in Leh. The first is contained in a gaily coloured clay tablet which was brought to us for sale. It was said to have come from Lhasa, and the official seal stamped on its reverse indicates that a homoeopathic measure of a Buddha relic was mixed up with the clay composing it. Mention has been made of another Buddha bone, that of Buddha in his elephant incarnation. With regard to the latter Munshi dPal-rgyas said that it was a tooth of the Buddha elephant on which the mystic syllable *Om* could be plainly read.

As I had suspected, Munshi dPal-rgyas turned out to be the writer of Dr. Marx's Manuscript C. Through Mr. Reichel's exertions I have come into possession of copies of the last two chapters of his *rGyalrabs*, and a comparison with Dr. Marx's translation shows that Munshi dPal-rgyas' text coincides with such passages of this version as are marked C-MS. As regards the "History of the Dogra war," Munshi dPal-rgyas has written no less than three different versions of it. He would perhaps never have thought of writing one, if Dr. Marx had not asked him to do so. The first account he wrote probably soon after the latter's arrival at Leh in 1886. This account was lithographed at Leh, and used as a school book. The Munshi seems to have soon found out that this account contained several mistakes, and therefore he wrote another version which he presented to Dr. Marx apparently in 1890; but the latter did not live to translate and publish the whole of this. As Dr. Karl Marx's text was believed to be entirely lost, the text and a translation of Munshi dPal-rgyas' first version of this account of the Dogra war was published. Mr. Reichel's manuscript contains the third version of Munshi dPal-rgyas' account. It is by far the best, and much fuller than his two preceding versions. I hope soon to be able to publish a translation of it. From what has been said, it follows that Munshi dPal-rgyas is quite an unusual man. Who else among the natives would have kept a certain subject of scientific interest in his mind for about twenty-five years, without being paid for it? Who would have continued his inquiries with so much patience and, discarding all his previous work, have started afresh, when more recent research showed him the truth in a new light? What a gain it would be to science if all historians were so conscientious !

Besides those already mentioned, it is necessary to refer to a few more buildings of importance at Leh. The mosque at the upper end of the Bazar is not the first of its kind at Leh. The first mosque is a very small building; but the time of its erection has not yet been fixed. The Christian church is situated to the west of the "Great Palace" of Leh, behind the Bazar. North-west of the New Bazar is a small temple, belonging to the Hemis monastery. It is said to have been erected at the same time as this convent.

The old kings had two pleasure gardens near Leh. One of them was the *bKar-bzo* garden. It is the present Joint Commissioner's compound. The other one is the *Mu-rtse* garden. It is situated south of Leh, near a ridge of rocky hills running acorss the desert. The latter garden contains the royal Polo ground (*Shagaran*). It is believed to have been planted by king Seng-ge-rnam -rgyal, c. 1600 A.D., Who brought the game of Polo from Baltistan.

Below Leh, at the Tewar gorge, is the longest *mani* wall in the country. It was built by king bDel dan rnam-rgyal and has the following measurements : Length : 1,931 feet 8 inches. Height : varying between 6 feet, 7 feet, 7.4 feet, 7.8 feet. Breadth 39.6 feet. The *mchod-rten* at both ends are built on square ground plans, each side of the square being 49 feet long.

In conclusion, let me say that the Wazir of Leh, Chaudhari Khushi Muhammad, a very well educated gentleman, and the Tahsildar, did their utmost to make me comfortable during my stay.

(From *Antiquities of Indian Tibet, Part I- Personal Narratives,1914)* painted by King Seng-ge-nam-gyal, c. 1600 A.D., who brought the game of Polo from Baltistan.

Below Leh, at the Taruar gorge, is the longest mani wall in the country. It was built by King Del dan nam-gyal and has the following measurements: Length: 1,931 feet 8 inches. Height: varying between 6 feet, 7 feet, 7.4 feet, 7.8 feet. Breadth 39.6 feet. The mchod-rten at both ends are built on square ground plans, each side of the square being 42 feet long.

In conclusion, let me say that the Wazir of Leh, Chaudhuri Khushi Muhammad, a very well educated gentleman, and the Tahsildar, did their utmost to make me comfortable during my stay.

(From *Antiquities of Indian Tibet*, Part I: *Personal Narrative*, 1914)

10

Journey from Ladhak to the Karakash River

By
Robert Shaw

Doorgoo — Price of Shawl-wool — Tankse — Difficulties about Ponies — Hire of Yaks — Enter the Chang-chenmo Plains — Wild Yak shooting — *Ovis Ammon* — Message from Mr. Hayward proposing a Junction — Reports of Country to the Eastward — Meeting with Hayward; his Plans — Objections to a Junction; Separation of the two Travellers — Singular Posture recommended for Sleeping in the Cold-Plain of Lingzee-Thang — The "Lavender-Plant," and its scanty Fuel — The *Guddee Servants* (from Kangra) — Lyre-horned Antelope — Lak-zung — Wild Yak shot — The Cook breaks down — Tibetan diet — Ice-lake — The Kuen-lun in sight -- The Karakash River — March down its banks — Warm Springs — Jade-quarries — *Kyangs,* or Wild Asses.

Extracts from Diary

"*September 23rd.* — Crossed the 'Chang-la,' a very easy pass out of the Indus Valley. For a mile or so from the summit the descent is stony, all the rest is good road, and easy gradient. After descending a series of terraces, like gigantic steps, the road takes along the side of a ravine (where there are old gold-washings). This ravine sinks more rapidly than the road, which at last turns off across a flat little plain, from which it drops down upon the village of Doorgoo. This flat is a triangle of lake-deposit left between two converging streams, and there are similar flat terraces opposite, showing that the Doorgoo River must have been dammed up at one time to form a lake.

"I asked my new Tibetan servant and guide, Tashee, what was the price of 'pashm,' or shawl-wool (which is produced in these regions). He said it had got cheap of late. I asked why ? Because the merchants had left off buying. I asked why they had left off? He answered: 'Because the "pashm" had got dearer !' In other words : pashm is cheap because it is dear. *Q. E. D.*

"*September 24th, Doorgoo to Tankse.* — Went over to Tankse to breakfast. Presented my order for ponies to the head-man. The head-man was very civil, but slow. He is a Panjabee Hindoo employed by the Maharaja of Kashmir to collect the taxes from the native Tibetans. I made all the remaining preparations for the journey here. Bought flour, parched barley, & c., for the men, and barley for the horses; two months' provisions; also a small flock of sheep. The afternoon was spent in trying to get ponies. The head-man is civil, but useless. All the lame and seedy ponies of the country are brought to choose from. I rejected all but four, and sent off for more to neighbouring villages. Awful obstructions (passive). I left them with a threat that I would get up in the morning with a stick in my hand!

"*September 25th.* — Eight or ten more ponies were brought in the morning, all of them very small and young. I at last agreed to take twelve altogether for the nine loads. Started finally about 1 p.m. Overtook the cavalcade, and found the ponies lying down at every step, being too weak and small even for the present diminished loads. They are hardly bigger than rats. Obliged to stop at Mooglib for the night; only seven miles! This is a promising start for Central Asia.

"*September 26th.* — Took on five 'yaks' in addition to ten ponies; reached Chagra, near the head of the Pangong Lake, and found the head-man awaiting me at the Tartar encampment there with more ponies, all small. The son of the Tibetan head-man (or 'Goba') had just arrived from the Karakash River, where he had been with the party of Mahammad Nazzar, the Yarkand envoy. He reports two horses dead of those belonging to Jooma, the Argoon who had gone with my man Diwan Bakhsh. Jooma's brother-in-law had also died on the road.

"I agreed to stop here to-morrow and next day, to complete arrangements which they ought to have completed three days ago.

"A message reached me from my Moonshee, Diwan Bakhsh, that I ought to be at Shahidoolla (on the Yarkand frontier) in a month from the date of speaking. Ten days gone, leaving twenty. Doubtful!

"September 27th, Sunday. — Halted. Wrote letters, and had the horses shod. Astonished the natives by showing them Rarey's method of casting a horse. I also placed a seal on the forelocks of all the ponies I had chosen, to prevent their being exchanged for worse animals, as seemed very likely. The grain and flour were also sealed up in sacks; and arrangements were made for serving out on each successive Sunday the provision for the ensuing week. The sacks were afterwards to be carefully re-sealed with my own signet-ring. This was necessary in order to prevent pilfering and waste, which might prove fatal in such a desert as we were entering upon."

I interrupt my diary to explain that I had here got into the direct route again, from India to Toorkistan. This is the place where I had met Dr. Cayley on his return from exploring the new route onwards, while I had traversed that part of it which goes direct to British India without passing through Ladak. My journey hence to Ladak, and back again, had been a mere surplusage caused by the necessity of making the arrangements detailed above. So from this point we resume the new direct route from India to Yarkand, which it is hoped will come into use more and more, to the exclusion of the old and more difficult route through Ladak, and over the Karakoram Pass, which merchants had hitherto been compelled to use by the Kashmir officials.

Leaving Chagra, the last Tibetan encampment, on the 29th September, we crossed the high but very gradual and easy pass of Masimik on the 30th, and entered Chang-chenmo. This district consists of open downs and plains at an elevation of about 14,000 or 15,000 feet. The small stream which drains it runs eventually westward into the great Shayok River, which is one of the sources of the Indus. At the head of the Shayok River, and separated from us by enormous mountains, is the Karakoram Pass (the old route into Yarkand). From the Karakoram Pass the Shayok runs nearly directly south towards Ladak, but, meeting a great range of mountains (one of the sides of the Ladak Valley), turns off abruptly west-ward, and runs for a dozen marches parallel to the Indus, and only separated from it by this great range, which it finally bursts through, joining the main Indus in Baltistan.

Having thus traced down the Chang-chenmo River into the Shayok, and the Shayok into the Indus, we will resume our march, which takes us up the Change-chenmo instead of down it. In this valley I stayed till the 16th of October; waiting for the faithless Argoon with my remaining things from Ladak, and also giving time to my Moonshee, Diwan Bakhsh, to accomplish his negotiations at Yarkand. I employed my time in shooting wild yak (a magnificent sort of wild cattle, twice the size of the tame ones used in Tibet), and also in exploring the heads of the various valleys to discover the easiest way northward.

The character of the Chang-chenmo Valley is a wide smooth shingly bed, amidst which the stream meanders from side to side. It is bordered by small cliffs of clay or conglomerate, sometimes several of them in tiers one above the other, divided by wide terraces, especially at the embouchures of side streams. Above these terraces rise the barren mountain sides. The soil is absolutely bare.

"*October 9th, Chang-chenmo.* — Returning down a valley, saw some objects in the distance. Made them out to be *Oves Ammon,* six fine males with enormous horns, coming towards us along the south-west hillside. Hid under a bank, and watched them into a side ravine, but did not see them come out. After a long watch, stalked the ravine. Looking round, to my horror, I saw a man standing in full view against the white snow in the middle of the main valley! Stalked on, but found the six *Oves Ammon* in full retreat. Went down to the man in a horrible temper. Found he was a messenger who had brought a note from Mr. Hayward, who wants to go to Yarkand. Proposes to meet me if I will wait from him. The man says the snow is now a yard deep on the Masimik Pass. (The ink is hard frozen in my pen every minute as I write this, and a water-wagtail has hopped in between me and the fire to warm itself! I am sitting not a yard from the fire in front of my tent.)

"I examined the messenger about his own country, which lies twenty marches eastward from Roodok (a small town near the Pangong Lake). We conversed through two interpreters, as his dialect was so different. He says his tribe's winter quarters are in valleys sloping eastward. To the north of these they yearly cross the snow-passes into a country sloping down to the north-east, whose streams get lost in sand. (Perhaps the same system as the rivers of Eastern Toorkistan.) These summer quarters are thirty days from their winter ones. To the east of his country lie the gold mines (down holes in the earth with galleries, & c.), where a sheep-load of rice sells for eight tolas of gold (?) — equal to over 12% sterling! Beyond are robber tribes endued with charms from the Grand Lama of Lhassa which make them invincible. Ten or twelve families of these robbers, driven away by their former comrades, are now established in Roodok (near the Pangong Lake). The Roodok authorities are bribed by them.

He describes a shrine two days' march this side of the Mansorawar Lake (one of the sources of the Indus). On the top of a pass there is a peak of which the lower half is precipitous rock, and the upper half ice. Pilgrims go round this worshipping; and take a day and a half in the circuit. Here is a fine specimen of campfire gossip!

"October 13th. — A letter from Hayward met me on the road, saying he was sent by the Geographical Society and must continue his journey, but did not wish to compromise me.

"October 14th. — Rode over to Hayward's camp. We dined together, and talked over plans. He said the Geographical Society had commissioned him to explore the route through Chitral (far away to the West on the borders of Kabul), and to try and reach the Pamir Steppes. The frontier was which has just broken out led him to try the more easterly route through Ladak, hoping to get permission at Yarkand to visit the Pamir Steppes. He proposed going in the character of an Afghan, having brought a complete Afghan dress, and having discarded most of the marks of European nationality, such as tents, & c. After some consultation, and seeing that I was going in the character of an Englishman, he determined to do so also. Indeed, it would require a most perfect acquaintance both with the Afghan language (Pooshtoo) and also with the Mahammadan religious ceremonial (an acquaintance only to be obtained by years of expatriation), to pass muster as an Afghan in a bigoted Mussulman country which swarms with Afghan merchants and soliders.

"The question then remained whether we should go together or not. On consideration it seemed better that I should appear on the frontier first and alone, in accordance with the announcement which I had sent on before. For if, after asking permission for one Englishman to enter, two were suddenly to appear together, suspicions would be aroused, and they would probably turn both of us back. It was determined, therefore, that I should go on before, trusting to the effect of my presents and letter for admission, while Hayward should follow shortly after in the hope that they would not turn him back after admitting me. If I saw an opportunity, I was to do what I could to obtain admission for him. This seemed the best solution of the difficulty caused by the unfortunate coincidence of our two attempts.

"Meanwhile, Hayward determined to explore the head of the Chang-chenmo Valley for a possibly better route in that direction.

"*October 16th.* — Hayward started on his way up the valley, and I on mine up the Hot-Spring Ravine. Some miles up came to an ascent of a terrace cliff some thirty feet high from the bed of the stream. Poor Schlagintweit, on his way to Yarkand in 1857, had built up a kind of sloping path-way, very steep. Great difficulties in getting the ponies up. They repeatedly tumbled back.

"In crossing the stream (which we did many times), a pony fell through the coat of ice which bordered the stream on both sides. Great difficulty in getting him out.

"*October 17th.* — Some time after sunrise, as we were packing up tents, & c., to start, we suddenly heard a noise like thunder coming down the stream. Found that the water was rising and bursting through the thick coat of ice that had bound it in the night. The stream was coming down full of fragments of ice, which it threw up high and dry on either side as it receded gradually into its proper channel. We had seen these heaps of ice six or seven feet high which lined both banks, but had not known the cause.

"Followed the tracks of the Yarkand envoy and his party. Towards the end of the day met the men and ponies he had hired, returning from escorting him. They gave me a letter in Hindostanee from my Moonshee *without date,* saying he would send some one to meet me at Shahidoolla in a month's time *from date.* I asked these men about a halting-place for the night. They said there was plenty of fuel and grass higher up.

I rode on alone to pick out a place, but found that, as usual with the Tibetans, they had told a lie. I rode back, and was in time to stop my caravan at the highest place where there was grass, some miles below where I had met my informants; rather an important matter, as the cattle could get no more grass for several days after this!

October 18th. — Followed marks of the envoy's party up a side stream from the north. Shingly bed of dry stream, gradually steeper and steeper, till we stood on the ridge. The depression of the 'col' is very slight indeed. View to south of glacier-mountains extensive but stormy. To north, very flat, downy country, nearly the level of our pass. One or two large patches of snow, our elevation being about 19,000 feet. Tashee and I walked on to keep ourselves warm, but, halting at sunset, had to sit and freeze for several hours before the things came up. The best way of keeping warm on such an occasion is to squat down, kneeling against a bank, resting your head on the bank, and nearly between your knees. Then tuck your overcoat in all round you, over head and all; and if you are lucky, and there is not too much wind, you will make a little atmosphere of your own inside the covering which will be snug in comparison with the outside air. Your feet suffer chiefly, but you learn to tie yourself into a kind of knot, bringing as many surfaces of your body together as possible. I have passed whole nights in this kneeling position and slept well; whereas I should not have got a wink had I been stretched at full length with such a scanty covering as a great coat. At last the camp arrived. We had brought a little fuel with us, and melted some ice for water. No grass at all for the cattle.

"*October 19th.* — Breakfasted as usual while camp was breaking up. Travelled through the high downs till we reached a little plain, bounded on the further side by a sandy ridge. Crossed this plain northwards. My Mussulman table-servant, Kabeer, was here quite done up with the rarity of the air at this great elevation, so I gave him my pony to ride. Ascended the sandy slope at the end (almost 100 feet high), and then saw another immense plain at our feet, about 400 feet lower than our own level. This has been christened by the Tibetans who have crossed it, 'Lingzee-tang.' To the east and west of it snowy mountains loomed in the distance, peering up over the edge of the plain like ships at sea that are hull-down. In front of us to the north, it was bounded far away by a long sandy ridge with the tops of smaller hills showing over it. Descending into this plain, we encamped about five miles out on it, under the lee of a small clayey rise. The soil is all clay, covered with flinty stones and rough agates. Not a vestige of grass; but a little fuel in the shape of the *lavender-plant*, as it may be called. This consists of a little bunch of shoots, three or four inches high, looking like lavender. These little bunches are scattered about seven or eight yards apart or more. They have a woody root, much more substantial than might be imagined from their insignificant appearance above ground; and these roots are a perfect god-send to the traveller. His men go out with little picks and dig them up, but it takes several hours, even where they are most plentiful, before a man can collect enough to light a fire with. The shoots are sometimes eaten by famishing horses, and to a certain extent stay their hunger where there is no grass, as here. So late in the season there was no water anywhere on this plain, but we found a few patches of snow, and melted enough to cook with and drink. There was not, however, fuel enough to melt any for the horses to drink, and they had for many days to content themselves with munching snow to allay their thirst.

"October 20th, Lingzee-tang. — A lovely morning to cross the plain. Marched straight for the opening between two hills which I called the 'dome' and the 'chorten' (a common Tibetan monument), from their shapes. Kabeer, as yesterday, was constantly lagging behind and lying down. I stopped the caravan for him, and made him keep up. He said, as an excuse, that neither his father nor his grandfather had been in such a country. There was really no reason to lag, within a mile of the start, as the walking was good and there was no cold to speak of. Of course the great elevation has its effect. But my

Guddee servants (the Guddees are a hardy and primitive race of hill men, living on the Kangra Mountains, who make capital and faithful servants), were swearing at the flatness of the plain and wishing for mountains again. Lots of mirage, but no real signs of water. After several hours across the plain we came to the rising ground about 100 feet high. Another flat on the top, then a descent into the mouths or upper ends of a lot of rocky-sided valleys. Took one leading to the right of the 'dome,' and camped about a mile down it near a rock. Fearfully cold wind; almost impossible to pitch the tents; a real hurricane, blowing the concentrated essence of east winds. Managed to get something to eat and get to bed *Third* night of no grass for the cattle. We give the ponies barley, but the yaks refuse it.

"October 21st, Lak-zung. — This is the name of that curious set of valleys leading down from the high plain of Lingzee-tang (which we have just crossed) into a lower one on the north. (They are both over 16,000 feet above the sea ! 1000 feet higher than the summit of Mont Blanc.) Saw a male Tibetan antelope, looking quite white in the distance, with very elegant lyre-shaped horns. We went down a broad valley, across which ran a line of curious granite rocks, which ought to have been the top of a range, but by some mistake have wandered across a shingly open valley. The chief one holds an ancient eagle's nest, below which the ground is covered with the horns and bones of antelope, killed by past generations of these birds to feed their young. Saw some more antelopes up a slope, but my fingers were frozen so stiff by the bitter wind that it was useless to go after them—I could not have pulled a trigger. This bit of country seems to have had two wills at the making of it. First comes a series of parallel ridges, with corresponding valleys running N.W. to S.E. (of which the granite rocks form one). Then a gigantic series of valleys were cut exactly at right angles to all this, leaving the eaglenest rocks in the middle of a valley as I said, and breaking all the other ridges across. Having come down one of these valleys, we turned into one of the first series to

our right, and found the yaks in the midst of lots of grass (such as it is, in Tibet) and the coldest of high winds. Camped, and presently the ponies came up also.

"*October 22nd.* — Halted in this place (called Lak-zung or 'Eagle's nest'), a our cattle wanted recruiting. Cold day, with bitter wind. Kabeer utterly incapable of 'making an effort.' Says he does not know what stones have fallen into his life !

"Tried to write, but the ink all froze in my pen a usual.

"I am convinced that the envoy's party and we also made a mistake in our route. We went off to the west from the hot springs, and after crossing the pass had to come back east, a day's march. We should have gone straight.

"*October 23rd.* — Still halting in Lak-zung; a finer day, *i.e.*, less wind, more sun, and thermometer nearly up to freezing-point in the tent at mid-day. Went out . . . . and shot another fine old wild yak. He measured ten feet from the nose to the insertion of the tail, and was five feet and a half high at the shoulder.

"*October 24th.* — Still halting and shooting. Day colder. Returned to camp after dark in the coldest of bitter winds. Kabeer is hopeless. He complains of no actual illness; but he cannot do anything but sit and warm his hands and groan. The other servants are indignant at him.

October 25th. — Tashee the Tibetan promoted to be cook, *vice* Kabeer, retired into private life. Had in the ponies from pasture, and shod those that wanted it. Also dabbed melted grease into their cracked heels.

"The Tibetans (or Bots, as they call themselves) tell me that they make preserved meat, by pounding and grinding it after drying in the sun. This is mixed with ground 'suttoo', or parched barely, and made into thick soup. The process is possible in this dry cold country, where everything keeps so well.

"*October 26th, Lak-zung to Tarldatt.* — Started the things off, and followed myself, but did not reach camp till ten o'clock at night, being detained by a long stalk after a Tibetan antelope, which I finally killed. Great difficulty in finding the camp in the open plain into which our route now led us. Sent out men to look for Kabeer, who was missing, and reported to have lagged behind on the road. Promised a reward for finding him.

"*October 27th.* — Kabeer was brought in during the night, having laid down by the side of the road. He had heard me and Tashee passing within a yard or two of him in the dark, but had not the energy to speak, fearing we might compel him to get up and come into camp ! Such are the natives of India. He would doubtless have died, exposed to that bitter night, had I not sent the men out to search for him.

"There is a curious ice-lake near this camp. An irregular solid sheet of ice, two or three feet thick, rests on the surface of the ground; some warm springs melt a way through the centre. Lower down, as I heard, the continuation of this ice-sheet floats on water, which further out is free from ice, and forms a small lake.

"*October 28th.* — Crossed a small 'col,' still going northwards. Coming after the caravan, I found one of our yaks which our men had been obliged to leave. The beast was tired and ferocious. However, there is plenty of grass here for it. Beyond the 'col' a gradual descent leads down a long valley into the plain of an old lake bed, with water-marks 200 feet up the hill-sides. One or two small brackish pools half-frozen, all the rest a bed of 'phoollee,' or coarse soda. Above is a very thin cake of earth, below which the foot sinks into the finest loose powdered soda, pure white, four or five inches deep. Below this is a sheet of impure common salt, or saltpetre, which you can hear crack like thin ice under fresh snow as you walk. In many places the coat of earth is absent, and the soda is hard and irregular. It was horrible walking for five hours over it; although we saw our halting-place from the first, we never seemed to approach it. Yaks hopelessly in the rear, but fine moonlight. Cold, but not much wind happily. Finally found a little dry ravine just big enough and deep enough to shelter our camp. Grass and ice near; pitched camp, and were thankful. Choomaroo (one of the Guddees) had his toe frost-bitten. No news of Kabeer or the yaks. But Tashee is ever to the fore and most useful.

"*October 29th.* — Halt. Kabeer arrived in the morning reporting that all the yaks had knocked up. Sent off men to help in with their loads. About the middle of the day two yaks arrived. The men report two others entirely *hors de combat,* one at the beginning of the soda-plain, the other near the salt-pool.

"*October 30th.* — The remaining men with the yaks' loads arrived this morning. We made a short march, the ponies being awfully knocked up. The north end of the soda-plain (rising a little) narrows into a valley. This valley curves off to the N.W., with a low broken granite ridge on its N.E. side. Beyond this ridge is the Karakash River (which we cannot see yet, of course), and beyond that a high steep shingly snow-topped range, a part of that which is known to European geographers a the Kuen-lun. Bitter cold wind. Camped in this valley at the last grass patches. Snow for water a usual, and a little *lavender-plant* fuel. The yaks did not come up.

"*October 31st.* — Continued N.W. along the valley which was now sloping downwards to the Karakash, leading to it by a rocky gorge some thirty or forty yards wide. Through this the soda-plain lake must at some time have disgorged itself. The Karakash was *soft-frozen,* flowing through a little round valley, enclosed to the north by a large old moraine. To the N.E. are high snow mountains and glaciers; the course of the stream comes down very steeply from them. I fancy its source is near. Down below we espied two black animals grazing in the bed of the stream. Query, wild yaks or tame? Question answered by a man driving them into our line of march, amid cheers from all our party. They were cattle abandoned (as some of our own had been) by the envoy's party which had preceded us.

"A perfect god-send. We were now able to unload the miserable yellow pony, and lighten the loads of the chesnut and grey ponies. Meanwhile the cattle all drank eagerly, breaking the slushy ice with their feet. This was their first real drink since the 16th; they have had nothing but snow since then.

"Beyond the point we had now reached, none of my men had gone. We were thus quite ignorant where we should find grass or wood, or how long to make our marches. It often depends on the distance of the next grazing ground whether you will encamp after a certain number of hours' marching, or continue. This is especially the case with exhausted cattle, for if the next place is near, it will not hurt them to go on, but if far, you would for their sake rest contented with your progress for that day. But we now had to do without such facilities. I had to feel the way by riding on ahead of the caravan, and towards evening surveying the route before us from some high point. The Karakash here has a broad valley quite flat and half a mile wide. The dry and shingly bed of what is sometimes a stream occupies the centre, with low terraces on either side, the barren mountains rising north and south of the valley, which itself runs westward. Anxiously I looked forward as each new vista opened out; every side-valley I examined with care. Imagine my horror, as the afternoon advanced, to find that this sterile soil did not supply even the *lavender-plant* for fuel, which had not hitherto failed us. Grass I entirely despaired of finding, and the bed of the stream was dry! The three great requisites for a traveller's camping-ground were all absent—fuel, grass, and water! Evening was beginning to close when I reached a high bed of shingle and *debris* which issued from a ravine on the north, and closed the view down the main valley. I mounted this to get a view, and at the lower end of a small plain I distinguished a dark strip of ground. Hope began to revive, but I could hardly believe that I saw bushes! However, my glass showed them distinctly, and, what was more, there was a glimmer of white ice visible amongst them. I pushed on, and after a seemingly interminable stretch of level in the valley I reached the first bushes that I had seen for a month. There was a horrible wind blowing up the valley, but I picked out a sheltered spot under a bank, collected a lot of dry branches for a fire (how often had I shivered and longed for this moment in the cold plains above!) and at down to wait. After waiting an hour, I began to fear that the caravan might pass me in the dark, so I commenced shouting. No reply. At last my pony showed signs of hearing something on the opposite side. I rode across, and presently was answered. They had actually passed me. Now, however, it was all right. I took them to my sheltered nook, and presently we had such a glorious blaze as gladdened our hearts. We found that the ice I had seen was on the banks of a stream of water, which came in through a narrow gorge from the left or south side of the valley, and filled the hitherto dry bed of the main valley. I had thoughts of exploring up this gorge the next day, as its stream seemed more important than that which I had come down. But it was necessary for the cattle's sake to push on to some grass.

"*November 1st.* — The yaks being still behind with the grain, we could not give the horses a feed. Luckily we found a little grass on the banks of a warm spring to the right. I rode on to a shingle ridge, about a mile further, to espy the valley, but could see nothing better, only brushwood. So I came back, and we camped at a warm spring. The water of the stream was slightly brackish, so we made tea, & c., from melted ice again. The stream here runs free between banks of ice. It is a few inches deep, and five or six yards wide. Plenty of wood, as the same brushwood jungle extends down to here. Tried to tin the saucepans, which are getting quite dangerous, but only succeeded in burning my fingers! There is plenty of snow scattered on the northern sides of the mountains, almost down to the level of the valley.

"The yaks arrived in the afternoon. One of our new acquisitions had given in.

"Glorious change of temperature. Thermometer up to 40^0 Fahrenheit at ten o'clock in the day. At day-break the temperature was 9^0 Fahrenheit.

"November 2nd. — Marched down the Karakash stream, which now flows freely between ice borders. It is fed by numerous warm springs, hence its freedom from ice. But these springs give the whole water a brackish taste. A couple of miles from last night's camp we crossed a little plain dotted over with small craters, each about four or five yards across, and two or three feet deep in the middle. The bottom of these craters is occupied by a deposit of common salt or saltpetre. The servants took a supply for common use, as their own was getting short. The valley is wide and flat, and the vista is only broken at intervals by great sloping tongues of *debris* issuing from the mouths of ravines (generally from the north side), and running nearly across the valley. More or less grass all along to-day's march, and plenty of brushwood. On the north side granite rocks now rise directly out of the valley. The granite is crumbling and disintegrated like that of Ladak. We found and brought on two more of the abandoned yaks, but had to leave our own yellow pony. Saw herds of 'kyang' (the Tibetan wild ass). Fine snow-peaks in sight down the valley, before which brushwood and grass cease.

"November 3rd. — Immediately on leaving camp this morning, the white pony broke down. Tashee professed to cure him by extracting a piece of cartilage from each nostril, making a cut and then tying a hair out of his tail to the cut piece, so that the animal pulled it out himself in attempting to rise. But I did not see the operation myself. They put his load on to two men and came along. At a corner on the south side there is a piece of path with a bit of wall built up to support it, and yesterday we passed a group of stone huts : all signs that this road was once in use.

"November 4th. — Men arrive late last night, and reported the white pony dead on the road. If this is true, I believe it was caused by the operation which was supposed to cure

him. This morning, at day-break, the thermometer was at 1^0 Fahrenheit.

"Pitched camp in the evening in a fine grassy meadow which occupies the whole width of the valley for several miles down. Picked up two more abandoned yaks, which had been luxuriating in this grass.

"*November 5th.* — A succession of fine meadow plains full of salt craters, larger than the former ones (some six or seven yards across). Some were full of concentrated brine (unfrozen in most), which on evaporating will give the usual salt deposit, I suppose. In this valley, wherever there is grass, there is also a saline efflorescence on the soil. I fancy both depend on the presence of moisture, and hence occur together. While crossing a swampy frozen meadow, I flushed a solitary snipe, and also what I took for a starling. Walked through some brushwood and shot two hares (of the blue Tibetan variety, with pure white tufts of tails). Whilst pitching camp, found the place occupied by a herd of nearly 100 'kyangs' (or wild asses), which stayed within 200 yards of us watching our proceedings till dark.

"Down the valley some snowy mountains are visible. On this side of them there is an opening in the northern range. According to Johnson's map, this opening ought to be the course of the Karakash turning towards Toorkistan.

"Picked up two more yaks, making nine altogether.

"*November 6th.* — Great part of to-day's march has been barren, but our camp is near a lot of grass; not a few blades scattered here and there, as in Tibet, but real grass covering the ground, so that you could cut a turf out of it. Near this camp are some 'jade' quarries, not abandoned. The workings were a little way up the hill-side, whence numerous rough fragments have rolled down."

(From *Visit to High Tartary Yarkand and Kashgar*, 1871)

11

Central Ladhak, Nubra and Zanskar

By
Drew F.

I

MOUNTAIN CHAINS OF LADHAK

In obtaining the general view which we wish for, a careful examination of both the General Map and the snow Map will materially help; in the latter, attention should especially be paid to the figures that mark the altitude of certain points in the valleys.

Commencing with the north-east part of the map, we see, first, the high table-land of the Kuenlun Plains and Lingzhithang—these two separated by a range of hills—the whole being surrounded by mountains. The plains are 16,000 and 17,000 feet high; the mountain chains around them reach to 20,000 and 21,000 feet; those which make the northern boundary are the Eastern Kuenlun Mountains.

West of the high plateaus is a space occupied by a great range of mountains, which is called both "Mustagh" and "Karakoram," or sometimes perhaps is called by both names according to whether its western or its eastern portion is spoken of. This is what intervenes between the line of the Shayok Valley and the upper part of the valley of the Yarkand

River. It consists of great mountain ridges, and of valleys which are never more than two miles in width. In the eastern part the summits are of the same level as those last spoken of — 20,000 and 21,000 feet; farther west they rise still higher; in the ridge separates the Upper Shayok (as it comes down from the north) from the Nubra River, are great peaks 25,000 feet high, rising out of a ridge of 20,000 or 21,000 feet; and among the mountains that lie to the north-west of this are several summits of 25,000 and some even of 26,000 feet. In this range originate many and great glaciers. As to the valley-levels; the Snow Map will show the position of the 15,000 feet level in the Changchenmo Valley, and of that of 14,000 feet by Pangkong. From these heights the descent along the Shayok is not recorded till we come to Nubra, where 10,000 feet is the altitude of the valley-bottom; thence there is a gradual fall to 9000 and 8000 feet, a little below which the Shayok River meets the Indus.

Next is the space between the Shayok and Indus valleys. The Indus Valley itself will be seen by the figures on the Snow Map to have a fall closely corresponding to that of the other. Between the two is a great ridge of mountains, which for convenience I will call the Leh Range. Of the summit of this, 19,000 and 20,000 feet is commonly the height, and the line is but little broken through; only down to 17,000 feet do gaps here and there exist.

Then comes the wide tract between the Indus Valley and the main watershed-range. Here is a mass of mountains whose ramifications are most complicated. As to height, we find the conspicuous summits varying from 20,000 down to 18,000 feet. In the South-Eastern part are flat valleys at 15,000 feet; to the North-West there are a few wide openings at 10,000 or 11,000 feet, but on the whole the valleys are narrow; they fall, with various degrees of slope, to the level of the Indus.

Last is the watershed-range itself. This makes another region of glaciers. Its summits for a long distance seem to average 20,000 and 21,000 feet, and the Passes through it are at very high levels. As we trace it north-westward we come to the Nun Kun Peaks, at which, coming from the other direction.

We now enter on the more particular description of successive districts.

II

CENTRAL LADHAK

By this name is denoted about 100 miles in length of the Indus Valley, from the borders of Baltistan up to 30 miles or so beyond Leh. I have followed the valley upwards from the village of Sanacha, a place within Baltistan, from which, nevertheless, we will begin the description.

In this part the bottom of the Indus Valley is a narrow rock-bound gorge. The river flows in it with an eddied but not uneven surface; its depth must be great to allow the body of water to pass along such a narrow channel, for I found that the width was in one place 65 feet and in another but 46 feet. The walls of this gorge are nearly vertical; above them rise other steep but more broken cliffs; above these the ground retires, but there are greater heights behind. All this is of granitic rock. Over this rocky ground the path is a difficult one; a laden horse cannot go along it, and with difficulty can an unladen pony be led. It is the same on both sides of the river. This difficulty of the road isolates the villages of this part of the valley, cuts them off greatly from intercourse, and it prevents the traffic between Ladakh and Baltistan from taking this route, which at first one would think to be its natural one. This, as it is the lowest, is also the warmest part of Ladakh. The level of the river is about 9000 feet, but even at this height the valley in summer time is hot. The unclouded sun heats the bare rocks that slope to meet its rays; the traveller, as he goes along the rugged way, exposes one side of him to the sun's direct rays and the other to a strong radiation from the ground , while the pent-up air itself becomes hot and gives no relief. But after a toilsome drag for some miles over this waste of heated rocks, he reaches one of the little villages that are made at the months of side ravines, if haply there can be found a few acres of flat ground for cultivation. These villages are to the traveller a most welcome and lovely sight; a space covered with crops of a brilliant green overshadowed by luxuriant fruit-trees in the midst of the barest rocks gives a relief equally to the eye, the mind, and the body of the wayfarer.

Garkon is the one of these villages most curious in its situation. It consists of very narrow strips or ledges of flat watered ground, between separate stages of a great river-cliff, so that on one side there is a precipitous fall of ground while on the other vertical cliffs overhanging the narrow fields, which, receiving their radiated heat, quickly ripen the crops; even at night the place does not lose its heat. Water is led over the fields from a ravine that comes from the high mountains. Apple-trees, apricot, mulberry, and the vine are cultivated, in company with the cereals, on the narrow space, and flourish well with the combination of moisture and warmth. In going from Garkon to the next village , called *Dah*, we have passed from Baltistan into Ladakh. The Baltis were in former times apt to make raids upon their more peaceable neighbours. Dah, as the frontier village, protected itself by the agglomeration of its houses together to form a sort of fort; on two sides protection is given by a steep cliff, on two by a wall, with a good tower to guard the entrance to the enclosure. Now that all are under one government, and perfect peace has ensued, the dwellings are scattered; but still in winter time the people from the outlying houses and hamlets join to live within the enclosure, for warmth and for mirth's sake. Within its walls the ground is almost all roofed over, hardly any space is left for alleys, passages from one house to another are led beneath the rooms of a third; the whole is a strange crowding together of hovels. In this part side valleys of various degrees of importance reach down to the Indus;

some are mere rocky ravines, others hold hamlets and villages. I visited the *Hanu* Valley. At the mouth of it the Hanu stream comes out of a narrow, deep, impassable gorge; one turns this by rising over the shoulder of one of the mountains whose spurs compose its walls; passing up the valley, still between bare mountains, we come to a strip of cultivated ground; then we come to another narrow rocky part, and then again to where a strip of cultivation occupies the bottom of the valley; this space between the mountains becomes wider, and the level is occupied by the village of Yogma Hanu or Lower Hanu. On the way, fruit-trees and willows and a few poplars had been passed, but at the higher level now reached hardly any trees were growing. Goma Hanu, or Upper Hanu, lies a few miles above; beyond that the road leads to a Pass over the Indus and Shayok watershed to the tract called Chorbat. It will be seen from the Political Map that this is the way of the route from Skardu to Ladakh, the difficulty of the valley-road, in the parts we have lately come from, thus deflecting the traffic to go over a Pass of 16,700 feet. The Chorbat Pass is the boundary of Baltistan in this direction; by this road also used to come Balti raiders, as the remains of a fort at Yogma Hanu prove , which the people of the valley had put up against them.

But we must return to the Indus Valley. One or two incidents of physical geography respecting this part of it may here be described. The lowest part, the bottom, of the valley has been spoken of as a narrow gorge. The gorge, not all along, but in places, is 600 feet deep; that is to say that the bottom part of the section of the Indus Valley is, for that height, specially narrow and steep; it seems as if, in the gradual cutting of the valley, this deepest part had been worked down under somewhat different conditions from the rest. I connect with this the narrowness of many of the side ravines where they join the main valley; the same causal difference (as, it may be, in the rate of downward denudation) affected the side valleys as well as the main valley. Thus the valley of the stream that comes down from Tsirmo, at the last, before reaching the Indus, closes to a narrow chasm with vertical walls of granite; this is quite impassable by man. We saw also that other side ravines had the same character at their mouths — that is, where they are on the same level as this gorge of the main river that they unite with. Again, in Rondu, below Skardu, I have observed the same combined phenomena, the bottom of the Indus Valley, for a depth of some 600 feet, being narrow and step-walled, and the side ravines having a similar character as they near the valley of the large river. Some other things connected with the doings of the river caught my eye. It can be imagined that a narrow channel, bounded by rocks rising to high mountains, must be exposed to chances of damming by falling debris, that is to say by the taluses, or even perhaps by the fans, made by the waste of the substance of the mountains. It seems to me most likely that such damming of a voluminous river should occur when sudden large falls of rock—such as would deserve the name landslips—happen; the material would be less likely to be carried away bit by bit by the force of the stream. Such sudden falls as I speak of would make taluses, or steep-sloping heaps, rather than the less-inclined fans. Looking now for evidence of such things having actually occurred, what do we see? Opposite Garkon there was a small recent talus, which I was told had dammed back the river for a time. Again, there is more than one place where the disposition of debris is as shown in the first diagram on the next page, where a continuation of the line of its slope (and in its formation the slope of the material must have so continued) would end against the opposite mountain at a vertical height of about 400 feet above the river. In these cases I do not see how the thickness of the debris could have accumulated without damming the river back and forming a kind of lake above and a rapid below. The next diagram is somewhat more complicated. It shows what occurs two miles above Garkon. There is a rock (marked C on the cut) bounding the river; the summit of it is 400 or 500 feet above the water; we can see that it formerly was separated from both the mountain sides, being now connected with one side by nothing but a mass of debris which has filled up the space. It seems to me that the space at B, equally with that marked A, must have been worn by the river. My theory is that B was excavated by the river before ever the hollow at A was made; next came the talus, filling up that then river-bed and damming back the river; and lastly occurred the re-excavation of the channel, not exactly at the same place, but *out of a fresh part of the rock,* that is to say, at the spot A, rather than through the loose debris. There are many instances of alluvial and lacustrine deposits at intervals, which I shall not here describe, as the subject of them wants to be treated in a technical way; a notice of these I hope to communicate to the Geological Society.

Of the inhabitants of the villages from Sanacha to Hanu I have purposely refrained from saying anything here. They have characteristics indeed of the greatest interest, but I keep back the description of these in order to bring it into connection with that of the other Dards, for to the Dard race the people here belong. From the next village, Achinathang, upwards, the people are thorough Ladakhis in race and language.

At Achinathang the Indus Valley begins to be rather less confined; the road along it is such that one can ride. Achinathang itself is a neat and pretty village, on a plateau of river-alluvium 200 feet above the water. Near this place, in the pebbly alluvium formerly deposited by the river, at a height of 120 feet above it, are to be seen shallow pits, from which Balti gold-washers had dug earth which they carried down to the water side to wash for gold. Every few miles , on each side of the river, are seen little tracts of cultivated ground. One was a continuous strip on a narrow plateau, a mile in length and but fifty yards wide. Sometimes, as at Skirbichan, is a wider expanse. Each tract has on it a collection of houses in proportion to the area, at the rate of a house to three or four acres. These white houses, half hidden by the foliage, and the spread of green fields, contrasting with the bare surrounding country, make each little village a charming sight. In this part the Ladakhis are well grown; they are taller than those of the neighbourhood of Leh. This I connect with the somewhat milder climate and the consequently less severe life experienced.

Besides the villages which we see along the Indus Valley there are several in the side valleys which join from both right and left. At the mouth of these valleys one sees but a narrow opening; from this they often stretch up for miles, and contain cultivated land and several hamlets. Of these the higher ones endure a distinctly more severe climate than do the villages of the main valley. Above the cultivation the ravines lead up into rocky wastes in the heart of the hills; those on the right bank lead to the watershed of the Leh Range; sometimes they lead to a more or less frequented Pass, as did the Hanu Valley, sometimes to a rocky ridge that man never reaches, for the reason that there is nothing to draw him, sometimes to ground so precipitous and impracticable that mortal foot cannot tread it.

Next above the part of the Indus we have been speaking of we come to a village mentioned two chapters back, Khalsi, the place where the road from Kashmir reaches the Indus Valley. But the route we followed in the march did not altogether keep to the valley, which now therefore remains to be spoken of. Along the valley is a succession of villages, but not a quick succession ; two on a day's march are as many as one meets. Nurla and Saspul are the most important of those we pass; they both are near the river. Of the hills that here bound the valley, those on the right bank are not lofty; a range of secondary height intervenes before the great granite mountains are reached. On the left bank the prominent mountains are 2000 feet or so high above the valley; these are but the ends of spurs from a range that rises 6000 or 7000 feet higher, namely, to 18,000 or 19,000 feet above the sea.

Above Saspul the river in places flows where the road cannot follows it, in narrow inaccessible gorges. The Zanskar

River, of great volume, here joins the Indus. As we approach Pitak we rise to the more open part of the valley.

I have described what kind of travelling it is to traverse the valley below Khalsi in summer time—toiling on foot along rough stony tracks or up rocky slopes under a powerful sun. This present part I have gone over both in summer and in winter; and, in spite of a severity of cold in the air far greater than I have ever experienced in England, I have been more comfortable on the winter journey. It was in January; the snow was falling lightly, keeping, as it fell, dry and powdery; the river was frozen in more than one place, so that we could cross, and choose which bank to go along, while near Nurla we were able to ride for a mile or two on the ice over the Indus itself. Thus by ice and snow the way made smoother; lambskin coats and caps and felt stockings kept out the cold, and the best houses of the villages afforded at every stage a shelter that in that season was welcome and comfortable.

Nearing Leh, we find that the ranges of mountains, on opposite sides of the valley, rise to about equal height, and for a considerable distance seem equal and parallel. But each has a character of its own. The one on the south-west rises, in a direct distance of nine miles, to a ridge which is commonly 19,000 feet high; just in front of the town of Leh is a peak of 20,000 feet, which retains perpetual snow; indeed there are on the range some fields of snow with small galciers leading down from them; the lower limit of perpetual snow here is 18,500 feet. This ridge is indented by ravines in regular succession that open to the Indus Valley; the spurs between the ravines rise, at the last, where they near the main valley, to greater heights than they have in the parts near the ridge; so there is a second line of eminences, overlooking the Indus flat; these (which are composed of strata of shale and sandstone, dipping inwards), when viewed from certain spots, appear to form a continuous ridge; but in truth they are separated from each other by the ravines, and are each joined by a neck to the range behind; looked at from the flat these heights are seen to rise along a well-marked straight line. The alternating ravines have narrow openings from which project alluvial fans, which meeting, form a sloping stony tract between the hills and the flatter alluvium of the main river. From the foot of these mountains, across the valley, to the nearest beginning of the opposite hills, is from two to three miles. These others are of a form different. The summit line indeed of this ridge also, as has been pointed out, is 19,000 or 20,000 feet in altitude; snow and small glaciers are found at the highest parts, but on the whole the ridge has a rocky surface. The difference of form lies in the character of the spurs. Sharp-ridged spurs descend from the central ridge to the Indus Valley; though possessing some irregularity of outline they decline without any great interruption, and project in long narrow ridges of granite, which lessen both in height and in width from far back, leaving between them space for alluvial deposits — sloping stony tracts — of the sort which I have called "confined fans." In colour this range contrasts with the opposite one, being of far less sombre tints; drab and yellow and light brown are the colours shown by this granite, of which sometimes the jointed rock itself, and sometimes the loosened material disintegrated from it, is shown; on both ranges the bare surface, untouched by vegetation, is exposed. At places the river itself, at palces the flat alluvium, ends the stony ground and touches the last points of the spurs; these are in some cases crowned with the white buildings of a monastery; at Tagna (or Stakna) are two isolated rocks, on the summit of one of which is built a monastery; between the two, in a rather narrow passage, flows the Indus.

The alluvial flat is of clayey soil, irrigated by watercourses from the Indus itself. South of Leh it is occupied by the village of Chushot, which, being near half a mile wide and some miles long, is the largest cultivated tract in Ladakh; it has over 200 houses, not concentrated into a village, but scattered over the plain singly, or in twos and threes, at intervals of a hundred yards or so. Chushot has not the picturesqueness of the villages which we have looked at lower down the valley; here fruit-trees do not grow, on account of the severity of the wind that blows along the length of the flat; still we see some poplars and small willows, and it is probable that plantations arranged in belts—one protecting the other—would flourish. The people of Chushot are Baltis, Bhots, and Arghauns, the first predominating. As we go up the valley the cultivation of the alluvi flat ends, and the surface of it is of rounded pebbles. Farther on, a little above Tagna, the river is bounded by high banks of alluvial matter, mostly belonging to fans that have been formed from the sides. Here, too, the fall begins to be greater, and the valley, narrowing, gets again the character it possessed lower down by Saspul and Khalsi. Besides the cultivation on the flat there are some villages in the tributary valleys on both sides, as Stok, Shan, Sabu, and Chimre; these are watered by the side-streams. In one of these tributary valleys is situated Himis monastery, the most noted one in Ladakh, which has 200 Lamas. The monastery is a large mass of buildings placed just beneath a cliff at a bend of the narrow ravine, and in that way well sheltered. The wide window spaces and open galleries, and the decorations and drapery and waving flags make it look quite gay. Close by is a grove of large spreading poplars, which must be of the oldest trees in the country.

The last point I have been to in this section of the Indus Valley is Upshi, a small village at the mouth of the Gya ravine. At that place we will count Central Ladakh to end. Above it is a narrow portion of the valley, which is called *Rong*, where the river flows between rocks along which it is difficult to find a practicable path; still, there also villages occur in the side valleys, and a small population finds cultivable just enough of land to get a subsistence from.

III

ROAD FROM LEH TO NUBRA

In going from Central Ladakh to Nubra (which lies along

the banks of the Shayok River and of a tributary to it) we must of necessity cross the Leh Range by one of two or three Passes. From Leh a direct road leads up along the stream whose waters irrigate the lands about that town. The Pass to make for is the Khardong Pass, which is 17,500 feet high; there is, therefore, an ascent to be made of 6000 feet. Not easily can this be done in one day; a half-way halt is almost always made, either at the last hamlet or farther up in the uninhabited part of the valley. The path is in palces difficult for laden ponies; they are generally relieved of their loads and are replaced for the Pass by yaks. The way leads for some miles up the bottom of the valley, rising at an angle of 5^0; then it continues in a branch valley of steeper gradient, till it reaches the watershed, which at this spot is a narrow rocky ridge.

A better idea of the form of the mountain range we are now going over than can be given in words will be got from the annexed section of it, made through a spot a little to the west of the road. The broken line represents where the path itself goes.

On the north of the Pass the road crosses a bed of ice which lies on the slope, and leads down a steep descent of some 1600 feet, to a small lake enclosed by a stony barrier which looked as if it might have been formed by avalanches. Thence an easy but long descent leads us for many miles down a valley between spurs from the main ridge. Several more little lakes are passed at different levels, which all seem to have been caused by either fans or avalanches damming the waters; there are, too, old moraine-mounds spread over a large space of ground. As we still descend we come to some grazing-grounds in the valley-bottom; then to some outlying hamlets, and then to a large village which is named Khardong. This place is on the remaining part of an alluvial plateau that has been much denuded. It is bounded in one direction by cliffs several hundred feet high, composed of alluvial matter. The onward path leads down to the stream at the foot of these cliffs, and continues along the bottom, where — rare sight for Ladakh—is a strip of brushwood jungle. From this narrow passage we debouch into the larger valley of the Shayok River. Crossing that river by a ford (if the season be favourable) we then keep along its right bank for the length of a day's march, till we reach the centre of the district of Nubra.

IV

NUBRA

This district consists of the valley of the Nubra River—which flows from the north-north-west—and of a portion of the valley of the Shayok River, with which it unites. There are the wide alluvial flats of the two rivers and the lofty mountains bounding them, with ravines, seldom habitable, that lead down from the heart of those mountains.

At the junction of the rivers the valley of the Shayok is some four miles wide; that of the Nubra River is from two to three. The flat is in part sandy and shingly, in part occupied by jungle-patches of a low growth of tamarisk and myricaria, or umbu. The line at the edge of the plain is sharply drawn; the mountains rise from it suddenly in rocky masses, and they rise to a great height. Sometimes one sees only the ends of spurs, but even these may tower above one with 7000 or 8000 feet of bare rock; sometimes the eye reaches to lofty yet massive peaks, may be rocky, may be snow-capped, of much greater height, with great spurs and buttresses coming forward from beneath them. The stupendous size and the suddenness of the mountains give a character of grandeur to the scenery of this district.

On looking at the two valleys which make the habitable part of it I find a cheerfulness in the general aspect of Nubra beyond that of the rest of Ladakh. This perhaps may be put down to the fact of the valley being so open that the eye reaches from village to village, and is able at the same time to overlook several green expanses of low jungle and of pasture. But it must not be thought that the cultivation bears any large proportion to the whole area. The villages occur each at the mouth of a ravine on the undenuded fan that projects from it; still it is only a small part of the surface of the fan that is tilled; much of the ground is impracticable for the plough on account of the masses of rock that have been strewn over the surface by the stream floods. The space occupied by the village is green and pretty. Groups of fruit-trees and many poplars and willows flourish, and there are generally some one or two buildings of a better character than the ordinary peasant's cottage — as a monastery and a village headman's house—which brighten up the place. A character of the villages here—which those of the rest of Ladakh have not—is the enclosure of the fields with dry thorn hedges; these are necessary for a protection for them from the ponies of the travellers who pass through this country on their way to Yarkand. Another peculiarity is that a large number of the fields are laid in for grass; the letting of the pasture to the travelling merchants being a profitable business.

For equal altitudes the climate of Nubra is nearly the same as that of Central Ladakh, except that probably the winter snow-fall is, as regards the valley, somewhat less. Between each fall of snow so much of it disapppears by evaporation and by the wind drifting it, that, throughout the winter, the cattle, sheep, and goats are able to graze in the low pasture grounds, only at night are they taken in under cover. Some of the villages have mountain pastures, to which the flocks are driven in summer time; but the climate is so dry that these afford but very scanty pasturage. The vegetable products are nearly the same as in Central Ladakh. The naked barley is the most general crop; wheat is grown in nearly all the villages; but not in large quantities, as the people themselves do not consume it. There is a little fruit-apples, walnuts, and apricots; of apricots the sueeter sort ripen only in the Shayok Valley below the junction of the rivers; in this part also melon and water-melon ripen. Unmaru, a village which has a southern aspect, is the best place for fruit in Nubra. The people of Nubra, under the head of Ladakhi, have been described in the last chapter. There is this difference in them when compared with those of the near neighbourhood of Leh, that they are taller and thinner. The difference seems to be due to local circumstances. I could not trace it to any admixture of other blood. The characteristics of high cheek-bones and elongated eye are found in almost all. The customs of the Nubra people, as far as I know, differ in no respect from those of the people of Central Ladakh.

I will now take the reader to a few palces in Nubra, in each of which something will be found that is worthy of note. At the village of *Chamshan* I got evidence of a flood, not a great one, the action of which illustrates the way in which some of the substance of the fans accumulates. The fans in Nubra are uncommonly perfect in form, that is, complete, undenuded. Chamshan is on a fan in front of a ravine that leads up to some of the highest mountains, which feed glaciers that occupy the head of the ravine. I have not gone up this side valley. I was told that it contained three lakes; whether these are confined by the glacier or by masses of debris I do not know. In many or June of the year 1866 one of these lakes forced its barrier, and a flood came down the ravine and over part of the fan. The flood lasted three or four days (while the lake was emptying). It came over some ten acres of cultivated land, which it spoilt by depositing on it a layer of coarse rather sharp sand. All villages on fans are subject to such floods as this *if no deep channel has been cut by the waters for themselves;* that is to say, there cannot be complete safety form such rushes of water and sediment, unless, since the accumulation of the fan, the stream has become a denuding one, and has worn down a channel for itself, from the mouth of the ravine, so deep that no possible flood can bring the waters over the bank. *Charasa,* on the right bank of the Nubra River, is about the most conspicuous village in the district. At one time it was also the most important, for here lived the hereditary rulers of Nubra, who ruled under the Gyalpo or Raja of Ladakh. The houses of Charasa are built on an isolated steep -faced rock, which stands up away from the mountain side; it is some 200 yards long and 150 feet high. All the upper part of it is covered with white buildings; the loftiest of them is the monastery; they were formerly defended by a wall — of which parts still remain — running along the rock at varying levels, and flanked by towers. With the exception of the Lamas, the people of the village live on the rock in winter only; for summer they have other dwellings scattered about by their fields, but for warmth in winter they crowd to their old fortress. Here the buildings are crowded so close together, the space occupied is so completely roofed over—pathways and all—that when filled with human beings and with cattle it must indeed be warm.

A great part of the rock on which Charasa is built is rounded, smoothed, and even polished. It is a *roche moutonnee*. On the smoothed surface there are in several places very distinct grooves or scratches which most clearly denote the movement over it of a glacier. The grooves are to be seen close down to the level of the alluvium and up for more than 100 feet above it. The very summit cannot be examined on account of the buildings; but I have no doubt that the ice of the glacier completely covered it and extended to an enormous thickness above, and at the same time occupied the whole width of the valley, a width, which both here and for some distance up, is abut 2½ miles. There is a slight difference in the direction of the scratches on the two sides of the rock. On the east side they are exactly with the run of the valley, namely, about north-north-west, while on the west they run north and south; this shows that the stream of the ice of the glacier separated, and part of it deviated a little, on coming to the obstruction of the rock.

This is by no means the only instance of ice-marks in the valley. A projecting rock about two miles above Charasa is very distinctly polished and striated. Two rocks projecting out of the fan by the village of Kuri have the form that denotes ice-moulding; and behind that village we see the same phenomenon extending for 700 feet up the hill-side. On the left bank, at Panimik, are low isolated hills, about 200 feet high, surrounded by the alluvium; they are of a dark metamorphosed slate; everywhere, except at the broken and weathered parts, are they ice-moulded and striated. In one of these little hills is a hollow occupied by a lake some 150 yeards across; this hollow is rock-bound on three sides, while the fourth is of debris, which doubtless is moraine-stuff. Other instances could be given to prove that ice had once filled the valley for a length of at the least the 70 miles from Charasa up to the watershed, and for the whole breadth of 2½ miles at the lower end.

It now remains to inquire to what depth was it thus filled; what was the thickness of the ice of the glacier?

We have seen that there are marks of ice-moulding up to 700 feet above the valley-bottom. It is possible that with further examination those marks could be traced still farther up the hill-sides. But we are not left to depend on this conjecture; there is other evidence of the ice having reached much higher up. Behind Charasa is an even hill-side, unbroken by ravines; up this a zigzag path leads for a height of 4000 feet above the valley. At that altitude (14,000 feet above the sea) the top of the ridge is reached. It should be said that the ridge here—and as far up the valley as the village of Ayi, 14 miles distant—is of altered shale or slate and of a crystalline rock which I count to be the result of further metamorphism; these rocks are of a dark colour. The mountains on the opposite side of the valley are of granite, of a light yellow or drab colour looked at generally; only at their very base a metamorphic rock occurs. Thus the composition of the two lines of mountain is very different. Above Ayi I have not traced the division of the two formations, but it is possible that there granite occurs on the right bank as well; the argument that is now to be developed will stand whether it does so or not. At the very summit of that ridge behind

Charasa I found blocks of the light-coloured granite and gneiss covering the surface; many of them had a diameter of eight or ten feet; they extend along the ridge for a mile and a half or two miles, at levels up to 14,500 feet. Where, farther to the north-west, the ridge rises above that height, it is free from boulders, and shows nothing but the dark metamorphic slate. The boulders must have come either from the opposite mountains, or, more probably, from the mountains on this side, more than 14 miles up. This transportation can only be accounted for by supposing that the glacier filled the valley to a depth of 4000 or 4500 feet — to have reached indeed up to the summit of the ridge at this comparatively low part of it, and there to have shed moraine matter; the position of this, on the very top, preserved it from subsequent removal by atmospheric influences.

It will be understood that with this enormous thickness the glacier could not have ended off at Charasa; it must have reached to the Shayok Valley, and there probably joined with other ice masses, and it may have extended far away down.

From every point on the ascent of this ridge, but especially from the summit, I obtained commanding views of the plain beneath and of the mountains opposite; these views gave so much more complete an idea of the form of the ground than could be got from below that it is worth while to dwell a little on what is seen from that height. We look down on the river flowing in an extraordinary number of channels, meeting and separating again so as to divide the bed into hundreds of curve-bounded pointed islands in form like the lights in a flamboyant window; a spread of brushwood jungle — in great part of red-berried Hippohae (which the natives call Tsarma)—shows where the wandering stream has for some years not reached to. Beyond this alluvial flat of the Nubra River are the fans at the mouth of each ravine; the completeness of the fan-shape of their outline is beautifully shown in this almost bird's-eye view. Looking to the opposite mountains we see the peaks of the central ridge between the

Nubra and Upper Shayok valleys, mountains which are not visible from below. There is a sharp serrated ridge of a height of about 20,000 feet. From out of this rise peaks which the trigonometrical surveyours have found to be from 24,600 to 25,180 feet high; they are grand masses of rock standing up bold and clear. Each mountain is an irregular mass 5000 feet higher than the lofty continuous ridge. Snow clothes their summits and lies in thick beds on some of their slopes, while other parts are rocky precipices too steep for it to remain on. The sketch gives the outline of the peak-masses with some exactness. It does not reach to the foot of the mountains in the valley, as the eye does from some points of view; when it does so there is in sight, in a distance of 18 miles, a vertical height of 15,000 feet. Farther along to the south-east other peaks rise for a thousand or two feet above the general level of the ridge, which seems to continue at 20,000 feet, till it ends suddenly at the corner where the Shayok makes the great bend. So much for the central ridge. The secondary ridges branch off from it with a height corresponding to its general level. Their edge is serrated, but not deeply so. They continue for many miles without any sudden fall to perhaps an average distance of three miles short of the edge of the valley, where in height they may be 18,000 feet. At these points they make the peaks which are seen when one is in the valley. From them there is a great and sudden fall down to the valley, the slope of which is about 35^0; this is remarkably regular for all the distance—of nearly 50 miles—that is within sight, with the exception that the ravines (some that reach to the central ridge and some that go but a few miles back) cut up the sloping face into triangular masses of which the base is from mouth to mouth of two ravines, while the apex is at the end of the intermediate branch ridge. The general colour of the mountains below the snow (and it is only the peaks, rising higher than the ridges, that are snowy) is a light greyish brown, from the hue of the granite they are mostly composed of A darker streak along the foot marks the position of the altered shale. The surface of the mountains is usually not so precipitous as to form great continuous cliffs, but is worn all over into numerous minor ramifying gulleys and ravines, whose sides are rugged slopes of rock.

V

ZANSKAR

Zanskar is a district of Ladakh which lies south-west of Leh, towards the Watershed Range; its extent nearly coincides with that of the basin of the large river, tributary to the Indus, which is called after the name of the country. Zanskar is closely united to the rest of Ladakh both by physical characters and by the close relationship in race, speech, religion, and character that exists between the people of the two countries. Till forty years ago, Zanskar was equally connected with Central Ladakh by political ties, being governed by a Raja, who was dependent on the Gyalpo at Leh; but now it belongs (as can be seen from the political Map) not to the Ladakh Governorship, but to the district of Udampur, in the Outer Hills, having been attached to this for, so to say, accidental reasons.

From all sides the approach to Zanskar, placed, as it is in a maze of mountains, is of considerable difficulty. To the south-west of it the wide Snowy Range makes a barrier, to cross which must be a laborious and may be a dangerous business. From the north-west and the south-east, indeed, roads lead in from Suru and from Rupshu respectively, to traverse which is less difficult, but these lead over long uninhabited tracts. That way which first one would look to for communication with Leh—by the valley of the Zanskar River—is quite impassable, except when the winter's frost makes a road over the waters of the river. Instead of this, in summer time, the traveller from Leh has to make a long detour by Lamayuru; he has to traverse fifteen stages in which several Passes have to be surmounted, before Zanskar is reached.

By far the greater part of the area of Zanskar is occupied by the ridges and the ravines of mountains, either of the Snowy Watershed Range, or of the more complicated mass lying between that and Central Ladakh. The inhabited region is nearly all included in the valleys of two streams and of the river they make by their union. These two streams come, one from the north-west, the other from south-east; uniting, they together flow away to the north-east. At their junction is a wide open space, which is the central part of Zanskar; it includes in itself the most important places. This space is a triangle, with a base of seven miles, and a perpendicular of five; on the three sides it is bounded by bare mountains. But a very small proportion of this plain is cultivated; the most of it is an expanse of stony ground; the rivers flow through it somewhat below the general level; where water from side valleys has been brought on to the alluvial terraces and fans, there only is land under cultivation. On the north and east are bare brown mountains 6000 and 7000 feet above the valleys; their surface is in part of irregular cliffs, in part of slopes of loose stones, either simply weathered off and remaining in the same place, or else fallen and formed into taluses. Some of these mountains are wonderfully clear examples of aerial denudation; their naked sides are scarred and cut in lines which mark either temporary watercourses, or the path of falling snow and rock, while below lie the heaps and the outspread fans, which are the next stages of the debris in its seaward course. Great and striking objects as are these mountains, the range on the south-west shows over them a great preponderance of height; it has a deeply-cut serrated ridge, a line of sharp peaks rising well above the limit of perpetual snow.

In the open triangular space are many remains of former extended glaciers. In front of the mouth of the ravine, coming from the south-west, where is marked on the large map Sani R., is an irregular moundy expanse made of stones, some angular, some rounded. Just south-west of Padam is another old moraine, which seems at one time to have reached across the stream a little above that place. The mound, also, on which Padam itself is built is due to a similar cause. But one cannot be sure how much of these old moraines were deposited by glaciers from the side ravines, or whether there was one large glaciers filling all the long valley from the south-east. The position of Padam, the chief place, now but a village—but perhaps in former days when a Raja ruled there deserving of a higher name—is very curious. As said above, it is built on a mound of moraine matter. The mound is about 80 feet high; it is of loose, heaped-up blocks of gneiss, blocks which look as if they had stayed just as they fell from the glacier—the interstices vacant, the whole mass seeming as if it might give way. On the very summit of this heap was the palace of the Rajas, of which some walls are still standing houses are built on the masses of stone all over the face of the mound. The place is dilapidated; ruin and decay are shown both in the substance of the hill — the waste of mountains — and in the human habitations that were built on it. Such instances of moraines could be multiplied. Not far from Padam is a conspicuous group of very large erratic blocks. Just south-west of Thonde, nine mile from Padam, where the valley is about a mile and a half wide, there stretches right across it — except for the channel that the river flows in—an irregular moundy tract of stones and sand. This is clearly a moraine; its width, measured in the direction of the run of the valley, is half a mile it contains pieces of gneiss, which must have come from the mountains south-west of Padam.

The climate of Zanskar is severe. The spring, summer, and autumn together last little more than five months, after which snow falls, and at once winter closes in, confining the people and the cattle within doors for the space of half the year. A much greater depth of snow falls here than in Central Ladakh. In the spring it causes avalanches from the mountains to such an extent that in the Nunak Valley the people cannot till a month has passed get about from village to village for fear of them. To clear the snow from the fields in time for the sowing requires special contrivance. During summer and autumn the people collect earth and store it in their houses in considerable quantities. In the spring, when they deem the time of snow-fall to be over, and the snow in the fields is partly melted and has begun to cake with the sun's rays, they spread the earth, which absorbs warmth from the sun, and melts the snow in contact with it. Sometimes snow falls afresh, and the labour is lost and has to be repeated. In 1869 there were three or four layers of earth and snow thus accumulated before the work was done. The villages of Zanskar are not so comfortable nor so picturesque in look as those we have seen in other parts of Ladakh. Trees are extremely rare; the continuance of snow and the force of the wind are much against their growth; there are a few plantations of poplars grown for the sake of timber, and lately the authorities have increased their number, but the trees produce nothing more then slender poles.

The people have, as has before been implied, the characters which were described under the head "Ladakhis." They have, indeed, the better of these characteristics in a higher degree than the rest of the Ladakhis. The Zanskaris are the old-fashioned ones among them, retaining their simplicity of manners and their honesty without stain. The language has a slight dialectic difference from that of Leh; even in the various parts of Zanskar recognizable differences exist; but none of these seemed — as far as I could gather—to be of great importance. The number of inhabitants is very small. I have a list of forty-three villages, which may contain ten or twelve houses each; the total may be 500 houses and 2500 souls. The tax paid to the Maharaja's Government comes to a very small sum; it used to be 300%., but in 1869 it was reduced to 200%. There is a trade, small in amount , but still important to the Zanskaris, which is carried on by three on four routes. First , the people of Rupshu bring salt, and take barley in exchange. Secondly, some of the salt brought by the last-mentioned route goes a Padar and Pangi (by very difficult Passes over the Snowy Range), and is there exchanged for rice, butter and honey, and for skins. Thirdly, other of the salt acquired from

Rupshu goes to Suru, whence comes in exchange pattu (woollen cloth), barley, and a little cash. Thus it seems that the Zanskar people export of their own productions only barley, if indeed they do that, for it is imported as well as exported . Their profit seems to lie in the trade for salt ; by acting both as carriers and merchants of this they increase its value enough to provide themselves with the luxuries that must come from outside. A fourth line of traffic is with Lahol, whence traders come with cash alone, and buy ponies, donkeys, sheep, and goats. It is only by this branch of trade that cash enough is introduced into the country to pay the Government tax. Nearly all the rest is done by barter: for instance, 7 lbs. or 8 lbs. of salt exchange in Zanskar for 1 lb. of butter; in Pangi 3 lbs. or 4 lbs. only of salt would be given. Again, in Zanskar the proportion in value of salt to that of barley is such that 2 lbs. of salt exchange for 3 lbs. of barley.

(From *Landmarksin Indian Anthropology — Jammu and Kashmir Territories, 1875*).

12

Mountains of Ladhak

By

Alexander Cunningham

I.— GENERAL REMARKS

The great Himalaya, which bounds India to the north, in one continuous chain of gigantic peaks, from the southward bend of the Brahmaputra to the holy lake of Manasarovara, is extended to the westward from the sources of the Sutluj to the magnificent peaks of Dayamur; and from thence to the sources of the Gilgit and Kunar rivers, where it joins the mountains of Pamer and Hindu Kush. Though less lofty than the eastern Himalaya, the western half of the chain is second to none else; and it is probable that some of its peaks may yet be found superior even to the most elevated of the Andes. A single glance at the map of India will show the reasons that have induced me to consider the Bara Lacha range as the continuation of the true Himalaya. It will be seen that the Eastern Himalaya divides the waters of the Tsang-po from those of the Ganges and its tributaries, while the Bara-Lacha forms the water shed between the Indus and its five affluents. It will also be seen that the western, as well as the eastern chain, separates the great Hindu family of India from the Botis of Tibet. Some mixed races are found to the south of each chain : the Lahulis and Kanawaris to the west, and the Gorkhas and Bhutanis to the east. Lastly, it will be seen that both ranges form the lines of demarcation between the cold and dry climate of Tibet, with its dearth of trees, and the warm and humid climate of India, with its luxuriance of vegetable productions. These facts, joined to the great elevation of the range, are, I think, sufficient to warrant the selection of the Bara-Lacha chain as the continuation of the true Himalaya. But there is one marked difference between the eastern and western ranges which can scarcely fail in striking the most casual observer. The inferior mountains of the eastern chain generally run at right angles to its axis, whereas those of the western chain are mostly disposed in subordinate parallel ranges. The general parallelism of the principal mountain-ranges of the world,-of the Himalayas and the Altai, in Asia,-of the Atlas, in Africa,-and of the Alps and Apennines, the Pyrenees and Carpathians, in Europe,-has already been noticed by Humboldt and others. But this parallelism also exists in the subordinate ranges of the western Himalaya. Thus we find no less than two distinct and independent ranges to the south of the western Himalaya, both stretching in the same general direction from south-east to north-west. These ranges I propose to call the *Mid-Himalaya,* and the *Outer, or Sub-Himalaya,* leaving the name of Sewalik unchanged for the lowermost sand-stone ranges.

Beyond the Himalaya the same system of parallel chains will be observed in at least three distinct ranges of mountains, which I propose to call the *Trans-Himalaya,* the *Chushal,* and the *Karakoram,* or *Trans-Tibetan* chains. These names are by no means intended to supersede any that may now exist, but only as descriptive appellations of extensive mountain-ranges which at present have no general names.

1. The *Trans-Tibetan* range is that which we call the Bolor and Karakoram, on the west; and which probably merges into the Kuen-lun, on the east. It is in fact the northern limit of the Tibetan people, and of their peculiar language. To the are the people of Balti, Ladak, and Chang-Thang, who were known to Ptolemy as the Byltee and *Chatal Scythal.*

2. The *Kailas,* or *Gangri* range, runs through the midst of western Tibet, along the right bank of the Indus, to the junction of the Shayok. Neither Moorcroft nor Vigne has given any name to this range, though both of them crossed it several times, and in different places. I have ventured to call it the *Kailas,* or *Gangri* range, because those names are equally celebrated by the Hindus and Tibetans. *Kailas,* or "Ice-mountain," is the Indian Olympus, the abode of Siva and the celestials. *Gang-ri,* or "Ice-mountain," is called *Ri-gyal,* or King of Mountains, by the Tibetans, who look upon Ti-se, or the Kailas Peak, as the highest mountain in the world.

3. The *Trans-Himalayan* range divides the head-waters of the Sutluj from those of the Indus, and extends to the western limits of Rongdo and Astor.

4. The *Bara-Lacha* (or Western Himalaya) has already been noticed. It is the main chain of this vast maze of mountains, and even on the banks of the Indus, where all the other ranges dwindle, the true Himalaya maintains its lofty supremacy in the magnificent peaks of Dayamur.

5. The *Mid-Himalaya,* or *Pir-Panjal* range, divides the valleys of Spiti, Lahul, Kashtwar, and Kashmir, on the north, from those of Kullu, Punach, and Chamba on the south, and terminates on the western bank of the Indus, in the celebrated peak of Mahaban.

6. The *Outer,* or *Sub-Himalaya,* stretches through Sukhet and Mandi, to the westward, between Kangra and Chamba, where it is called the *Dhaola Dhar,* or White Mountain. Still further west it forms the Ratan Panjal, and terminates in the well-known peak of *Gandgarh.*

These different ranges form the principal features, and consequently the natural boundaries of the hill states of the Panjab. The whole mass of mountains, from the crest of the Karakoram range to the plain of the Panjab, has an average breadth of 250 miles. The breadth of the Himalaya, from the crest of the Bara-Lacha range to the plains, is about one-half of the whole breadth; for though not more than ninety miles broad from Lahul to Hushiarpoor, it is nearly 150 miles broad through Kashmir to Jammu, on the south. Its length, from the source of the Indus to the source of the Gilgit river, is 600 miles.

II.—1ST. TRANS-TIBETAN RANGE

The *Karakoram,* or *Trans-Tibetan* chain, forms the natural boundary of Ladak, and the small Musulman districts of Balti, Hunza-Nager, and Gilgit on the north. Nothing whatever is known of this range to the eastward of the upper Shayok river, and of the northern portion we know but little. At the head of the Shayok river, it is called Karakoram, which is a Turki word, signifying the "Black Mountains." To the north of Balti it is known as the Bolor range: but this name is only the common appellation of Balti, amongst all the races of Dardu origin. It is, however, of some value, as it enables us to state precisely that the Bolor mountains, which have hitherto occupied an uncertain position in our maps, are no other than the mountains of Balti. As this district formerly included Hunza-Nager and Gilgit, the Bolor mountains may now be defined as extending for 300 miles from the source of the Gilgit and Yasan Rivers, in east longitude 73^0, to the source of the Nurba river, in east longitude 77^0. From the latter point eastward, as far as the most remote sources of the Shayok River, the continuation of the chain, about 150 miles in length, is best known as the Karakoram range. The whole length of the chain, from the eastern sources of the Shayok to the head of the Gilgit river, is 450 miles, the general direction being from east to west.

The learned Humboldt supposes the Bolor mountains to be the transverse chain, running from north to south across the Indian Caucasus, and dividing the sources of the Oxus from those of the Yarkand and Kashgar rivers. But that chain is universally called Pamer, a name which it has borne for many centuries. In A.D. 632-40, the Chinese pilgrim Hawan-Thsang mentions the district of *Pho-mi-lo*, or Pamer, which he makes 167 miles in length from west to east. To the south or Pamer he places *Po-lu-lo*, or Bolor, of which he says that the south-eastern part of the district is inhabited, and that the country produces much gold. Both these facts are true of the present Bolor or Balti; the higher mountains, moreover, abound in rock-crystal, which is consequently called the Belor-stone, or simply Belor. The transverse north and south range of mountains is called *Belut-Tagh*, or the "Cloudy Mountains;" and this name has, I believe, been confounded with Bolor. Marco Polo is the next who mentions Pamer and the neighbouring districts : I have two copies of his works before me, but they differ so much that I feel quite puzzled which to follow. After the mention of Pamer, the earlier copy has the following-"From hence, the way to Kathay leads for forty days' journey between the *east* and the north-east, through mountains, hills, and valleys, in which there are many rivers, but no villages, except that some huts and cottages are to be seen amongst the mountains. * * * * The country is called *Palow*." The other copy thus renders the above- "Leaving this place, he (the traveller) has to go on forty days between *north* and north-east, and passes many rivers and deserts; and in all this journey finds neither verdure nor habitation. This country is called Belor. The people live in very lofty mountains." In the later copy, the editor (Huge Murray) has apparently corrected the Palow of the older copy to agree with his own identification, and has moreover changed the direction from north-east by *east*, to north-east by *north*, perhaps with a view of bringing it nearer to the true bearing of Kashgar, which is the next place mentioned. Now it is evident from Hawan-Thsang's statement, that the district of *Pa-lo-lo*, or Bolor, must, in his day, have extended to the north of the Karakoram range, and that the northern portion from Sir-i-kol to Khafalun, was then, as now, almost uninhabited. This, therefore, in my opinion, is the country which Marco Polo describes.

The Karakoram Pass was traversed by the Chinese pilgrim Fa-Hian, in A.D. 399. He calls the range *Tsung-Ling*, or "Onion Mountains," a name which they must have received from the number of wild leeks that grow upon them, and scent the air in all directions. They were found by Dr. Thomson on the elevated plateaux to the south of the pass. Mir Izzet Ullah no doubt alludes to the strong and unpleasant smell of these wild leeks, when he ascribes the headache and difficulty of breathing that are usually attendant on ascending great heights, to the *Esh*, which is a Turki word, signifying "smell."

The actual height of only one point in this range has yet been ascertained, namely, the Karakoram Pass, which Dr. Thomson found to be 18,660 feet above the sea. Vigne was ot opinion that the height of this pass would be found "somewhat under 15,000 feet," and Mr. Thornton argues, in favour of this opinion, that it was sufficiently depressed to permit Mir Izzet Ullah's passage in the end of October. But though this argument will hold good for the southern Himalayas, it will only mislead when applied to the northern ranges of Tibet, on which the snow falls so scantily that many of them may be crossed even in December. A single peak to the northward of Sassar was estimated by Dr. Thomson at 24,000 feet. The estimate may perhaps be a little too high, but I have great confidence in the accuracy with which a practised eye may measure heights.

To the eastward, this range maintains its superior elevation, as Captain H. Strachey found several of the passes, on one of its ramifications to the northward of Ruthog, to be between 18,000 and 19,000 feet in height. To the westward, the same general loftiness may be inferred, from the known heights of some peaks in the neighbouring ranges of Hindu Kush and Pamer (or Belut-Tagh). The average height of the peaks may be estimated at 21,000 feet, and that of the passes at upwards of 18,000 feet. To the eastward of the Shigar valley, Dr. Falconer crossed a pass 16,200 feet, on a spur of the Karakoram.

Vigne was informed by the Yarkandi merchants that "the snow does not remain upon Karakoram for the greater part of the year." But my informants, who wee also yarkandi merchants, stated exactly the reverse; and we know that Izzet Ullah, in the beginning of November found snow and ice the whole way over the pass. It is always difficult to ascertain the snow limit from the information of travellers and merchants, who, though they generally discriminate sporadic falls of snow, yet very rarely make any distinction between beds of snow sheltered in ravines, and the mass of exposed snow on the mountains that braves the noon-day heat of a whole summer. I believe that the Karakoram Pass is rarely, if ever, entirely free from snow, although at no period of the year does the snow accumulate upon it in any great mass. There was of course much snow on the pass when Dr. Thomson ascended it in July 1848, and it was lying much lower on the northern than on the southern face. The probability is that the Karakoram Pass has about the same elevation as the snow-line of the range, and this would at once account for the discrepancies of the different authorities. I would therefore fix a height of 18,500 feet as the snow limit on the southern face, and of 18,000 feet or even less, for the northern face. For the snow-line, which in Rukchu is about 20,000 feet, has already begun to descend, and in the Pamer range to the north of the Karakoram has been estimated by Wood at rather more than 17,000 feet.

In the Shayok and Nubra valleys, the prevailing rock is limestone. Granite occurs in the ridge between the rivers, and clay-slate towards the source of the Shayok. The limestone continues towards Ruthog, and the waters of the Pangkong lake hold a sufficient quantity of lime to form a calcareous deposit, which cements the pebbles together in patches of concrete at the bottom of the lake. But the mass of mountain is composed of granite and gneiss, which in this, as well as in the other lofty ranges of India and Tibet, form the highest peaks and crests of the ridges.

III.—2nd. KAILAS RANGE

The *Kailas* or *Gangri* range runs through the midst of Western Tibet along the right bank of the Indus, from its source to the junction of the Shayok. At this point it is cut both by the Indus and by the Shigar river; beyond which it stretches to the north-west, dividing the two valleys, and is terminated at the junction of the Hunza and Nager rivers. The general direction is from south-east to north-west, and the whole length of the range from the celebrated peak of Kailas to Hunza-Nager is not less than 550 miles. In many of our maps the main stream of the Indus or Singgechu, is laid down to the northward of the Kailas mountains, and the Garo river or Higong-chu is degraded to a mere tributary, which falls into the great river at Tashigong. But all my informants agreed in stating that the Garo river was the *Singge-chu* or Indus, and that the stream which joined it at Tashigong was not larger than the Hanle river. The Kailas or Gangri range therefore extends in one unbroken chain from the source of the Indus to the junctions of the Shayok. It forms the natural boundry between Ladak, Balti, and Rongdo on the south, and Ruthog, Nurba, Shigar, and Hunza-Nager on the north.

This range has been often crossed by Europeans, but always on the same high roads, which generally lead over the lowest and easiest passes. We have the heights of six of these passes in different parts of the range.

Passes	Feet	Authority
1. Tsaka-la	15,000	Trebeck.
2. Kongta-la	15,495	Moorcroft, MS.
3. Chang-la	18,105	Ditto do.
4. Lazgung or Sabu-la	17,666	Dr. Thomson.
5. Le Pass	17,600	Ditto.
6. Hanu pass	16,890	Col. Bates.
Mean height	16,792 or 16,800 feet.	

As the average height of these passes approaches 17,000 feet, the general elevation of the range may be estimated at not less than 20,000 feet. The height of the celebrated Kailas peak has been determined by Lieut. R. Strachey at 20,700 feet. A peak which I measured on one of the spurs of the range to the north of Mahe was 18,500 feet. In this part, as we may see from the heights of the Kongta-la and Tsakala Passes, the range is much depressed, but in the neighbourhood of Le, wherever I could see the ridge, it was entirely covered with snow in the beginning of October. As the lofty passes to the northward of Le are said to be always clear of snow at the end of summer, the snow-line on the Kailas or Mid-Tibetan range may be estimated at 19,000 feet, or more, on the southern face; and at 18,500 feet on the northern face. In the south-eastern portion of the range, between the elevated tablelands of Chang-Thang, Rukchu, and Ngari, the snow-limit will of course be higher than in the north-western portion, which divides the valley of the Indus from the Shayok. In the neighbourhood of Le, therefore, we cannot estimate the height of this range at less than 20,000 feet; and although it may be somewhat depressed between the Pangkong and Tshomoriri lakes, yet it rises again towards the south-eastern extremity, where the lofty peak of Kailas towers over the holy lakes of Manasarovara and Raw-an Hrad. On this part of the range the snow never disappears, and this fact has originated the name of the mountain both in Sanskrit and in Tibetan, in which languages Kailas and Gangri respectively mean the "Ice Mountain."

The geological structure of this range is chiefly clay-slate, gneiss, and granite. In the neighbourhood of Le it is wholly of granite of a very coarse texture.

IV.—3rd. TRANS-HIMALAYAN RANGE

This range is a branch of the lofty *Ri-Gyal,* or King of Mountains, which it certainly equals, and perhaps surpasses in height. It branches off from the Gangri mountain to the south of Garo, and extends in one unbroken chain through the districts of Chumurti, Rukchu, and Zanskar, to the junction of the Zanskar river, which rushes dark and turbulent through a vast chasm in the mountain, where human foot has never trod. From this it extends to the junction of the Dras river with the Indus, where it is again cut through by the Dras river at a narrow gorge called the Wolf's Leap; but beyond this point it stretches in one unbroken chain to the great southward sweep of the Indus at the junction of the Gilgit river. Its general direction is from south-east to north-west, and its extreme length is upwards of 350 miles. It forms the natural boundary between Ladak, Balti, and Rongdo on the north, and Rukchu, Zanskar, Purik, Dras, and Astor, on the south.

This range is much better known than either of the preceding chains. I have the measurement of four peaks determined by myself in 1847, and of no less than eleven passes, of which I have myself crossed five. The following are the heights of peaks in the neighbourhood of Hanle, and in other parts of the range.

Peaks	Feet	Authority
1. Rongo Peak	20,786	A. Cunningham
2. Changlung, N. Pk.	20,357	Ditto.
3. Changlung, S. Pk	20,141	Ditto.
4. Hanle Peak	20,650	Ditto.
5. Lanak Peaks	20,000	Ditto.
6. Tshomoriri Peaks	21,000	Ditto.
7. Gya Peak, W. of Gya	21,000	Ditto.
8. Tok Peak (S. of Le)	21,000	Ditto.
Mean height	20,616 feet.	

The mean height of the peaks in the eastern part of the range, is therefore not less than 20,500 feet.

The following table shows the height of different passes in the eastern half of the range.

In the same month, the four peaks, which I measured in the neighbourhood of Hanle at different heights between 20,000 and 21,000 feet, and averaging 20,483 feet, were all partially covered with snow. The general height of the ridge was about 20,000 feet, and the snow was lying along nearly the whole line of crest to the west. On the eastern face it evidently descended lower, as on the Lanak peaks. I estimate the snow-line of Rukchu at not more than 20,000 feet on the western and southern slopes, and at 19,500 feet, or even less, on the eastern and northern slopes.

The great height of the snow-line on this range is caused chiefly by the radiation of heat from the elevated plains of Rukchu and Garo, and by the reverberation of heat from the bare sides of the mountains. It is in part also due to its situation in the midst of lofty snowy mountains, which intercept the ascending vapours, on all sides, and prevent the precipitation of moisture within this ice-bound region. As the mass of land rises, the snow-line recedes higher and higher, notwithstanding the increase of the latitude. This is shown clearly in Plate 1, which exhibits a section of the mountains from the southern base of the Himalaya to the northern foot of the Karakoram. In this section the snow-line is seen to rise with the mass of land until both attain their greatest elevation in Rukchu. From this tract the snow-line descends as the country falls to the northward towards Yarkand and Kotan. But the fall is less rapid than the rise. From the eastern peaks of Kullu in latitude 31½^0 to the Lanak and Hanle ranges in Rukchu, the rise of the snow-line is fully 4,000 feet, while the increase of latitude is only one degree; but from Rukchu to Pamer the increase of latitude is five degrees, while the fall of the snow-line is only 3,000 feet. We must therefore attribute the greatest part of this difference to the influence latitude.

Of the geological structure of this range I can only speak generally. The Lanak ridge consists of a core of granite nearly overlaid by clay-slate. To the west of the pass, the plain of Dongan is strewn with rolled boulders of granite for several miles. Thence to the Thung Lung Pass the higher ridges are of gneiss, and the slopes of mica and clay-slates. Throughout Zanskar from the Lachalang Pass to the Singge-la the chief formation is limestone, and beyond that the ridge consists of mica and clay-slates crested by granite, which is the prevailing rock on the table-land of Deotsu. Trap occurs in the volcanic district between Hanle and the hot-springs of Puga.

V.—4th THE WESTERN HIMALAYA

The great Himalaya forms a natural boundary between India and Tibet. On the east it presents the lofty peaks of Kanchinjinga and Dhwalagiri, which rise to the vast height of more than 28,000 feet. To the westward it is less known, but the peaks that have been measured between the sources of the Sutluj and the Chenab give an average elevation superior to that of the Andes.

The general direction of the western Himalaya is the same as that of the other chains which have just been described, from south-east to north-west. The whole length of the chain from the peak of Monomangli to the sources of the Gilgit and Kunar rivers is not less than 650 miles. It is pierced in three places by rivers, by the Sutluj and Para at the base of Porgyal, and by the Indus at the foot of Dayamur. Its greatest elevation is the lofty peak of Nanda Devi (Jawahir) 25,749 feet, and its greatest depression, the pass of Seoji-la, 11,700 feet, between Kashmir and Ladak. Throughout its whole extent it forms the boundary between the races of Hindu origin and the pure Tibetans of Ladak and Balti. To the south-east it divides the Tibetan district of Garo from the Indian province of Kumaon. Midway it separates the Ladaki districts of Rukchu, Zanskar, Purik, and Dras, containing only pure Botis or Tibetans, from the provinces of Spiti, Kullu, Lahul, Kashtwar, and Kashmir, whose inhabitants are chiefly a mixed race of Indo-Tibetans. To the westward it was once the boundary between the Dards of Chelas and the Tibetans of Astor and Gilgit; but the Dards have since penetrated to the northward, and the Gilgitis of the present day are a mixed race of Dardo-Tibetans.

To the south of the Sutluj the heights of many of the loftiest peaks have been determined by Webb, Hodgson, and the Gerards, but to the north of the Sutluj, no heights were ascertained by them, except only that of Porgyal by Alexander Gerard. Beyond this, not more than five peaks have been measured, with more or less precision, but the general accuracy of these measurements is proved by the ascertained elevation of several passes. The following table gives all the heights to the south of the Sutluj.

Peaks	Height	Authority
1. Monomangli or Gurla	23,900	Lieut. R. Strachey.
2. Kunlas Peak	22,513	Trigonometrical. Map.
3. Gula Ghal Peak	21,258	Ditto.
4. XX	20,479	Ditto.
5. XIX	22,707	Ditto.
6. XVIII	22,511	Ditto.
7. XV	22,491	Ditto.
8. Nanda Devi	25,749	Ditto.
9. XIII	22,385	Ditto.
10. XII	22,385	Ditto.
11. A No. 1	23,531	Ditto.
12. XI	20,758	Ditto.
13. A No. 3	23,317	Ditto.
14. N	23,482	Ditto.
15. L	22,266	Ditto.

Contd....

Peaks	Height	Authority
16. K	22,570	Ditto.
17. I	23,300	Ditto.
18. IX	21,383	Ditto.
19. VIII	23,236	Ditto.
20. Badrinath Peak	22,954	Ditto.
21. VII	23,441	Ditto.
22 ...	22,754	Ditto.
23. H	21,894	Ditto.
24. G	22,556	Ditto.
25. U	21,612	Ditto.
26. Kedarnath	23,062	Ditto.
27. M	22,792	Ditto.
28. St. Patrick	22, 798	Ditto.
29. St. George	22,654	Ditto.
30. Rudru Himala	22,390	Ditto.
31. Swarga	22,906	Ditto.
32. The Pyramid	21, 579	Ditto.
33. Jaonli Peak	21,940	Ditto.
34. E. C.	21,772	Ditto.
35. F.	21,964	Ditto.
36. G. Srikanta	20,296	Ditto.
37. Rock Peak	21,076	Ditto.
38. Windy Peak (Kyobrang)	20, 169	Ditto.
39. Glacier Peak	20,544	Ditto.
40. Raldang or W. Kailas	21,103	Ditto.
Mean height 22,274 feet.		

The distance from Monomangli to the Raldang and Kyobrang Peaks, is only 175 miles, and between these points we find no less than forty peaks, whose well ascertained heights exceed 20,000 feet, and which yield an average of more than 22,000 feet. The passes are less known, because only the most frequented have yet been measured. The heights, however, of nine of them, have been ascertained chiefly by the Gerards and Stracheys.

Passes	Height	Authority
1. Lankpya	17,750	Capt. H. Strachey.
2. Lakhar	18,300	Lieut. R. Strachey.
3. Unta dura	17,700	Ditto.
4. Kyungar Ghat	17,700	Ditto.
5. Balch dhura	17,700	Ditto.
6. Deo Ghat	18,000	Trigonometrical Map.
7. Niti Pass	16,570	
8. Kyobrang	18,331	Capt. A Gerard.
9. Gangtang	18,295	Ditto.
Mean height	17,816 feet.	

The average height of this part of the range, by taking the mean of the greatest elevation, and greatest depressions, is not therefore less than 20,000 feet.

To the westward, the heights of the following peaks and passes have been ascertained, with more or less accuracy.

Peaks	Height	Authority
1. Pyramidal Peak	20,106	Capt. A. Gerard.
2. Porgyal	22,700	Ditto.

Contd....

Peaks	Height	Authority
3. Chang-Razing Peak	20,500	Dr. Gerard.
4. Gyu Peak	24,764	A. Cunningham.
5. Parang Peaks	19,500	Ditto.
6. Zanskar Ridge	20,000	Dr. Thomson A.C.
7. Ser and Mer	20,000	Hugel and Vigne.
8. Bal Tal Peak	19,650	Jacquemont.
9. Dayamur	20,000	Vigne. Col. Bates.
10. Peak to N. of Peshawur	20,493	Macartney.

Mean height 20,771 feet.

Passes	Height	Authority
1. Meyung La	17,700	Capt. Gerard.
2. Parang La	18,500	A. Cunningham.
3. Bara Lacha	16,500	Ditto.
4. Umasi La	18,123	Dr. Thomson.
5. Seoji La	11,634	A. Cunningham.
6. Gutumi Pass	12,000	Vigne corrected.

Mean height 15,743 feet.

Taking the means of the greatest heights and greatest depressions, the average elevation of this portion of the range will be upwards of 18,000 feet; and as that of the other half was found to be upwards of 20,000 feet, the mean height of the crest of the western Himalaya, from Monomangli to the source of the Gilgit river, may be assumed at 19,000 feet.

On this range the snow-line can be determined within very narrow limits. On the three passes crossed by Lieut. R. Strachey, each about 17,700 feet, no snow was found in September. The Lakhar Pass, 18,300 feet, and the Jayanti Pass, 18,500 feet, were also free from snow. "But the line of perpetual snow was evidently near, for though the Jayanti ridge was quite free, and some of the near peaks were clear, to perhaps upwards of 19,000 feet, yet in more sheltered situations, unbroken snow could be seen considerably below the ridge:" and Lieut. Strachey concluded "that 18,500 feet must be nearly the average height of the snow-line at that place."

Alexander Gerard found no snow on the Kyobrang Pass (18,313 feet), even in July, and it was equally bare when visited by Jacquemont. On Porgyal, in October, the Gerards found no old snow below 19,400 feet, and their station on the Chang-Razing mountain, 20,400 feet, was also clear; but as Dr. Gerard mentions a range due north, and a peak to the westward, while he is perfectly silent regarding the lofty peaks to the south, it seems certain that their station was on the northern exposure of Porgyal. I can myself vouch for its southern faces being covered with masses of snow in the end of August and beginning of September 1847, when the northern side seemed generally bare. The absence of snow on the Pyramidal Peak of Porgyal, 20,106 feet, is more to the purpose, as it is certain that the Gerards could only have seen this peak from the south and west. On crossing the Manerang Pass, on the 30th of August, Alexander Gerard found the last half mile was over the perpetual snow, which he distinguishes from the fresh covering of the former night, in which the foot sank from three to twelve inches. On descending the Pass to the north, he "travelled over the snow for a mile." On recrossing the Pass, on the 7th September, he found that "the snow had not descended above 400 feet; but the great field of ages had a new and deep covering." The snow, therefore, remains for the whole year on the Manerang Pass.

From the Manerang Pass, Alexander Gerard observed "very distinctly the Paralasa (Bara Lacha) range, covered with snow." I estimate the height of this part of the range at 19,500 feet. On the 8th September, 1847, I found no snow on the southern face of the Parang Pass, 18,500 feet, but there was a glacier one mile and a half in length, on the northern face, on which the snow was frozen hard. Snow was lying in patches on many of the peaks, at about 19,000 feet, but chiefly on the western and southern faces. The exposed faces to the north and east were bare. In September 1846, I crossed the Bara Lacha Pass, 16,500 feet, twice; and on both occasions found in entirely free from snow. The Umasi-la, 18,123 feet, was crossed by Dr. Thomson, in June, at which time it was, of course, covered with snow: but it was not clear in October 1846, when traversed by Vazir Gusaun, the minister of the Mandi Raja. In this part of the range, therefore, the snow limit does not exceed 18,000 feet, and is probably not more than 17,500 feet. On the Baltal Peak, 19,000 feet, close to the Seoji-la, the snow remains throughout the year. Dayamur, or Nanga Parbat (the bare mountain) is, as its name implies, free from snow; but this is owing entirely to its precipitousness, which prevents the snow from finding any resting-place. Snow, however, does lie in the hollow between the peaks.

The following are the different heights of the snow limit on the western Himalaya.

Snow Limit	Height	Authority
1. On the Kumaun Range	18,500	Lieut. R. Strachey.
2. Pyramidal Pk. of Porgyal	20,106	A. and J. Gerard.
3. Manerang Range	18,000	A. Gerard.
4. Parang Range	19,000	A. Cunningham.
5. Bara Lacha to Umasi	17,500	Ditto.
Mean height 18,021 feet.		

This height agrees so closely with the elevation deduced by Lieut. R. Strachey, that we may conclude, with some confidence, that the snow-line, on the southern face of the western Himalaya, is between 18,500 feet and 19,000 feet. On the northern exposure, the snow limit is somewhat higher. The Gerards, as we have seen, found the northern face of Porgyal bare, to a height of 20,400 feet. In September 1847, I observed very little snow on the northern faces of the Parang Peaks, about 19,500 feet, while in September 1846, the crest of this range, as I saw it from the banks of the Tshomoriri lake, was sheeted in snow. To the westward, as the ridge diminishes in height, with the general fall of the country, the snow-line falls somewhat lower, and in the neighbourhood of the Bara-Lacha Pass is not more than 18,000 feet. The mean of those observations is 19,133 feet, or in round numbers, upwards of 19,000 feet.

The mass of the western Himalaya, from the Sutluj to the Indus, is limestone. The ridges of Kyobrang, Parang, and Umasi-La, are all limestone, while the sides are chiefly overlaid with clay-slate. At Scoji La, the formation is mica-slate, but the mass of the northern mountains of Kashmir, and the peaks of the magnificent Dayamur, are all of limestone.

VI.—5th THE MID-HIMALAYA, OR PIR-PANJAL RANGE

This chain consists of four distinct masses of mountain, which may be styled the Bisahar, the Lahul, the Pir-Panjal, and the Swat ranges. The Bisahar range is an offshoot of the western Himalaya, extending for about sixty miles, from the lofty cluster of Jamnotri peaks to the Sutluj, below Shatul. It is continued to the north of the Sutluj by the Lahul range, which stretches to the north-west for 160 miles, to the great southward sweep of the Chenab, in Kashtwar. Beyond this again, it is continued in the same direction by the well-known Pir-Panjal, to the great southward sweep of the Jehlam, at Mozafarabad, and across the Jehlam to the Indus, at Derband. To the west of the Indus it terminates in the Swat mountains, which extend for about seventy miles to the Junction of the

Swat and Panjkora Rivers. This portion of the chain, though not remarkable for its height, is worthy of most particular examination, for the sake of identifying the celebrated Aornos, which was beyond all doubt situated in this range, and which I believe to have been the well-known mountains of Mahaban.

The whole length of the Mid-Himalaya or Pir-Panjal range, from the Jamnotri peaks to the Swat river, is about 470 miles. Between the Jumna and the Indus the direction is from south-east to north-west, as in the other ranges; but beyond the Indus the Swat mountains run almost due east and west.

The general elevation of this range can be determined with tolerable accuracy from the ascertained heights of a considerable number of points. The following tables show the heights of the principal peaks and passes in the different portions of the range.

BISAHAR RANGE-PEAKS

Peaks	Feet	Authority
1. Jamnotri, Great E.	20,916	Trigonometrical Map.
2. Ditto. Black E.	21,155	Ditto.
3. Ditto. Lower E	20,122	Ditto.
4. H. left	20,501	Ditto.
5. H. right	20,668	Ditto.
6. H. middle	20,668	Ditto.
7. The Cone	21,178	Ditto.
8. a No. 39	19,481	Ditto.
9. L	19,512	Ditto.
10. The Needle	19,044	Ditto.

Contd....

Peaks	Height	Authority
11. J	17,425	Ditto.
12. l	17,331	Ditto.
13. h	17,337	Ditto.
14. g Shatul Peak	17,035	Ditto.
15. d or Pyramidal	17,174	Ditto.
16. b	16,982	Ditto.
17. a	17,044	Ditto.
Mean height 19,033 feet.		

BISAHAR RANGE-PASSES

Passes	Feet	Authority
1. Nalgun Pass	14,891	A. Gerard.
2. Rupin	15,460	Ditto.
3. Nibrang	16,035	Ditto.
4. Burang or Buranda	15,179	Ditto.
5. Yusu	15,877	Ditto.
6. Shatul	15,556	Ditto.
Mean height 15,499 feet.		

By taking the mean heights of the peaks and passes, or greatest elevations and greatest depressions, we obtain the average height of the Bisahar range at 17,250 feet.

LAHUL RANGE-PEAKS

Peaks	Feet	Authority
1. Western F.	18,798	Trigonometrical Map.

Contd....

Peaks	Feet	Authority
2. Kotgarh Peak	17,353	Ditto.
3. No. 9 Black	16,203	Ditto.
4. k Peak	17,730	A. Cunningham
5. j Obelisk Peak	18,062	
6. f	19,310	
7. e	19,366	
8. d	19,922	
9. c	19,948	
10. b	20,064	
11. a	21,786	
12. Kali Debi Peaks	18,500	

Mean height 18,920 feet.

LAHUL RANGE-PASSES

Passes	Feet	Authority
1. Rotang Pass	13,000	Moorcroft, Dr. Gerard, A. C.
2. Kali Debi Pass	16,700	A. Cunningham.
3. Saj Pass	15,500	Dr. Thomson.

Mean height 15,066 feet.

The mean height of the Lahul range is therefore close upon 17,000 feet, and that of the united Bisahar and Lahul ranges upwards of 17,000 feet.

PIR-PANJAL RANGE

Of the Pir-Panjal itself we know much less than of the other portions of the Mid-Himalaya. The height of the loftiest peak was ascertained by Jacquemont to be 15,000 feet, and that of the lowest pass 9,690 feet. The mean of these two gives 12,345 feet for the average heights of the crest, which is certainly not too much, as the heights of two of the most frequented passes, approach 12,000 feet. The Pir-Panjal Pass is 11,970 feet, and the Mirbal Pass is 11,400 feet; and the mean height of the three measured passes is 11,020 feet. The following are the heights of different points in the Pir-Panjal.

Points	Feet	Authority
1. Highest Peak	15,000	Jacquemont.
2. Tata Kuti	14,000	A. Cunningham.
3. Dydyum	13,000	Vigne.
4. Kol-Narwah	12,500	Ditto.
Mean height	13,625 feet.	

The mean of the mean heights of the peaks and passes is 12,322 feet, which agrees with the mean before deduced from the greatest elevation and greatest depression.

Of the height of the Swat range I cannot speak with any certainly. The peak of Mahaban, as seen from the Yusufzai plain, at different distances between twenty-five and thirty miles, I estimated at 6,000 feet, or rather more, and the highest point in the range is probably not more than 7,000 feet.

On the Pir-Panjal and Swat ranges, the snow entirely disappears; but it remains throughout the year on the lofty ranges of Bisahar and Lahul. Of the glacial lines of the Bisahar ranges, we know but little, although the Gerards made a special excursion to most of the passes in this range for the purpose of ascertaining the snow-limit. The following passages, however, bear upon the subject and corroborate each other.

In describing the Buranda Pass (15,179 feet), which they visited in October, 1818, the two brothers, Dr. John Gerard and Captain Alexander Gerard, state that "the eastern wall rises with a considerable inclination for 500 or 600 feet; thence starting backwards, it terminates in a crown of snow, perhaps 1,500 or 2,000 feet higher." * * * "Its western side rises to a towering summit deeply clad in show, and corresponds with the opposite or eastern one, being about 2,000 feet in height." From these statements, we learn that both flanks of the pass were certainly bare of snow to 15,179+600 = 15,779 feet, and most probably much higher; for the eastern peak is said to terminate in a "crown of snow," and the western peak in a "summit deeply clad with snow." Now, as the height of the peaks on both sides is stated at 17,000 feet or somewhat less, we may fairly estimate the snow-line on the southern faces of the Bisahar range at about 16,000 feet.

Another passage leads to a similar conclusion: "Tufts of moss and grass with a light soil are seen all the way to the top (to the Buranda Pass), and even rise on each side to 200 and 300 feet, while higher up on the rugged cliffs that are doomed to sustain perpetual snow, animated nature finds a habitation." The snow-limit by this account was therefore certainly as high as 15,179 + 300 = 15,479 feet, which was the boundary of vegetable life, and was no doubt somewhat higher.

Again, some days later, on the Rupin Pass, 15,460 feet, at the head of the Pabar River, Alexander Gerard describes the strata of the range to the south of the Pabar as vertical, and that above the summit of this "mural portion," which "preserves an elevation of between 15,000 and 16,000 feet, to near Jangleg," the "rocks slant towards the summit, and upon the slope lie banks of congealed snow and ice, having a perpendicular brow of packed appearance, so much resembling blocks of marble and quartz, that I doubted for some time of their reality." This account is more explicit than any other that I have seen in Alexander Gerard's travels. From the Rupin Pass to near Jangleg, a distance of about eight miles, banks of snow lay upon the slope of the ridge, while the summit was entirely covered with packed snow. This agrees with the other statements that no exposed snow was seen below 15,500 feet; that above that line it was observed in banks or patches; and that everywhere at 17,000 feet the snow was lying undisturbed masses.

The Rupin Pass, 15,460 feet, was crossed by Captain Herbert and Captain Patrick Gerard, on the 30th September, 1819. In his map, Herbert writes along the upper course of the Rupin river, "all snow in September;" but Patrick Gerard describes the snow which they found on their way to the Rupin Pass in detail. "Distance from encamping-ground to large snow-bed 2¼ miles, where crossed a dangerous chasm. Steep ascent through patches of snow (half a mile), fresh and melting fast. A quarter of a mile farther on, *no snow*. To pass over snow, *soft*, knee-deep, thigh-deep, and neck-deep, 3½ miles across eternal snow." The soft knee-deep and neck-deep snow was of course freshly fallen. We have thus another independent and distinct proof that the Rupin Pass (15,460 feet) was clear of old snow on the last day of September.

These different observations of the Gerards on the Bisahar range may be taken as sufficient evidence to prove that there is no perpetual snow below 15,500 feet, and that the actual snow-limit is somewhere about 16,000 feet.

On the 17th September, 1849, I took from Simla the bearings and altitudes of several peaks and snow-lines in the Lahul range with a very good theodolite, reading to half minutes. To test the performance of the instrument, I first took the altitude of the Shali Peak, which gave an elevation of 9,629 feet above the sea, or six feet in excess of that determined by the trigonometrical survey. I next turned it upon the Tural Peak, which is the highest in the Dhaola Dhar or Kangra range, with a result equally satisfactory; the deduced altitude being 16,167 feet, or ten feet less than the mean altitude obtained from my former observations at Kangra and Nurpur.

Lastly, I took the altitude of the Kotgarh peak beyond the sutluj, to the north of Rampur. The altitude obtained was 17,353 feet, or eight-one feet less than Captain Herbert's elevation by trigonometrical survey. These altitudes do not of course pretend to any very great accuracy, but they may be depended upon as near approximations to the truth. Their errors will arise chiefly from the difficulty of obtained the correct distance of points that have not yet been laid down by a regular trigonometrical survey. The following table gives the heights of the snow-lines on the Lahul range as observed from Simla.

	Height of Pk.	Lower Edge of Snow	Mean.
1. On c	19,948	17,650	
2. On e	19,366	16,837	17,297
3. On f	19,310	17,399	
4. On g, Kotgrah Peak	17,434	15,983	
5. On j, Obelisk Peak	18,062	16,179	16,034
6. On k,	17,730	15,940	
	Mean height		16,665

The difference between the heights of the snow-line is simply accounted for by the difference of position in the observed points. The first three are situated in the Kullu range, and are fully exposed to the action of the south-west monsoon, which blows direct up the valleys of the Parbati, Gomati, and Sainj rivers. The other points are situated at the intersection of the lofty transverse chain which forms the watershed between the valley of the Byas and Sutluj rivers, and which runs in the same direction as the monsoon. In its passage along the ridge, the heat of the blast is gradually abstracted, until when it reaches the snow it is reduced to the temperature of the surrounding atmosphere.

We have thus four distinct and independent observations for the height of the southern snow-line in different parts of the Mid-Himalayan range.

	Feet	Authority
1. In Kumaun	16,000	Lieut. R. Strachey.
2. In S. Bisahar	16,000	The Gerards.
3. In N. Bisahar	16,034	A. Cunningham.
4. In E. Kullu	17,297	Ditto.
Mean height	16,333 feet.	

On the same range, but farther north, I found the Kali Debi Pass, 16,700 feet, covered with snow in July, and I was assured that the snow never disappeared from the crest of the Pass. On the whole, therefore, the mass of observations agree in fixing the snow-limit on the southern exposure of this range, at 16,000 feet and upwards.

On, the northern exposure, the snow-line is probably about 17,000 feet. On crossing the Rotang Pass, in the end of August, 1846, I observed that the snow on the northern face of the Lahul range did not generally descend below 17,000 feet, although on particular peaks it was lying in masses as low as 16,500 feet. On the Bisahar range, as we have already seen from the observations of the Gerards, the snow remains throughout the year; and as the mean height of the peaks which came under their observation, does not exceed 17,200 feet, it is certain that the northern snow-line cannot be higher than 17,000 feet. From the correspondence of these observations with my own, we may conclude that the northern snow-line of the Bisahar and Lahul ranges is somewhat under 17,000 feet.

According to Herbert, the great mass of the Bisahar range is gneiss. The same rock occurs is the Lahul range, on both flanks of the Rotang Pass: but beyond this it is succeeded by limestone, which forms the crest of the Kali Debi ridge, flanked by silicious schist on the north and by trap on the south. Beyond this, at the Saj Pass, Dr. Thomson found mica and clay slates; and limestone at the Banahal Pass, on the Pir-Panjal. But the mass of the Pir-Panjal, according to Vigne, is basaltic.

VII.—6th. THE DHAOLA DHAR OR OUTER HIMALAYA

The outer, or Sub-Himalaya, stretches from the bend of the Byas, at Mandi, to the well-known peak of Gandgarh, on the Indus. In attains its greatest height between the Byas and Ravi, in the Precipitous range of hills called the *Dhaola Dhar*, or White Mountain, to the north of Kangra. The general direction is from south-east to north-west, as in the other ranges, and the whole length is nearly 300 miles. The Sub-Himalaya is pierced by the Ravi, the Chenab, the Punach, and the Jehlam rivers, which divide it into several distinct ridges.

The most easterly of these separate ridges is the Dhaola Dhar, which forms the natural boundary between Kullu and Mandi, and between Chamba and Kangra. It is about eighty miles in length, and is of sufficient height to be covered with snow for about eight months of the year. I have observed this range for four sucessive years, and I can state positively that the snow entirely disappears from it every year, although the crest of the ridge has an average height of 15,000 feet. In the end of November, 1846, I marched from Kangra to Nurpur, and observed these mountains daily, and they were then entirely bare of snow. On the night of the 30th November, snow fell in considerable quantities, and did not disappear until the end of the following rains. In september and October, 1848, when I was at Simla, I observed this range carefully with a telescope, and could not discover a speak of snow on any part of it. Again, on the 16th and 17th of September, 1849, before leaving simla, and when not a patch of snow was visible with a telescope sufficiently powerful for observing the occultation of Jupiter's satellites, I took the bearing and altitudes of several peaks and passes, for the purpose of verifying the measurements which I have formerly made from Kangra and Nurpur. The following table gives the results of all these measurements.

		Nurpur	Kangra	Simla	Mean Height
A	Balen Peak	13,783ft.	—	14,138	13,960
B	Cleft Peak	14,981	—	—	14,981
C	Andrar Peak	15,612	—	—	15,642
D	Tural Pass	—	—	14,808	14,808
E	Tural Peak	·16,145	16,210	16,167	16,174
F	Thalan Peak	—	15,220	—	15,220
G	Sangar Peak	—	14,529	—	14,529
H	Satmaru Peak	—	13,575	—	13,575
K	Peak	—	14,240	14,701	14,470
L	Peak	—	15,109	14,244	14,676
M	Surai Peak	—	15,644	15,207	15,425
N	Peak	—	—	15,975	15,975
P	Thamsar Peak	—	—	15,826	15,826
	Mean height of the range		15,020.		

The discrepancies which appear in these results are mostly attributable to the difficulty which I experienced in identifying the peaks from the different stations. I had taken the precaution of making outline sketches of the crest, as seen both from Nurpur and from Kangra; but from simla, at a mean distance of eighty-five miles, and at a much greater elevation, the ridge presented such a different appearance that I could not satisfy myself as to the identity of more than two or three points. The Tural peak, which is the highest in the range, was of coursé, readily recognised, as well as the Tural Pass to the westward. Two other peaks, K and M, agreed tolerably well with the outlines, and with the bearings on the map: but the others were all doubtful. One, L, which I thought I had recognized, was most probably not the same peak, but I have retained it in the table because its height, as determined from simla (although it is so much below the other), does not decrease the average elevation of the range by more than thirty-four fact. By striking out this one observation, the average height will be 15,054 feet.

The elevation of this range is of considerable importance is determining the long-upsettled question of the snow-line, which, on the joint authority of the great Humboldt and the learned Colebrook, had been fixed at 13,000 feet between 30½ and 32^0 of latitude. Lieut. Richard Strachey, of the Engineers, was the first to correct this error, and to determine by observation that "the height of the snow-line on the more prominent points of the southern end of the belt, may be fairly reckoned at 16,000 feet, at the very least." This conclusion is fully borne out by my own observations, one half of which were made before the publication of Lieut. Strachey's paper. The ascertained height of the Dhaola Dhar, which rises abruptly from the low plains of Kangra, 3,000 feet, to a mean elevation of 15,000 feet, and of 16,000 feet in its loftiest peaks, proves most clearly that the snow-line, in the southern Himalaya, cannot be under 16,000 feet.

The geological structure of this range is almost unknown. In 1839, when I descended the valley of the Ravi, along the northern spurs of the Dhaola Dhar, I noted that the whole of the formations, at from 3,000 to 8,000 feet, were of clay and mica slates,and mostly of a very fine description, well adapted for roofing. The crest of the ridge is, however, most probably granite and gneiss, both of which I found on crossing the Chuari Pass to the south of Chamba. Between Chamba and Chuari, the gneiss was overlaid by chlorite and mica slates.

On the south of the range, the same fine roofing-slates (both mica and clay) and found to the north of Kangra, and to the north of Mandi. Both on the north and south of the range, the beds of some of the small streams are washed for iron-sand, which, after washing, yields as much as 90 per cent of pure metal. The same iron ore is worked at Kuman, near Mandi, where it occurs in thin black, sparkling ribands, in a soft grey sandstone. The sandstone is pounded with a hard round boulder, and after washing yields about the same quantity of metal as the other.

The second portion of the Sub-Himalayan range extends from the Ravi to the Chenab, a distance of fifty-five miles, and forms the natural boundary between Chamba and Bhadrwar, on the north, and the small districts of Chaneni, Bandralta, and Balawar, on the south. Between Bhadrwar and Chamba, the passes of Bhadr Dhar and Chatr Dhar are upwards of 10,000 feet in height, and the ridge may therefore have an elevation of 12,000 feet, or even more. To the south of Chaneni it breaks into remarkable triple-peaked mountain, which is held sacred by the Hindus, under the name of Tre-Kuta Devi (the three-peaked or trident goddess).

The central portion of the Sub-Himalaya is the well-known Ratan Panjal, which is crossed by the Bhimbar road to Kashmir. The pass of Ratan Pir, from which the mountain (*Panjal*) derives its name, has as elevation of 7,700 feet, and the highest peaks rise to about 11,000 feet. It is clothed to the very summit with magnificent trees, and its glens are not surpassed in beauty by anything that I have seen in the Himalaya, always excepting the lovely valley of the Byas. The length of the ridge is eighty miles, from the neighbourhood of Chaneni to the southern bend of the Punach river.

The fourth portion of the Sub-Himalaya is altogether unknown. It extends from Koteli to Dhangali, the Ghakar capital on the Jehlam, a distance of twenty-five miles.

The fifth, and most westerly portion of the Sub-Himalaya, stretches from the Jehlam to the Indus, a distance of nearly seventy miles. It rises to an elevation of more than 7,000 feet, and is well clothed with trees on its northern slopes.

In this general survey of the mountain-ranges that bound the Panjab to the north, I have purposely omitted all mention of the vegetable products that occur at different heights, as this subject naturally forms a part of Dr. Thomson's botanical labours. I have also omitted all notice of glaciers: not that I am unaware of their existence, but because I have seen so few of them that I have nothing to say of them which is worth recording. In 1839, I traversed a magnificent glacier which spanned the valley of the Cheli rivulet, below the Kali Debi Pass (16,700 feet). It was fissured in all directions, and down the main fissure, which was five feet wide, I saw the stream trickling at a depth of more than 300 feet. The surface was covered with hardened snow and imbedded stones; but the mass, as seen in the fissures, was clear transparent ice, filled with white specks. This glacier was about one mile long, and a quarter of a mile broad, with an average depth of 200 or 300 feet. In the same range, Dr. Thomson saw a similar glacier to the north of the Saj Pass, about thirty miles to the north-west of Kali Debi. In 1817, I crossed a second and larger glacier, to the north of the Parang Pass, 18,500 feet. In extended down the head of the Para river for 2¾ miles. At its termination is was fifty feet high, but a quarter of a mile upward it was fully 150 feet thick. Its upper end was covered with hardened snow, but the lower end was half-hidden in fragments of stone, which were mixed into the ice for several feet in depth. It was fissured in many places. A still larger glacier was observed by Dr. Thomson, on the northern side of the Umasi-La, on crossing into Zanskar. It extended from the top of the pass, 18,123 feet, down to a level of 14,500 feet, and cannot have been less than three or four miles in length. All these glaciers are mere still masses of ice, that are only dangerous when one has to cross them; but both above and-below Sassar there are several gigantic glaciers that span the noble valley of the Khundan river. At different times, the river has been completely dammed for several months by these mighty barriers, until the accumulated waters have burst their icy chains, and swept away all traces of man and his puny labours, for several hundred feet above the river.

The following table gives a summary statement of all the information collected regarding the great mountain-chains in the north of the Panjab.

No	Chains	Length in Miles	Elevation highest Peak	Mean Height of Chain	Snow-line South	Snow-line North
1	Karakoram, or Trans-Tibetan	450	24,000?	20,000	18,500	18,000
2	Kailas or Gangri, or Mid-Tibetan	550	20,700	29,000	19,000	18,500
3	Trans-Himalaya or Tshomoriri	350	21,000	19,300	20,000	19,500
4	Western Himalaya, or Bara Lacha	650	25,749	20,000	18,500	19,000
5	Mid-Himalaya, or Pir-Panjal	470	21,786	17,000	16,000	17,000
6	Outer Himalaya, Dhaola Dhar	300	16,174	15,020	the snow disappears annually	

(From *Ladak—Physical, Statistical and Historical, 1853)*

13

Village Life

By
Ernest F. Neve

The villages of Kashmir are full of human interest as we study the people in their natural environment.

The chief village population is found all round the valley on the higher ground which shelves up to the mountains, on the slopes below the foot-hills, the deltas of the tributary valleys and the sides of the karewahs. Here enormous areas of terraced rice-fields are to be found, stretching from the alluvial plain up to the base of the mountains. And as we go a little higher we find whole slopes covered with maize. The flat tops of the karewahs are used especially for wheat, barley, mustard and linseed, early crops which come to maturity before the scorching heat of summer parches the soil.

The life of Kashmir depends upon its agriculturists. The population of the Kashmir Province is 1,295,203 and of these probably more than a million are engaged in agriculture. In olden days the interests of the villagers were largely subordinated to those of the inhabitants of the city of Srinagar, many of whom were influential and all of whom were more immediately under the eye of the rulers.

Rice for the city was taken from the villagers at low rates. They were liable to frequent calls for forced labour. Every year the levy of coolies for Gilgit placed in the hands of the Tehsildars (the district magistrates) great powers of oppression. And from the chief of the local administration down to the humblest peon of the Tehsil this was an unfailing source of income. Meanwhile, the poor and friendless, or those who had incurred the wrath of the authorities, were seized and sent off on the hated task of carrying loads a thirteen days' journey, over rough mountain tracks to Gilgit. Their condition was indeed little better than that of slaves.

"In May 1888 I was on cholera duty in Islamabad. Just as the epidemic was reaching its height, and hundreds were dying every day in all the districts around, a levy of 5000 or more coolies was called for. The villagers were almost distracted with fear. Who would do all the agricultural work? What would happen, during their long absence, to their wives and children? To what perils of pestilence and inclemency of weather would they themselves the exposed in the crowded bivouacs and snowy passes of the deadly Gilgit district? I was present at a sort of farewell service on a maidan outside Islamabad, when nearly 1000 men were starting. And when they took leave of the friends who had accompanied them so far, loud was the sobbing of some, fervied the demeanour of all as, led by the mullah, they intoned their prayers and chanted some of their special Ramzan penitential psalms. Braver men might well have been agitated at such a time. It is certain that cholera clung to the camp, and that unburied corpses of hundreds of these poor 'begaris' marked the whole line of march from Srinagar to Bunji."

In the year 1882 the State tried the remarkable experiment of auctioning the villages for revenue purposes. The purchasers in many cases did amounts which were absurdly greater than the value of the village revenue, and after wringing all they could out of the unhappy villagers they absconded without paying the State a single rupee. This was bad enough. But to aggravate it the State actually professed to regard the sum offered at the auction as the real value of the village tax, and year by year put pressure upon the unfortunate cultivators with a view to realizing this fictitious revenue!

The great land settlement, initiated by Sir Andrew Wingate in 1887, and carried through by Sir Walter Lawrence from 1889-1895, changed all this, and from that time the condition of the villagers has been one of increasing prosperity. Two among many evidences of this are the large areas of new land being annually brought under cultivation, and the numerous shops, which are springing up in the villages, stocked with cotton piece goods and other luxuries or necessities of civilization.

The abolition of the old method of a special low rate for rice, fixed by Government, was, however, effected too abruptly. It had been going on for generations, and the life of the poorer inhabitants of Srinagar was largely dependent upon cheap food thus obtained. When the market was thrown open in 1902, the price of rice rushed up to more than fourfold, and thousands in the city were threatened by starvation. The Government was compelled to readjust the situation and dor a time to make grants of cheaper grain to those who were really poor.

Kashmiri villages are conspicuous in the landscape. There is usually a group of chenar trees, with light grey trunks, mottled with pale yellow, and massive curved limbs, with dense foliage forming dark green masses in summer and brilliant splashes of light red in the late autumn. Close by are two or three lofty poplars and lines of young saplings, bordering orchards of pear, apple and apricot, or market gardens enclosed by wattle fences. Mounds covered with large purple and white irises, brilliant and fragrant in the sunshine, mark the sites of the old village graveyards, and the hamlet itself shows as a collection of large high-pitched, straw-thatched gables, peeping out from among the mulberry trees.

These homesteads embowered in trees are surrounded by thousands of acres of arable land, terraced squares and crescents of rice-field, irrigated from small channels.

Rice ripens up to an altitude of about 7000 feet. It is the staple crop of Kashmir. There are at least sixty different varieties with distinct names; but there are two broad division viz., white and read. The former is considered greatly superior.

The successful cultivation of rice entails enormous labour. First of all the fields have to be constructed in terraces so as to allow of effective irrigation. Channels have to be dug for the distribution of the water. It is essential, when the rice has been sown or planted out from the nurseries, that the soil shall never again get dry. The weeding alone is a tremendous task. Rows of peasants may be seen standing in mud and water, bent down, scooping out all the adventitious plants and grasses, and plastering mud round the stalks of the young rice plants. This goes on day after day under a hot sun, and the fields have to be carefully and completely weeded no less than four times a year. Where, however, the rice plants have been transferred from nurseries, instead of being sown broadcast, twice is sufficient. This special weeding is called khushaba.

The Kashmiri is an absolute expert in rice cultivation, and unless early frost steps in, continuous rain at harvest-time, or one of the disastrous inundations to which Kashmir is so liable, there is usually a splendid harvest.

Throughout the valley there is very extensive irrigation. The water can be taken off at great heights from the tributary valleys, and there are also a large number of springs. The distribution is very wide and is said to be conducted on a system introduced by the Moghuls.

In and around Srinagar and the larger towns and villages lift irrigation is also carried on largely by means of a long pole acting as a lever and working on a pivot upon a cross-piece resting on two uprights, or on the forked branches of a tree. The short end of the pole carries a large stone as a counterpoise, and on to the long end like the line of a fishing-rod hangs a thick rope with an earthenware bucket attached. This is rapidly lowered into the river or well by pulling on the rope and dragging down the end of the pole. When this is released the weight of the stone raises the bucket which, as it reaches the level of the ground, is emptied into a long boat-shaped tray of wood which acts like a funnel and conducts the water in the required direction. This form of irrigation is especially useful for market gardens. All the land really belongs to the State. But hereditary rights of occupancy have been granted to cultivators who pay their taxes regularly. They are not, however, allowed under any circumstances to sell or mortgage their land. This rule saves them from the clutches of the Hindu banias and middlemen. And if it is necessary for a villager to raise money, he can usually do it in advance on his standing crops.

A certain number of high officers and privileged persons, such as the Mian Rajputs, the clan of H.H. the Maharajah, hold estates in Kashmir, which are revenue free and not under the control of the Forest Department. These are called Jagirs.

The land revenue actually collected in Kashmir in 1890 was twelve and a half lakhs of rupees (£83,715). This is about what it was in the time of the Emperor Akhbar.

Of recent years, however, although the taxation has been reduced from fifty to thirty per cent of the total crops of the cultivators, the land revenue has greatly increased, and it is now more than half as much again as it was in 1890.

Entering the village, we usually find a broad track with grassy borders bounded by a rippling stream. Grateful shade is cast by large walnut trees, the deeply fissured and gnarled trunks of which rise from spreading roots which encroach on the path. Some of these trees have a girth of 18 feet and more. The houses are mostly two storied, and they have a framework of wood which is filled in with sundried or, in the better houses, with red kiln-backed bricks. Under the thatched roofs in an airy space with stores of grass and firewood, and sometimes silkworms. The eggs of the latter are imported from France and to a less extend from Italy, and about 30,000 ounces are distributed annually to villagers, who place them in the roofs or rooms of their houses and hatch them. The young are then fed on the leaves of the mulberry trees which are so common. The cocoons when ready are purchased by the silk factory. In this way as much as 32,200,000 lbs. may be brought in by the villagers in one year, for which the Department of Sericulture pays over Rs. 600,000 about (£40,000). This goes to about thirty-five thousand villagers, giving them on an average nearly Rs. II/each, which makes it quite worth their while, as this is equivalent to at least two months' wages for an ordinary Kashmiri cultivator.

Most of the houses have a front verandah to the upper story in which the people live for the greater part of the year, and at one end of which is a little kitchen with clay fireplace. The inner rooms, chiefly used in winter, are dark and almost unventilated. The ground floor is often set apart entirely for cattle and sheep. If this arrangement secures warmth for the dwellers above, it is at some sacrifice of sweetness. Every village has several granaries, small square wooden buildings, the floor of which is raised a few feet above the ground. And not far away is sure to be a village shrine (Astan) often on an eminence and usually with fine old trees in the vicinity. The Mosque is probably near by, and in its roof may be seen the wooden bier in which the dead are carried to the graveyard to be interred without a coffin. At daybreak and at sunset the voice of the muezzin sounds out, calling the faithful to prayer, and soon a small congregation gathers and the Imam conducts the Namaz. In some mosques the congregation chant their prayers almost in Gregorian style.

Often the sides of the houses are festooned with bright rows of red chillies or split turnips, golden maize cobs and dried apples.

In the courtyard in front of a house we see two women busily engaged in pounding the unhusked rice in a large wooden mortar with pestles 5 feet long. First one straightens herself, lifts the pestle as high as she can, and then bending suddenly brings it down with a crash. Then the other woman facing her does the same. This is perhaps one of the commonest sights in the village. On a stretch of green, there is a row of upright sticks at intervals of 2 feet. These are for weaving purposes. One of the villagers may be seen walking up and down rapidly winding from a spindle a unread of cotton in and out of these stakes. In the verandah an old woman is seated with masses of snow-white cotton-wool in front of her, from which, with the aid of a curious old wheel, she is spinning excellent thread. A peep through the window of another house shows a rough loom in which woollen blankets are woven. This is one of the staple village industries. A common arrangement is for the local shopkeeper to advance money on the promise of repayment in blankets and garden produce.

According to the Kashmiris there are six seasons in the year, each of two months. "Wandh," with a somewhat similar sound, corresponds to our English winter, or at least with the time from 15th November till 15th January. During this period and on till the end of March, the first ploughing for wheat and barley is done. Then rice, maize and the other autumn crops are threshed; and when the snow falls towards the end of December the people weave woollen blankets, and attend to their sheep and cattle. "Sont" is the period from 15th March to 1st May. This is an extremely busy time. The fields have to be ploughed and manured for rice and maize. And then these are sown. In many villages the rice is sown in nurseries, and the seedlings are planted out when they are nearly a foot high. Broadcast sowing gives better crops but entails considerably more labour in weeding. The wheat and barley harvest begins in the valley at the end of May, and during the whole summer the harvest goes on at the various altitudes. Linseed is a little later than wheat. From July to September the peasants are busy in the fields weeding the rice, maize and cotton.

The last is a very pretty crop, with its large yellow flowers followed by snowy tufts. The real harvest of Kashmir comes on the September and October, called by the Kashmiris the season of "Hard." It is then that the rice and maize, millet, sesame, amaranth and other autumn crops are gathered in. And now the fruit trees are laden, and before long from all parts of the valley strings of ponies may be met, and lines of coolies carrying baskets of apples and pears and sacks of walnuts, most of which will find their way to Baramula and be exported from there by cart to the plains of India.

At harvest-time all round the valley, but especially near the fringe of the forest, the villagers are troubled by the depredations of bears. The fields of maize and the fruit on the trees are a great attraction. To guard their crops the people erect "machans"—little roofed platforms twelve to twenty feet above the ground. Here they sit and watch at night and blow trumpets, beat drums, old kerosene tins, or anything else which will make a noise. And at the same time they emit blood-curdling yells, or piercing whistles, all with the object of terrifying the nocturnal robbers. The combined effect of fifty or a hundred people thus engaged at night over a comparatively small area of cultivated land is somewhat suggestive of pandemonium.

Kashmir is particularly rich in fruit trees. Many of these are indigenous and found wild in the forests. The people are quite clever at grafting. The stock is cut off rather low, and into the end three or four scions are wedged and supported by clay surrounded by birch bark. Ring budding is also successfully practised. In addition to the ordinary fruit trees, currants, raspberries and gooseberries are found wild. Apricots are also common. The fruit has been all immensely improved by cultivation and the introduction of choice varieties.

The grapes are rather disappointing. In the valley, rapid night radiation in the autumn, and the heavy dew, together with the great sun heat in the day, appear to favour blight and other disease. At the mouth of the Sind valley there are some good vineyards producing delicious white and red dessert grapes.

On the east side of the Dal Lake there are about 400 acres of wine grapes, and at the distillery, under M. Peychaud's skilled supervision, wines of the Barsac and Medoc type are produced. The vintage varies much from year to year. It is said that the soil is deficient in iron and phosphates, and that the frequent difficulty in obtaining perfectly ripe grapes affects both the quality and keeping powers of the wine.

Hops grow well in Kashmir. In the summer the growth is very rapid. A market is found for them in the Murree and other breweries.

A large number of sheep are kept by peasants who live in the valley. These all have to be sent up to the hill pastures in the summer to escape the intense heat and get fresh grazing. They are entrusted to shepherds who bring them back again in the autumn and receive two per cent of the flock if it is intact. They are also paid in rice and are allowed all the butter made from the sheep's milk.

The cows, which are numerous in the villages, are small, and they usually appear to be half starved. They seldom give more than six pints of milk a day. A cow may be bought for about twenty rupees.

In the sides of some of the houses in the villages we see a circle with a hole in the centre into which bees are seen to be crowding. These are the Kashmir hives.

They are merely earthenware cylinders, about 2 feet long, and built into the wall. The outside end of the hive has a central hole about an inch across, or sometimes a series of small holes in a circle. The inner end has an earthenware lid fitted over it and sealed on with clay. No artificial feeding is done in the summer, but in winter the bees are supplied with food. No special measures are, however, taken to protect them from the cold, and the mortality is often very great. In many village's after a severe winter, when the temperature sometimes falls to zero Fahrenheit, more than three - quarters of the colonies will perish. Under favourable conditions strong colonies are formed. Early in May the swarms issue. One hive may give off as many as six, weighing from two to four pounds each. The villagers usually expect the swarms to settle and hive themselves in one of the numerous empty wall hives. The bees are not accustomed to English hives, and it is extremely difficult to retain them. In many cases it appears advisable to fit a strip of queen excluder zinc across the entrance to prevent the queen from leaving. Usually this can be safely removed after two or three weeks. But I have frequently lost swarms in spite of this precaution. One colony left the hive and deserted its brood two months after it had been introduced. This was, however, due to persistent attacks of bee-robbers. Where Kashmir bees are kept in wooden hives there seems to be an unusual amount of fighting and robbing. The local earthenware hives do not appear to attract outsiders. Hornets, however, are often seen attempting to get in. The wooden hives perhaps emit an odour from their joints, for they are pestered by hornets, worried by robbers and sometimes in the spring a swarm will descend upon as already occupied hive.

The Kashmiris understand something of the management of queens. They sometimes secure a restless queen by tying a fine thread to one of her legs and pinning her to the comb. Sometimes, too, they change queens, and they cut out queen cells quite cleverly.

Two harvests may be obtained, one in June and the other in October. The back of the hive is opened and smoke is blown in, and the combs are rapidly cut out. The bees are gentle, so comparatively few are killed. No proper care is usually taken of brood comb, and insufficient supplies are often left for the survivors. Sulphur is, however, not used.

The bees are wonderfully tame. I have often manipulated them without the use of any subduer. As in Europe, there appear to be two chief varieties—the yellow bee and a darker kind. In the yellow variety there is a fairly broad transverse stripe on the back, with four parallel pale yellow bands below.

The ventral surface of the abdomen is yellow, and the thorax is covered with light brown fur. The lowest stripe is a little broader at the middle, which makes the bee look as if it had a white tail. The wings when folded reach to the lower margin of this stripe.

Wild bees appear to be yellower and to have slightly longer bodies than the domesticated varieties. I have seen them as high as 12,000 feet above sea-level. The favourite altitude for wild colonies is between 5500 and 7000 feet. It is too hot for them in the valley in the summer; but all round the hills in the mountain villages they thrive. The forests are full of wild balsams and the slopes are covered with wild sage. So great is the attraction of the mountain and forest flowers that many swarms desert the valley in the spring but return to their village hives again in September.

Both hornets and ants are troublesome enemies. When hornets threaten the hive the bees come out and form compact groups, and as the enemy approaches they lower their heads and, with a peculiar quivering movement, turn their tails with the sting exposed towards the intruder, who usually veers off. Hornets, however, sometimes carry off one or even two bees at a time. Occasionally a bee with bold spirit takes decisive action. Perhaps, like Sir Nigel Loring, she regards the hornet as a "courteous and worthy person with whom some small bickering may be had." Or possibly, Marcus Curtius like, she seeks, by sacrificing herself, to save the whole community. I have seen a bee suddenly dash out from the armed circle of defenders and pierce a formidable hornet four times her own size, inflicting a fatal wound. But all are not so courageous, for one day I placed a dead hornet on the alighting-board when the sentry had gone in-for a moment. A casual bee coming out for an evening walk suddenly and unexpectedly caught sight of the orange-coloured monster, gave a most dramatic start, and then hastened back to her own quarters. Whether she spread the alarming news I know not, but almost at once a fierce and stalwart worker emerged and, single-handed, seized the unwelcome intruder and threw him off the platform. In their behaviour toward ants bees seem rather timid. Ignoring them unless they come quite near, they even then appear to chase them with some apprehension lest the ant should turn and seize them by the nose.

Large ants are the most formidable of all foes. They will sometimes raid a hive like a band of Masai warriors attacking a village. There is a large black variety half an inch long with powerful mandibles, with which they literally cut off the bees' heads. Should an invasion of these occur, the bees will leave the hive, but not before large numbers have been massacred. Fortunately the defence is easy, as it is only necessary to stand the legs of the hive in water.

No one in Kashmir has yet succeeded in getting bees to work properly in the upper sections of a standard frame hive.

It will be interesting to see whether the introduction of English or Italian queens will result in greater industry, or whether their progeny, to, will succumb to the somewhat enervating influence of the climate and the summer and autumn droughts.

As the autumn draws on in Kashmir the days remain bright and hot, but the cold at nights becomes increasingly intense. Early in September excellent snipe-shooting is to be obtained, and large numbers of duck begin to fly over the valley. On some of the lakes wild waterfowl are very abundant. In 1906 Lord Minto and the Viceregal party shot 1500 duck in one day on the Hukra Jheel. When shooting is going on, the duck rise from the lakes and marshes in clouds and wheel round in tens of thousands, some at a great height.

After the middle of October the leaves rapidly change their colour. Poplars and mulberries become lemon-yellow, chenars a pure light red, and apples and pears orange and crimson. At this season the willows are pollarded and their saplings and leaves stored for winter fodder for the flocks. In the hedges blackberries are abundant. In the evenings at this time of the year a blue mist hangs over the valley and round the foot of the mountains, which take on exceedingly rich orange-coloured tints as the sun sets.

In the winter snow usually falls in the third week of December. After that, sometimes for six weeks, the whole country is snow-bound, clouds settle down upon the mountains and there is no sunshine. The cold then becomes very great. Occasionally the Dal Lake is frozen sufficiently to bear. I have on two occasions skated from the distillery at the south end to beyond the Nassim Bagh, 3 miles to the north-west. It is not, however, very safe, as there are warm springs.

Every morning, during the winter, thousands of jackdaws leave the city and fly in dense clouds out into the country in search of food. About five o'clock in the evening they return. In fine weather they fly high. If, however, the weather is threatening, they skim just over the tops of the houses and trees. It is interesting to watch their flight. The whole army appears to be composed of divisions. As they advance, a cloud of scouts is thrown out in front. On reaching the outskirts of the city the front battalions settle on groups of trees in such numbers that the whole tree becomes black and the branches are weighed down. When the rear divisions arrive there is much wheeling and maneuvering and evidently different clans occupy distinct trees, for which sometimes active skirmishing is carried on. When, however, the last stragglers have arrived, the whole force rises in a dark cloud and makes its way to the city, where the night is spent roosting in trees and under the eaves of houses.

The valley of Kashmir is remarkably calm. With the exception of thunderstorms in the summer and occasional gales early in March, it is extremely rare to have a windy day. The rainfall varies much from year to year. It is usually between twenty-five and thirty-five inches. The heaviest rain is ordinarily towards the end of July, corresponding to the full development of the monsoon in North India, and it is then that there is great danger of floods.

One of the commonest of Kashmir birds in the village is the white-cheeked bulbul. These have a graceful feather crest curving forwards and nearly 2 inches long. They are quite domesticated and often come indoors, perching on tables and chairs or even on the edge of a tea-cup, the sugar at the bottom of which has special attractions for them. With a little trouble they can be taught to catch crumbs thrown in the air, and they will perch on the back of one's hand. Swallows are exceedingly common. They usually arrive in March and build their nests in April and May.

Small game is not nearly so common in Kashmir as might be expected. There are no hares nor wild rabbits in the valley. On the hills the chikor partridge is common. It belongs to the genus of rock or sand partridges, and is found usually just above the line of cultivation among the rocks. Coveys are often seen in the fields at harvest-time, and they are met with up to an altitude of 9000 feet. The monai pheasant is the most handsome of all Kashmir birds. The cock is magnificent, with rich peacock-blue plumage with golden-red sheen. These pheasants are not very common. They live chiefly at the upper margins of the forests.

The valley is infested with rats. In the summer they live in the fields and farmyards. In the winter they crowd into the houses and to immense mischief. They would be still more numerous were it not for the large number of half-wild cats which take up their abode in the roofs and basements of the houses and do valuable service. It is an interesting fact that when Kashmir was attacked by plague there was no evidence of any rat infection.

As we walk through the village we notice the little shop, the tawny-yellow or black dogs stealthily walking about, the flocks of ducks busy gobbling in the stream and the little bathing-houses close by.

Ploughing is done with small bullocks and the ploughs are small, for deep furrows are unnecessary. Rice cultivation is the great interest of most of the inhabitants of the valley. It speaks well for the fertility of Kashmir that although there is only one annual rice crop, in good year excellent rice may be bought at a halfpenny per pound.

It is in the villages that we see the real Kashmir life. The language, dress, complexion, manners and customs of the people are quite distinct from those of any other country. Probably few people have undergone less change in the march of the centuries than this nation, in its isolated valley, separated by gigantic mountain ranges from all the countries around and, until the last quarter of a century, connected with India only by a rough bridle track more than a hundred miles long.

(*1915*)

14

Leh

By
Marco Pallis

A belt of willows standing in rather dry ground marks the outskirts of the city. As we came to the houses, our baggage animals turned off the road abruptly. The ponies stepped over a wooden bar at the base of a gateway, and we followed, thinking it must be some short cut, and found ourselves all at once in the main bazaar, a broad and stately street, flanked by rows of immense pollarded poplars. The vista is closed by the prodigious castle of the Ladak kings, its lower stories of Egyptian severity, while the upper ones are pierced with larger windows leading out on to wooden balconies. The scale of the building is colossal, dwarfing the rest of the town; through most of it is unoccupied, it is in a fair state of preservation. It is built at the end of a rocky spur, at the foot of which nestles Leh.

Immediately below the castle is the mosque—for there is a large Mussulman community—built in the usual Ladak style of architecture. Later on, it became one of our regular pleasures to walk down to it at night and wait for the muezzin's call. The first time that we happened to be there, standing in the darkness of the unlighted street, we heard from the balcony of a house a tenor voice of rare sweetness singing a melancholy rhapsody. The man now and then paused in his song and then began to sing again. His mellow notes floated out into the surrounding stillness; he seemed to be expressing some deep joy that lay close to tears. In style his songs reminded me of those of Greece, so that I at first suspected Turkish influence, for many Turkish traders come down from the north to Leh; but on inquiry the house proved to belong to a Panjabi.

Eventually he ceased; spellbound we lingered in the hope of hearing him sing again. A bell changed somewhere above our heads, and then the *Azan*, or Call to Prayer, resounded in ringing tones through the night, making known that: "There is no God but God and Muhammad is the Prophet of God ! God is greatest !" It was the first time that we had listened to these words; we fell, for the moment, under the spell of the directness and simplicity of the Mussulman faith, which proclaimed, in terms that clove like a sword, the unity of the Principle of all Being and the dependence of all created beings upon It, its Prime Cause.

But this is anticipating: on that first day, as we rode into the bazaar in the noon sunlight, we could overhear the remarks of the people. "They must come from Lhasa." "I hear them speaking the dialect of Tsang." We passed through the crowd to the far side of the town, where we sought out a secluded lodging in a garden to which we had been directed: it belonged to a native Mussulman called Ghulam. We pitched our tents, whilst our host, who proved to be the kindest and most attentive imaginable, regaled us with bread, a long untasted luxury, and tea prepared in the Turkish way, with plenty of sugar forming a thick syrup, and scented with roses. Among teas it corresponds to our after-dinner coffee and is too sweet to be thirst-quenching.

In Leh one can buy three kinds of tea, Turkish, Tibetan and "Lepton"; the last-named is the denomination under which all brands intended to be brewed in the English manner are sold, whether they be the most expensive or really packets sent out by the late owner of the yacht *Shamrock.* We had been in our garden only a few moments when Khan Muhammad Din came to call and invited us to a tea-party at his office, where we were to meet the principal merchants of the town. There were two of these; one was an old Mussulman of seventy-five called Hadji Muhammad Siddiq, who traded with Lhasa and Gartok and knew the former city well, a humorous and hearty old man with a large family—the second one was also a Lhasa merchant, a Ladaki Buddhist, Nono Tonyod Sha, quiet and courtly; we used to see him almost every day and we owe much to his kindness. They both asked us to their houses at once, so the next day was occupied entirely with visits.

The interior of the better Ladaki house is usually extremely elegant, with spacious chambers bordering on a courtyard, windows with translucent paper in fretwork frames after the Chinese, fashion and attractive painted woodwork, on which floral and dragon motives are applied with an almost endless power of invention. The ceilings are of unsquared poplar logs laid across the main beams. The furniture does not differ in principle from that used by the peasants, except in its greater richness and finer workmanship. There are carpets, Yarkandi, Tibetan and best of all, Chinese, divans round the walls, and painted chests and cupboards; apart from these there is little else. In the old Hadji's house there were also Turkish pipes. He and his family wore the usual costume of Tibet except for the head-dress which, in their case, was a turban or red fez. We have sine heard the sad news of the Hadji's death: it is surprising, for he seemed in such good health. It is difficult to imagine Leh without his merry presence.

Nono Tonyod, the other merchant, possessed a magnificent house, but his taste appeared to have been affected by his journeys to Kashmir; in the midst of many beautiful things we saw much worthless junk. A cabinet contained, for instance, some lovely chased silver stands for teacups from Lhasa, side by side with cheap English earthenware adorned in the style favoured by third-rate landladies at the seaside. A painted tea-table, a perfect specimen, stood side by side with a packing-case stencilled with the name of Messrs. Brown & Co., Bombay. Appalling modern Yarkand carpets swore loudly against the soft texture, the warm browns and blues of the Tibetan products. It was a curious, untidy medley, an indication of the mental confusion that follows interference with the traditional sense. In fact Tonyod was a typical transition case. In theory he was still a faithful adherent of the old ways; whenever he pronounced judgment on something that fell within the scope of his knowledge, he was a faultless appraiser of quality. But in regard to novelties, his standard was chaotic and he could tolerate things that most of us would have been ashamed to possess, and allowed them to disfigure his house. The symptoms were those of aesthetic indigestion.

He showed us his treasures, not forgetting to serve delicious Tibetan tea and trays of dried kernels and sugar-candy. He had a prodigious collection of teapots, magnificent examples of the silversmith's art, also teacup-stands, one of which, made at Lhasa, was a real marvel. Later on we asked him if he would part with it—it is quite in order to offer to buy things seen in a private house—but he said we could only have if it he first sent it to Lhasa to be copied. He had also some fine jewellery of gold filigree set with choice turquoises. Strangely enough, the central jewel of a magnificent pendant was only a cheap piece of red glass that might have come out of a Christmas cracker; but though this was intrinsically unworthy of its setting, the effect was not inartistic.

Nono Tonyod proved a kind friend to us throughout our stay. He had all the polished manners of the Lhasa-bred man. One day he invited us to lunch and served a kind of spinach, with meat cakes which we, as vegetarians, could not take, and excellent *chapattis,* like huge muffins but of almost paper thinness. He started by apologizing that his cook had unfortunately spoiled the dinner. Not yet being accustomed to Tibetan etiquette, I answered naively that to my taste, far from having spoiled it, he had excelled in every dish, "No," he said, "it is not good to-day". We later discovered that it is good form to disparage the food that is set before a guest. This was always our host's custom when entraining us; eventually we realized the position and made suitably ceremonious replies. This custom has probably reached Tibet from China.

The merchant had manager called Ishe Gyaltsan, a young man of energetic appearance, much more like a Tibetan than his master, who was a typical Ladaki of mixed blood. The manager looked after the Tibetan part of their business, while Tonyod himself dealt with the Indian side. Ishe Gyaltsan usually wore yellow shirts which matched his face, so that we called him the "Yellow Man." Occasionally he wore vivid magenta, which suited him equally well-I envy those who have a complexion that enables them to wear so strong a colour. We were surprised that he should wear yellow, for he spent some months each year in Tibet and had, so he said, lived there without a break for fifteen years, and it is forbidden for any but members of the clerical Order to be clothed in that colour. "But I am of the clerical Order," he protested, "I was brought up as a novice at Tashilhunpo and I still can stay there whenever I like, though I have taken to trading." There are many similar cases in Tibet. He also wore his four-eared cap in a queer way, with three of flaps tucked in, out of sight, and only the left ear sticking up asymmetrically. It gave his face a peculiarly comic air: again we asked the reason for this and were told : "It is the privilege of anyone who has served tea before the two great Lamas. As a boy I served the Panchhen Lama and now I always wear it thus, for if I did not, people in the road might say to themselves 'What sort of a man is this?' -now they know."

He told a story with great animation, and his face and hands helped to act the part, so that one could picture the whole scene. His description of an unworthy treasurer making off with the monastery plate to sell it on the quiet was a screaming farce-one could see the teapots being stuffed under his robe and the man slipping out to meet the foreign art dealer to dispose of his ill-gotten wares. Yet though he was so amusing, we never saw even the flicker of a smile cross his face. He was a curious, self-sufficient character, extremely concrete in outlook and of untiring industry in his work, for which he had a passion that had little to do with the mere making of money. Rather did he treat trade as an adventure; he spent a large part of his life in solitary expeditions with only his own picked servants, all pure Tibetans, for company, going first to Gartok to the great fair which takes place there every autumn, and then east-ward to Shigatze, Gyantse and Lhasa, a three months' journey on horseback.

He was just then organizing a caravan of forty ponies with Yarkandi merchandise such as carpets, green jade cups and felt rugs, also Indian cotton, to take to Lhasa, whence he would return with the precious brick tea, grown in West China, which the Tibetans in the remotest places love to drink in preference to more easily obtainable Indian-grown varieties. Ceaseless tying up of bales continued all day long on Tonyod's veranda, while piles of saddles were ready stacked in the porch. The Yellow Man himself had not had his taste upset like that of his employer. He was quite clear in his mind about the excellence of his own country's customs and of the undesirability of exchanging them for ours. All his mind about the excellence of his own country's customs and of the undesirability of exchanging them for ours. All his private possessions were of the highest quality, from his sturdy horse splendidly caparisoned, with high peaked saddle and fine blue pile saddle-cloth, to his boots, riding-whip and other personal objects. He had a critical eye for quality of material and workmanship. His own servants were picked men from Shigatze, a more vigorous and lively type than the heavy, mild Ladakis. They were employed under a similar indenture to the one described in connexion with the boy T'hargya at Lachhen, that is to say, they earned pocket money, not wages, but were kept, fed, clothed and treated familiarly; if they married, their families were also adopted into the household.

They appeared entirely contented and devoted to their semi-feudal employer.

The Yellow Man had another amusing characteristic. Whenever he felt excited, he would repeat the last word of a phrase many times at great speed, for emphasis. He might be asked: "Do you think this is an excessive price?" "No, it is quite reasonable, not excessive at all, at all, at all, at all, at all . . ." Or he would say, "To sell the sacred books to foreign collectors is entirely unlawful, unlawful, unlawful, unlawful . . ."

He and I became fast friends; he seemed to make the overtures soon after we met. One day he explained himself, "You know, I loved you from the first moment, because it is plain to me that you really love and understand our Tibetan customs and know how to do things just as if you were one of us."

Another friend in Leh, of whose generous help we cannot speak too gratefully, was a Christian called Joseph Gergan who, however, in spite of his change of religion, had not attempted to become like a European, as is too often the case with converts. He was a man who truly deserved the name of Christian; for never have I come across anyone in whom the love of Christ and the imitation of His life were more manifest. There was no attempt to slur over the inconvenient portions of Christ's teaching; in him was seen the simplicity of a child, side by side with the wisdom of a cultivated, well-read mind. When very young he came into contact with missionaries and felt impelled to embrace the Christian faith. At that time his brother, in un-Buddhist fashion, had attempted to bully him. When Joseph reached the age of full discretion, he decided that so serious a step required to be taken with open eyes, so he proceeded to devote some years to a careful study of the other two Traditions possible for him, namely, the Mussulman and the Buddhist. After three years he decided against the first but it took him eight years fully to make up his mind about the second. His Christianity, as may well be imagined, had both justified itself and remained free from bitterness : for a man who so impartially tried to weigh up alternatives and to find out the good in them all, was not of the stuff that bigots are made of. We always spoke of him as "Gergan the Translator," borrowing the term from St. Marpa and the other eleventh-century importers of sacred books into Tibet, for Joseph too was a man who only tried to impart to others a doctrine which he had first practised himself. He had been occupied for years on the tremendous task of turning the Bible into colloquial Tibetan and had actually reached the end of St. John's Gospel.

In the summer, when caravans from India and Turkistan enter or leave Leh almost daily, the scene in the bazaar is most picturesque. Here can be seen tall, thin, hawk-nosed Kashmiris in their unbecoming Euro-Indian rags. Across the way saunter some stocky Baltis in thick grey-brown homespuns and close-fitting caps. Tall Turks, fair as Englishmen, but with narrow slits of eyes and rather unintelligent faces, stalk about the market, clad in white shirts, sheepskin caps and high Cossack boots. Some of them add a Bolshevist touch in their drab Russian semi-uniforms, probably exported from the factories of the Five Year Plan. Their women wear fine orange or rose embroidered dresses and are closely veiled, while their Ladaki sisters move about freely, for their position is high in society and stands in no need of protection. A few red-cloaked lamas are always to be seen and occasionally a true Tibetan, or an Afghan youth of great beauty, with white skin and long eylashes and oval face, an amorous prince from the brush of Persian Bihzad come back to life.

Huge yaks ruminate contentedly in the courts of the Turkoman caravanserais, over which, like a shower of wool, floats the clinging white down of the poplars. The average condition of the animals is quite good, but many ponies or mules employed on long-distance traffic show the usual sore-marks from the hard pack-saddles, suffered during the protracted journey across the Karakoram. I have heard that many animals fall from fatigue and are abandoned on the passes there, where wolves put an end to their sufferings. the Turks are extremely callous and frequently inflict cruelties out of sheer stupidity. I cannot say that I have witnessed any cruelty in Leh itself, even from Turks, or heard an animal abused; so I am prepared to believe that insensitiveness, rather than actively sadistic instincts, is responsible for the evil.

The Ladakis, on the whole, treat their animals well and in their attitude do not differ from other Tibetans. The only form of ill-usage that is common among them is the chaining of watchdogs. Most large house, and even monasteries, have one or more mastiffs chained up in kennels by the entrance, and never let loose, so that their friendliness becomes perverted to the point of extreme ferocity. When a stranger approaches, they bark savagely and strain with all their might at their chains in a mad impulse to fling themselves at his throat. Although all Tibetans are born dog-lovers, they have come to treat the presence of a chained dog as a piece of household furniture and are no longer conscious of the cruelty involved. In a peaceful country like Ladak, this practice is absurd as well as unkind. In parts of Tibet there might be an excuse on the score of defence against robbers, but even that is inadequate when one remembers that the dog, if well trained, could do its work just as well unchained. We tried several times to draw people's attention to this evil, but without much effect.

An over-simplified interpretation of the injunction to avoid inflicting injury upon sentient creatures sometimes leads to cruelty, as when an injured or incurably sick animal is allowed to suffer, because no one wishes to shoulder the responsibility of putting it out of its pain. We were told that sometimes when a goat has to be abandoned in the mountains the herdsman will cut off a horn to bring as evidence to the owner, but is quite unwilling to take the life of the animal first. At Gangtok, in Sikkim, we had been much distressed by the sight of scores of pariah dogs, mangy and underfed, that infested the bazaar. People meant to be kind to them and fed them with scraps, but to put them out of their misery would, to the majority, have seemed unthinkable.

We had occasion to discuss the ethics of killing in order to spare suffering, with our servant, Norbu, who was an intelligent and kindly man and must be regarded as typical of his class. One day we came across a small black kitten in the bazaar, which had an injured paw as if someone, possibly some mischievous boy, had given it a blow with a stone. The poor little thing took refuge in a shop, running on three legs, so we inquired who was the owner and the shopkeeper said, "No one owns it. If you want it, keep it by all means." We carried it to our tent in the garden and there Dr. Roaf examined it. He thought that the limb was not fractured, but it had received severe injuries which might or might not be curable. It was decided to try to treat it, putting the paw in plaster of Paris; but we also said that if the doctor later pronounced it a hopeless case we would kill it painlessly. "That would be a great sin," said Norbu, "I would never do that." He much approved of the efforts to nurse it, but had they failed, he would certainly have left the animal to its fate, while continuing to feed it. We endeavoured to explain to him our point of view, saying that after all the Buddha enjoined the non-infliction of suffering generally, not only with reference to killing; but we failed to convince Norbu. One must remember that this common attitude of Hindus and Buddhists towards compassionate killing, derives from the same motive that debars Europeans from relieving human suffering in extreme cases by inflicting death. The story of the kitten has a happy ending, for the injured paw was duly put in plaster, to the great interest of our landlord's son, a delightful boy called Aziz, who promised to give the kitten a good home. It was solemnly adopted and given the name of Dolma, the equivalent of our Mary. I have since heard that the limb healed up satisfactorily and that the kitten grew into a fine cat.

From Nono Tonyod we managed to collect a good deal of information about the local craftsmen. The principal metal-worker of Ladak, who was the maker of many of the best examples in our friend's possession, did not live close to the capital, but in a village a couple of days' journey away, in a subsidiary valley on the south side of the Indus. The place is called Chhiling, and one large family, probably including cousins and brothers as well as children of the master, supplies most of the high-class copper and silver work for all Ladak. The master makes periodic visits to the capital for a few weeks to take orders and carry out repairs. He luckily happened to be at Leh at the same time as ourselves and Tonyod took us round to a hose on the outskirts of the town where he was at work. He had set up his furnace under a huge tree and was busy mending teapots, assisted by a pupil. Later he came over to Tonyod's house to discuss with us the price of a new brass teapot. Several examples from his own hand were shown to us, in every degree of elaboration, from one covered with silver applique to a plain copper one tinned inside, with a particularly fine dragon for a handle; it spout was inserted into the mouth of a tusked marine monster. We decided on one of the latter pattern as the proportions were the best and the price was very reasonable. This teapot reached me in 1938 and proved to be a masterpiece of the art of the hammer. The same smith was also asked whether he could make a faithful copy of Tonyod's best silver teacup-stand, to save sending it as far as Lhasa for reproduction; but, after thinking it over, he said that though he might possibly manage it, he was not sure: and it would necessitate the forging of a large number of special tools. The fact was that he was not keen on the commission; he was too honest to disguise his doubts as to whether his own skill could quite rise to the heights required for producing a replica of a work by a still greater master.

Though the Chhiling silversmith was so renowned, it was generally admitted that for more finicky jobs, such as jewellery and filigree, he was surpassed by a Moslem jeweller who lived in the city itself and worked on a veranda, assisted by his young son. We paid him a visit, in company with Tonyod, having seen one brilliant example of his work, a gold filigree necklace with turquoises. He showed us one or two minor things in the making and we noticed that the workmanship fell far short of the standard of the necklace. It was only another example of these people's attitude—for good material, good workmanship; for good workmanship, great care over the details of the design, and *vice versa*. To them the material forms a relatively high proportion of the price, while the work counts for little. Everything is sold by weight; for gold so much, for silver so much, for copper so much. The time is not reckoned separately.

We wished to purchase a couple of small tea-tables of carved and painted wood called *chogtse*. Nono-Tonyod made us a present of an old one carved in the Tibetan province of Purang near the source of the Satlej. For the other, he indicated to us the best woodworker in Leh, whose house was situated on the edge of the city, looking out across the forest of *chortens* which rises out of the surrounding sands. He was a large man of cheerful appearance, with very little of the Tartar in his features. He came to us in our garden, holding an adze in one hand and a baulk of wood in the other, which he had hastily carved to show what he could to. The moment we caught sight of him we cried: "One of the Mastersingers of Nurnberg!" The price for a carved and pierced folding table, with dragons and birds, came to about three pounds. We impressed on him that there was no hurry, and that he could take his time; one of our friends would post it to us later. He also promised to see that no foreign paint was used on it, but only the regular traditional materials. He said that he would not carry out the actual painting himself, but would get a specialist in the colouring of furniture to do it, who lived at Sabu, a village some six miles away.

It is instructive to note the distribution of the leading artists in Ladak. The chief woodcarver and also the best jeweller lived in Leh itself. The silversmith with the greatest reputation dwelt at Chhiling, but the potter whose wares were most valued belonged to the Likhir valley. Rigzin, the leading painter, came from down the Indus, while at Kalatze, where we had crossed the river four days short of Leh, lived the only man with any reputation for weaving rugs. Besides these there were many assistant craftsmen and painters, both lay and monastic.

We were given an introduction to another merchant, this time a born native of Lhasa, who was married to a Ladaki lady and lived out of the town in a country house at Sabu. I rode out to pay him a call across a stretch of desert which, being free from stones and not too heavy going, gave the opportunity of an enjoyable canter. The house, which was on the usual plan with the family apartments on the first floor, was approached through a courtyard in which three chained dogs, veritable hell-hounds (but made so by man's folly), growled threateningly as I entered.

The squire—for such a title seemed to fit him better than that of trader—received me hospitably and accepted my present and a white scarf, offered in accordance with etiquette. I had chosen for him a silver ring with a cornelian; it had been designed to slip over a finger of normal size, but he had great difficulty in discovering one thin enough to take it. He was huge and burly, and surely one of the ugliest of men; he was dressed in a dirty old shirt and greasy gown, with high velvet boots such as are affected by smart Lhasa society, all smeared with mud. On his head he wore a pointed hat of violet silk, also in the latest fashion. He was rough of speech and hearty, and he certainly might, but for the clothes, have figured as the typical squire in the days when John Bull was John Bull. He had two sons, eighteen and twelve years old respectively, both of them exceedingly beautiful and well brought up. They waited on me at table with the grace of medieval esquires, bringing a basin and pouring water over my fingers from a ewer between the courses : and when it was time to leave, they ran out to hold my stirrup. Our servant Norbu was given food in the same room; he squatted in a corner and interrupted the conversation when he thought he had a useful comment to offer. After a pleasant afternoon's small talk with the worthy squire, we returned to Leh, which we reached at sundown, when a light breeze was rising after the torrid heat of the afternoon. A soft thinkling, as of elfin bells, was wafted towards us; we found that it came from tiny peals attached to the pinnacles of the *chortens.*

Next morning we had hardly finished breakfast when who should appear but the squire himself! Had we been more versed at that time in Tibetan customs, we would have known that it is conventional to return a call at the earliest possible opportunity. Luckily we managed to behave as though we had been expecting him all the time. "Please sit down," we said, "thė tea is nearly ready," — meanwhile hastily whispering to Norbu to make the tea. While our guest drank tea we had a breathing space in which to cook lunch. Actually someone had to be sent post-haste to the market to buy bread and eggs, so that omelettes, always so handy in such emergencies, could be prepared. In a few minutes lunch, or rather brunch, was served, to which, after the polite show of refusal prescribed by custom, he did full justice. When he had enough of a dish, he passed his plate to his own servant to polish off the leavings. At the end we gave him a stiff tot of the medicınal brandy, so we felt that, though nearly caught napping, we had not fallen short of Tibetan standards of hospitality.

I must not take leave of Leh without mentioning yet another kind friend, the principal Kashmiri officer of the province, who bore the title of Wazir. In former years, officials had been posted to Ladak who regarded their stay there as banishment among savages, which could only be compensated for by doing as little work as possible and feathering their nests at the expense of the inhabitants. However, reprehensible this may sound morally, it actually worked out to the advantage of Ladak, for the institutions of the country were not tampered with through over-zeal, and the officials did not spend precious money upon "progressive developments." In circumstances where a district of intact culture happens to fall under the government of an Occidentalized suzerain, the best one can wish for it, is that it should be treated with indifference and be preserved from the conscientious and active, but unimaginative, functionary. However, in our year, the office of Wazir had at last been entrusted to a sympathetic and enlightened official, a Hindu of the name of Rao Rattan Singh, who was doing much for the country in really useful directions, such as extending the plantations of trees so as to shade new sources of water. That is the greatest material service that can be rendered in a desert country, and has from time immemorial been held to confer special merit on the man who undertakes it. Everyone to whom we spoke paid an enthusiastic tribute to the integrity and justice of the present Wazir and contrasted him with his self-seeking predecessors. To us he was always most kind and encouraging, and took a great interest in all our doings.

(From *Peaks and Lamas, 1940*)

